God and *Eros*

God and *Eros*

The Ethos of the Nuptial Mystery

EDITED BY
Colin Patterson
and Conor Sweeney

CASCADE *Books* • Eugene, Oregon

GOD AND *EROS*
The Ethos of the Nuptial Mystery

Copyright © 2015 Wipf and Stock Publishers. All rights reserved. Except for brief quotations in critical publications or reviews, no part of this book may be reproduced in any manner without prior written permission from the publisher. Write: Permissions, Wipf and Stock Publishers, 199 W. 8th Ave., Suite 3, Eugene, OR 97401.

Cascade Books
An Imprint of Wipf and Stock Publishers
199 W. 8th Ave., Suite 3
Eugene, OR 97401

www.wipfandstock.com

ISBN 13: 978-1-62564-933-1

Cataloging-in-Publication data:

God and eros : the ethos of the nuptial mystery / edited by Colin Patterson and Conor Sweeney.

xviii + 250 p. ; 23 cm. —Includes bibliographical references and index(es).

ISBN 13: 978-1-62564-933-1

1. Marriage—Religious aspects—Catholic Church. 2. Sex—Religious aspects—Catholic Church. 3. Human body—Religious aspects—Catholic Church. 4. John Paul II, Pope, 1920–2005. Theology of the body. I. Patterson, Colin. II. Sweeney, Conor. III. Title.

BX1795.S48 G63 2015

Manufactured in the U.S.A.

In memory of
Professor Nicholas Tonti-Filippini KCSG
(1956-2014)

Whose vision was the catalyst for this volume, and whose contributions to the life of the John Paul II Institute were immeasurable

Contents

List of Contributors ix
Preface xi

PART I: Approaching the Mystery

1 The Church and Human Sexuality: An Introduction 3
   MOST REVEREND PETER J. ELLIOTT

2 The Culture Wars: Saint Pope John Paul II—
   Pope of the Civilization of Love 19
   TRACEY ROWLAND

3 The *Theology of the Body* in Outline 38
   ADAM G. COOPER

4 Communion with God: Marriage as Metaphor
   in the Old Testament 60
   ANNA SILVAS

5 God and Communion: Marriage as Sacrament
   in the New Testament 73
   ANNA SILVAS

6 The Story of God and *Eros* 91
   ADAM G. COOPER

PART II: Applying the Mystery

7 Bodily Love and the *Imago Trinitatis* 107
   CONOR SWEENEY

8   A Constructive Approach to Secularism   123
    COLIN PATTERSON

9   The Role of Natural Law in Bioethics:
    Anthropocentrism or Theocentrism   136
    NICHOLAS TONTI-FILIPPINI

10 The Family in the Life and Mission of the Church   162
    OWEN VYNER

11 God and *Eros*: Six Implications for Religious Education   177
    GERARD O'SHEA

12 Priestly Formation for Celibacy:
    Nuptial and Trinitarian   191
    ANNA KROHN

13 Co-operators of the Truth of the Human Person   212
    MARC CARDINAL OUELLET

Bibliography 227
Index of Themes 235
Index of Magisterial Documents 244
Index of Persons 245
Index of Scripture 248

Contributors

Adam G. Cooper is Senior Lecturer in Patristics, John Paul II Institute for Marriage and Family, Melbourne. Among his published works are *The Body in Saint Maximus the Confessor: Holy Flesh, Wholly Deified* (2005), *Life in the Flesh: An Anti-Gnostic Spiritual Philosophy* (2008), and *Naturally Human, Supernaturally God: Deification in Pre-Conciliar Catholicism* (2014).

Most Reverend Peter J. Elliott is the Director of the John Paul II Institute for Marriage and Family, Melbourne, and Auxiliary Bishop to the Archdiocese of Melbourne. He is author of *What God Has Joined: The Sacramentality of Marriage* (1990), *Ceremonies of the Modern Roman Rite* (1994, 2004), and *Ceremonies of the Liturgical Year* (2003). Bishop Elliott also served as the General Editor of the religious education text series *To Know, Worship and Love*.

Anna Krohn is a doctoral candidate and Academic Skills Counsellor, John Paul II Institute for Marriage and Family, Melbourne. Her research interests are centered on the thought of Dietrich von Hildebrand.

Gerard O'Shea is Senior Lecturer in Religious Education, Catechetics and Family Ministry, John Paul II Institute for Marriage and Family, Melbourne. He has recently published *As I Have Loved You* (2011), a parent resource for training children in sexuality according to the mind of the Catholic Church.

Marc Cardinal Ouellet is the present prefect of the Congregation for Bishops. He was a member of the Faculty of the Institute in Rome. Among his works translated into English is *Divine Likeness: Toward a Trinitarian Anthropology of the Family* (2006).

Colin Patterson is Lecturer in Moral Theology and Psychology, John Paul II Institute for Marriage and Family, Melbourne. He has published on the interface between science and ethics.

Tracey Rowland is Dean of the John Paul II Institute for Marriage and Family, Melbourne, and Professor in Theological Anthropology and Political Philosophy. In 2014 she was appointed by Pope Francis to the International Theological Commission. Her publications include *Benedict XVI: A Guide for the Perplexed* (2010), *Ratzinger's Faith: The Theology of Pope Benedict XVI* (2008), and *Culture and the Thomist Tradition after Vatican II* (2003).

Anna Silvas is Lecturer in Patristics and Medieval History, John Paul II Institute for Marriage and Family, Melbourne. Her works include *Macrina the Younger: Philosopher of God* (2008) and *The Asketikon of St. Basil the Great* (2005).

Conor Sweeney is Lecturer in Sacramental Theology and Continental Philosophy, John Paul II Institute for Marriage and Family, Melbourne. He is the author of *Sacramental Presence after Heidegger: Onto-Theology, Sacraments, and the Mother's Smile* (Cascade, 2015).

Nicholas Tonti-Filippini, until his death in November 2014, was Associate Dean, Professor of Bioethics and Philosophy, Sexuality and Fertility Awareness. He was a widely published scholar, his last major work being a series of four volumes titled *About Ethics*.

Owen Vyner is a doctoral candidate, John Paul II Institute for Marriage and Family, Melbourne. His research is in the area of liturgical theology. He has a Licentiate in Sacred Theology from the Liturgical Institute (Mundelein, Il.).

Preface

THE PONTIFICAL JOHN PAUL II Institute for Marriage and Family was founded by St. John Paul II on May 13, 1981—the same day as the assassination attempt made on him in St. Peter's Square. The mission of the Institute reflects John Paul II's personal convictions regarding the central importance of marriage and family in the life of the Church and in society at large. In his encyclical *Familiaris consortio*—promulgated in the same year the Institute was founded—the pope spoke of the urgent need to proclaim to all people God's plan for marriage and family. John Paul II was a man acutely in tune with the desires of the human heart, particularly aware that at the core of human experience is the desire for love. As he put it in the first encyclical of his pontificate, "Man cannot live without love. He remains a being that is incomprehensible for himself, his life is senseless, if love is not revealed to him, if he does not encounter love, if he does not experience it and make it his own, if he does not participate intimately in it." His own pastoral experiences with young people and married couples made this intuition concrete, and his concern with marriage and family—especially within the "dark shadows" of a secular context—reflects his conviction that the fate of love is closely linked to the way it is experienced and nurtured within the nuptial and familial context. The work of the various sessions of the Institute around the world—including our own session, in Melbourne, Australia—is thus to study and proclaim this call to love which the vocation of marriage and family gives specific form.

A graduate of the Institute receives formation in what the subtitle of this volume describes as the *ethos of the nuptial mystery*, which enables them to contribute to the building up of a civilization of love. While ensuing chapters will provide the reader with more comprehensive working definitions of this phrase, we can state here that the phrase identifies love, gift, communion, fruitfulness, participation, and relation as constitutive marks of a sacramental existence received as gift from a God who is a Communion of Persons. This perspective—which is often spoken of in shorthand as a "Trinitarian anthropology"—grounds original reflection on the many themes, perspectives, and issues studied at the Institute. The John Paul II Institute in Melbourne offers graduate courses in the Theology of Marriage and Family, Bioethics, and Religious Education.

A faculty project, *God and Eros: The Ethos of the Nuptial Mystery* arose from a sense that there was a need to publicize and clarify more widely the important developments that have occurred in the areas of the theology of marriage and family, and thereby to more accurately and comprehensively propagate the full ethos of the nuptial mystery. Since the book's initial conception in late 2012 and early 2013, this conviction has only deepened. The tumultuous events and conversations that have accompanied the 2014–2015 Synod on the Family have revealed the extent to which the ethos of the nuptial mystery has not yet been adequately internalized. Though written well prior to the Synod, the attentive reader will notice that every chapter offers something of a preemptive response, as it were, to recently articulated positions that have sought to downgrade the significance of what it means to participate in that mystery. In this context, perhaps the unique and long-term value of this volume lies precisely in the ways its contents transcend current polemics. Of special importance throughout is the work inspired by the Wednesday audiences of John Paul II, commonly referred to as the "theology of the body." A *theology* of the body deepens reflection on themes associated with marriage and the family, by rethinking the body itself as the bearer of a specifically personal and sacramental meaning—John Paul II argued that the "body reveals the person," and that it "transfer[s] into the visible reality of the world the mystery hidden from eternity in God, and thus [is] a sign of it." What John Paul II adds to the Church's already robust historical defense of the goodness of the body is a much keener sense that the body is not just the natural backdrop to our existence, but is in fact firmly set at the center of our identity as children of God called to love.

Against a theology of the body, some have recently suggested that what we need today is a "theology of love" as though it is possible to bracket out the body and its significance from love. John Paul II's answer to them is that in Christ the body and love receive their definitive, integrated, and sacramental meaning. A theology of love is necessarily a theology of the body, just as a theology of the body is necessarily a theology of love. What the pope has given us, then, is precisely a theology of *embodied* love that fully immerses the person in the sacramental ethos of the nuptial mystery.

Beyond recent conversations provoked by the Synod, it should come as no surprise that the theology of the body has seen a massive groundswell of popularity, especially among young people and married couples. The married have in particular been gratified to see a renewed emphasis on the dignity, perfection, and sacramentality of their one-flesh communion in Christ. John Paul II's ability to think the mystery of love "from above," so to speak, has restored and deepened appreciation for the fact that marriage is a "communion of persons," a total, personal "gift of self," a real participation in the mystery of Christ and the Trinity. "Man becomes an image of God not so much in the moment of solitude as in the moment of communion," said the pope, who underscored the fact that the "communion" of marriage is one of the main avenues wherein this call to communion can be realized in this life. Marriage, no less than the consecrated state of life, is a state of perfection, a way to realize the universal call to holiness, and a path to eternal communion with God.

This remains one of the perennial achievements of John Paul II. But what we would also like to accent in this volume is the fact that the ethos of the nuptial mystery is not just about marriage. John Paul II's catecheses are more than a marriage manual or an ethics handbook for all things sexual. A common misperception of the theology of the body is that it is only for those who are married or who have an interest in marriage, or for those who have struggles with chastity. We may even, in our eagerness to make it relevant to such concerns, obfuscate its deeper sacramental grounding. For in fact, *a theology of the body is for everyone*: before it is a "theology of body and sex," it is the sacramental marking of our capacity and restlessness for the Love that exceeds the horizon of this world. To be a body is to be marked by the sign of the other—to be from somewhere, some*one*—and to have one's existence only fully realized through being gift for the other. It is thus to be "aimed" toward God in the most concrete, constitutive, liturgical, and existential way possible. The burden of John Paul II's claim that the body bears a "theology," is to say that to be human is to be sacramentally inscribed from "the beginning" with the call to communion with God. The body thus proclaims or "preaches" our destiny in an adoptive, filial belonging with God the Father, through the Son, in the Spirit (Gal 4:4–7), in the nuptial consummation of the

Bride and the Bridegroom (Eph 5), in the Wedding Feast of the Lamb (Rev 19:6–7, 9).

This is the total context and purview of the theology of the body—a theology for all believers, young or old, married or unmarried, capacitated or incapacitated. For even if life and vocational circumstances may mean that not all of us are called to the "normal" realization of the call to love in the sacrament of marriage, *all of us*, by virtue of being a body, are called to what this sacrament em-bodies; that is, a self-giving, communional love that is not only biologically but ultimately *spiritually* fruitful. All of us are called to live the spiritual "language" of the body, no matter what circumstance or vocation we find ourselves in. John Paul II made this spiritual perspective of the resurrection of the body quite explicit:

> Marriage and procreation do not definitively determine the original and fundamental meaning of being a body nor of being, as a body, male and female. Marriage and procreation only give concrete reality to that meaning in the dimensions of history. The resurrection indicates the closure of the historical dimension.

Far from denigrating marriage and procreation, this passage places what they signify in the here and now of created existence, within the perspective of the coming kingdom where they will be fulfilled. And so, what we seek to offer in this book is an account of the ethos of body and the nuptial mystery that makes this perspective more thematic.

This ethos can never be thought of as existing in an historical and cultural vacuum. Another aim of this text is to read the mystery against the backdrop of its mediation in history and culture. After all, a theology of the *body* bids us to be attentive to the incarnate conditions that necessarily accompany and influence our being in the world. The conditions that we presently face include a secular context hostile to the ethos of the mystery we present here, perhaps best summed up in Nietzsche's famous claim that Christianity poisoned *eros*. In the first encyclical of his pontificate, Pope Benedict XVI took up a conversation with Nietzsche on this question, expressing the philosopher's complaint thus:

> Here the German philosopher was expressing a widely-held perception: doesn't the Church, with all her commandments and prohibitions, turn to bitterness the most precious thing in life? Doesn't she blow the whistle just when the joy which is the

Creator's gift offers us a happiness which is itself a certain foretaste of the Divine?

Nietzsche voices a profound cultural dissatisfaction with and hostility to the Church's ethos of marriage and family. In a move that surprised many, Benedict's response to Nietzsche was a gentle but firm exegesis of the profound unity of love that forms the basis of the Church's account of *eros*. Our cultural task includes presenting not only the truth of the ethos but also its beauty and goodness—the way it captures the imagination and calls the heart, the way it connects with our experience of and desire for love. The perspective of love can both engage and transcend the context that it confronts, provoking the encounter with the Person who gives life a new horizon and decisive direction. This volume expresses this intuition, embodying a positive rather than a merely reactive approach to contemporary malaises, one marked by gentleness but also open-eyed to the realities and challenges we face.

We hope that readers of this text discover something to suit all levels and interests. The book is divided into two parts, the first designed to provide entry into the broad contours and features of the nuptial mystery, with a particular emphasis on providing a coherent account of the major themes and foundations of the theology of the body. Part II reflects more systematically on discrete themes and topics, revealing the far-reaching scope of this ethos. Each respective contribution can be located within a common vision shared by our faculty, but also reflects the contributor's own personal interpretations and emphases. Each brings something unique to the understanding and application of the ethos of the nuptial mystery. Our aim was to present accessible pieces that nevertheless retained a certain level of scholarly depth, while covering a range of different themes. Each chapter can be read on its own but will clearly benefit from an exchange and dialogue with the others.

Part I opens with Bishop Peter Elliott's straightforward and highly accessible historical and thematic summary of the classical themes and concerns associated with the Church's approach to the body and sex. In the next chapter, Tracey Rowland clarifies some of the foundational theological convictions that motivated John Paul II's thinking, bringing the intellectual and cultural context of his teaching into sharper relief, while paying special attention to the importance of a "civilization of love" in the pope's thought. With chapter 3, we move to Adam Cooper's systematic and concise introduction to the theology of the body. This chapter is a must-read for those wishing to acquaint themselves with the form, structure, and terminology of the theology of the body. Chapters 4 and 5 feature Anna Silvas's account of the scriptural foundations of marriage—an essential element for a full appreciation of the way the ethos of the nuptial mystery is firmly grounded in Scripture. Finally, in the last chapter of Part I, Adam Cooper considers the curious pairing of the two words that form the title of this book—God and *eros*—picking up the extraordinary discussion of the theme in the encyclical of Pope Benedict XVI, *Deus caritas est*.

Part II begins the shift from basic foundations and overviews to more applied and focused analyses of the nuptial mystery in relation to specific themes with Conor Sweeney's creative account of John Paul II's consideration of the body as the bearer of love. This chapter focuses on the specific link between bodily love and the Trinity. Colin Patterson's chapter offers in fairly abbreviated form an analysis of some elements of secularism—the backdrop against which the fate of God's plan for marriage and family is played out today—and the current relationship between Catholic believers and the state; it suggests some tentative pointers toward how that relationship might be re-envisioned. In chapter 9, Nicholas Tonti-Filippini considers the status of natural law in contemporary moral theology, situating it within his own experience as a bioethicist and arguing that employment of natural law discourse in the public forum cannot eschew the properly theocentric orientation of natural law in our tradition. Owen Vyner's chapter accents the ecclesial mission of the family as a domestic church. He situates the origin of the domestic church in the spousal communion and develops this communion along the axes of worship and mission. With an eye firmly on the crucial role that education plays in the re-evangelization of our culture, Gerard O'Shea's chapter takes up a number of key theological anthropological principles and finds some very concrete and practical applications for them in the field of religious education. Also dealing with education but in a quite different setting is Anna Krohn's contribution to that urgent question faced by the Catholic Church today: how are our priests to be formed and educated in the demands and the freedom of celibacy so that their ministries are enlivened by this aspect of their vocation? Krohn responds by developing a nuptial and Trinitarian account of priestly celibacy, concretely demonstrating how the vocations and the theologies of marriage and consecrated celibacy are not to be pursued in isolation, but must rather be allowed to mutually enrich each other.

To bring the collection to an end, we are pleased to be able to include a chapter prepared by His Eminence, Cardinal Marc Ouellet, prefect of the Congregation for Bishops. Ouellet is a former professor at the John Paul II Institute's session in Rome and a significant figure in the further development of the theology of the body and in the ministry of leadership in the Church, both in his Canadian homeland and in Latin America and Rome. His close knowledge of the Institute and his ability to situate its mission within the broader ecclesial and cultural currents are well expressed in his piece.

What is common to all the contributions is a commitment to an approach that respects the theological traditions that have shaped Catholic "faith seeking understanding" over the centuries, but that aims to continue and develop the conversation and to avoid at all costs a certain stagnation and rigidity that has characterized the dominant pre-conciliar approach. We hope that with what we offer here, readers will come to share in our appreciation and enthusiasm for the riches and potential of the ethos of the nuptial mystery to which that challenging juxtaposition—God and *eros*—invites us.

PART I

APPROACHING THE MYSTERY

chapter 1

The Church and Human Sexuality: An Introduction

MOST REVEREND PETER J. ELLIOTT

INTRODUCTION

A SPECIFIC MISSION OF the John Paul II Institute for Marriage and Family is teaching, with the mind of the Church, that sex per se is good. Preferring the wider term "sexuality," we interpret human sexuality as part of the creation that God looked upon and saw as "good." This created reality from the hand of the personal God is intrinsic to marriage and the procreation of children, for from the very "beginning," God created the embodied person. "So God created man in his own image, in the image of God he created him, male and female he created them" (Gen 1:27).

Sexuality is therefore all about being a man or a woman, not merely the biological reproductive capacity or the erotic drive or a libidinous instinct. At the center of the creation of male and female is marriage, a created reality from God the Father. Marriage was raised to be a holy sacrament by his incarnate Son, Jesus Christ, who is called the Bridegroom of his beloved Church. Sacramental marriage may thus be understood as "eros redeemed."

In his encyclical on love, *Deus caritas est* 3–5, Pope Benedict XVI hit back at the assertion of the German philosopher Friedrich Nietzsche that Christianity poisoned eros, a view that is widespread today among those secularists who depict Christianity as a sex-hating religion. The pope refuted this opinion in a Christian perspective, honestly admitting problems, but developing the meaning of the word for love that predominates in the Greek New Testament, *agape*.

Agape is self-giving love, the selfless love often attributed to Jesus Christ, although Jesus also expressed filial love for his apostles; *eros* in the sense referred to by Pope Benedict XVI expresses the desire to be loved, such as when Jesus repeatedly requested the company of the apostles when he prayed at Gethsemane, or wanted the gratitude of the other lepers he had cured. His love is not otherworldly or ethereal; rather, it is concretely human, which is captured in the Latin equivalent word, *caritas* (charity). All of us are capable of receiving and giving this kind of love, and *eros* is redeemed in and through such love.

BUT WHO AM I?

This conversation on *eros* and *agape* presupposes a Christian understanding of the human person, a Christian response to the basic question, who am I? The understanding of the person or anthropology consistently taught in the John Paul II Institute reflects the teaching of St. John Paul II himself. This approach may be summed up in six principles:

1. The bodily nature of the person;
2. The person as the image God in terms of moral responsibility, sexual difference, and complementarity;
3. The effects of original sin on sexuality;
4. Marriage as the norm for human sexuality;
5. Procreation as inseparable from sexuality;
6. Sexuality as a sacred mystery.

First, the human person is an embodied spirit or an enspirited body. This is the first basic principle. "Bodiliness" is essential to our nature and sexuality is intrinsic to being a living body. Catholics are not dualists, those who see the soul alone as good. The body is good. All its natural functions are good and form part of its intrinsic order, design, and finality. I will return to this question of the body because it is a major challenge.

Secondly, the human person is created in the image and likeness of God. This is the biblical principle. Thus the person, having received the divine breath, is a responsible rational agent. He or she is called to participate in the divine freedom, in the divine creativity of choice, decision, self-direction, and self-awareness. Male and female persons are therefore moral agents. At the same time, in their sexual difference and complementarity, they are called to reflect God by being in harmony with his will, that is, with the moral order he has established within human nature: the Natural Law.

Thirdly, the human person inherits the effects of original sin. Understood as a privation of freedom, the effects of original sin are evident in disordered passions, desires, instincts, and drives; sexuality is perhaps the weakest point of this problem of concupiscence, that is, disordered desires. Because sexuality is such an important part of our created nature, it seems to be a target for the forces of evil. But this is not to say that sexuality per se is corrupted by original sin. As with human nature itself, it remains good; nevertheless it is often disordered, hence prone to misuse, a focus of sin and suffering as well as joy and fulfillment.

MARRIAGE AS *EROS* REDEEMED

As a fourth principle, the Church places the Sacrament of Marriage at the heart of her teaching on sexuality. Faithful to the sources of Revelation, she relates all sexuality to marriage and proposes the right use of sexuality in the vocations to marriage or to celibacy or virginity. In different ways these are "spousal" or "nuptial" vocations, and all are fruitful. She also finds the redemption of human sexuality here, in lives lived as a response to a divine call, lives understood as bearing a personal plan and purpose for each one of us.

Therefore, marriage is something deeper than the "remedy for concupiscence" of medieval theologians who relied heavily on St. Augustine before he was corrected by St. Thomas Aquinas. Marriage is a raising up of human sexuality within the sacrament so that sexuality is fruitful in two ways: as grace-filled love and as the means of bringing children into this world within the family. In marriage, sexual union becomes spousal union, the "one flesh" of reciprocal self-giving, of the distinctive interaction of complementarity between the two sexes. The act of consummation in marriage is thus the beginning of self-giving love. It establishes the indissoluble spousal bond (*vinculum*) and it is exclusive, demanding fidelity until death. True sexual freedom is found in mutual fidelity. This matrimonial focus on sexuality underlines the fifth principle: that procreation is never to be separated from sexuality. As is evident in her teaching on contraception, the Church holds together the two natural meanings of the marriage act, unitive and procreative. They are not to be separated, nor are they to be seen as if they were in opposition to one another. The Church sees the finality of sexual union not in terms of biology, as "reproduction," but rather as procreation, that is, as a cooperation of spouses with their Creator in transmitting new life to build the kingdom. John Paul II explained this principle in terms of the vocation of a married couple to participate in and give witness to Divine love that is both unifying between the Persons of the Trinity, and between God and humanity, and also fruitful as the Creator of the entire universe. Scripture refers to marriage as an analogy for Divine love. Marital love participates closely in Divine love and a deliberate suppression of either the unitive or procreative dimension of the marital act is a rejection of that vocation to give witness to Divine love. John Paul II refers to contraception as contradicting the language of the body which should express the truth of the sacrament—the eternal plan of divine love revealed in the body in our femininity and masculinity.

The sixth principle affirms that, in spite of the effects of original sin, human sexuality is a sacred mystery and is worthy of reverence. This balance between the mystery of sexuality and human weakness is set out in the Vatican guidelines for education in human sexuality, *The Truth and Meaning of Human Sexuality*, 122. Consciences should be formed properly to cultivate respect for the mystery and to encourage a sense of responsibility, self-respect, and, especially, respect for others. Yet we live in an age that has demystified sexuality, reducing it to erotic sport and detaching it from abiding and binding relationships.

THE GREAT SOURCES

Based in the *ressourcement* school of post-Vatican II theology, the John Paul II Institute constantly draws on the sources of Church teaching. As is evident in this book, the faculty of the Institute start with the Sacred Scriptures and Tradition, the sources of Divine Revelation that provide ample guidance for a Christian understanding of human sexuality.

The Old Testament sexual ethic is centered on marriage, childbearing, and hygiene, the latter linked to ritual purity. While polygamy was tolerated, it was not seen as the norm. Divorce was allowed under some circumstances, but adultery, homosexual activity, and prostitution were rejected. Romantic and faithful love are extolled in the stories of Ruth and Tobit, in the Song of Songs, and through images of God as spouse in prophetic literature. The wisdom tradition rejects recourse to prostitutes and fornication. In the Hebrew Scriptures we see development, refinement, but always a healthy positive attitude to human sexuality.

A clear change takes place in the New Testament, but it is a further development. It is most important to understand how Jesus Christ deepens and fulfills the Old Testament perspective on sexuality. He does not merely repeat it; he builds on it, and in the area of divorce corrects it (cf. Matt 5:31; 19:3–11; Mark 10:2–12; Luke 16:18). He personalizes sexuality and indicates its interiority, so it is not what goes into a man that corrupts him but what comes from his heart (Matt 15:17–20; Mark 7:20–23). The evil thought of adultery "in the heart" matters just as much as the sinful act (Matt 5:28).

Our Lord's sexual ethic is more personal, hence more demanding. But he is realistic—for example, in his teaching on celibacy, which he says is only for those able to receive the gift (Matt 19:10–13). Moreover, his greatest anger is directed against proud people, and he is merciful to the adulterous woman, while firmly telling her to go and sin no more (John 8:10–11). Yet he searches the conscience of the woman at the well and mentions her five "husbands" (cf. John 4:16–18).

The whole Catholic discipline of chaste thoughts, pure intentions, and purity of heart thus springs directly from the historical Christ of the Gospels. St. Paul was the faithful transmitter of his teaching, undaunted by the unenviable task of evangelizing the pagans of the Greco-Roman world. These men and women for the most part lacked Jewish sexual discipline, and they lived in places like Corinth and Ephesus, notorious seaports that were cult centers of permissiveness. Paul made it clear that unrepentant sexual sinners cannot enter the kingdom (1 Cor 6:9–10). But he constantly insisted that once you are baptized the misuse of sexuality belongs to the past. Having put behind them past vices and deviant practices, the baptized are new creatures. Living "in Christ" and "in the Spirit," they are called to reject fornication, perversions, and impurity. They are called to find their fulfillment in Christian marriage or Christian celibacy—grace-filled vocations lived for the coming kingdom of God.

This quality of sexual discipline, chastity, purity, and fidelity characterized Christians from the earliest centuries. In the *Letter to Diognetus*[1] we read that a Christian will share his table but not his marriage bed. Marriage in the early Church was centered on procreation, fidelity, unity, harmony, and strong family life, and this consciously contrasted with the pagan lifestyles that surrounded Christian families.

PREOCCUPIED WITH SEX?

When we go to the sources, we see also how unfair it is to accuse the Church of having a "preoccupation with sex." It is the world that is preoccupied with sex. The Church has a broader and richer approach. Moreover, the Church has been consistent in her sexual ethic, even if a more rigorist approach was evident in some centuries. This has been unfairly attributed to Saint Augustine, whereas it was more closely linked to the rise and deep influence of monasticism in the centuries following the fall of the Roman Empire. But when the Church fought for celibacy and virginity against permissive trends in brutal ages when tribal customs used women as chattels, she always strenuously supported marriage. As will be outlined below, she was firmly set against the Albigensians and other dualists and ascetical extremists who regarded sexuality as evil and having babies as unclean.

Therefore, the official responses given by the Magisterium to questions relating to sexual morality show a consistent ethic, faithful to Scripture and Tradition but pastorally sensitive to the fact that serious sin is found in any misuse of sexuality. At the same time, across the centuries and more clearly in recent times, there has been a steady and consistent development in Catholic teaching which values sexual love in marriage, while rejecting a view of marriage based only on erotic pleasure. That balance is evident in this book.

The most extensive magisterial teaching on human sexuality was proposed in the era when the John Paul II Institute was founded. This is a pastoral response to a changing situation, generally described as the "sexual revolution" that emerged in mid-twentieth century. To understand this response we first focus on the theology of the human body because today the body is often misunderstood, abused, and misused.

---

1. The *Letter to Diognetus* is an early example of Christian apologetics, written by an unknown Greek author circa AD 130.

THE BODY

Christians have long wrestled with the value and meaning of the human body. We know that the body is important because at the heart of our faith is the Incarnation, the core doctrine that God took our flesh, our human nature, in a real human body in a historical Person, Jesus the Christ. He was born of the body of the Blessed Virgin. He died in that same body he took from her flesh, and in that body he rose again. The tangible, historical Incarnation is extended first in the visible Church, which, following St. Paul, we call "the Body of Christ," and then through her sacraments, all of which are bodily acts.

In the Mass, the central mystery of our religion, the priest speaks the words of Jesus Christ: "This is my body which will be given up for you." The seven sacraments are received and celebrated in and through our bodies. We worship as embodied beings and we carry out works of charity and mercy in our bodies, often to meet the bodily needs of others, especially those who are afflicted by poverty, as well as the frail, marginalized, or suffering. We are called by God to respect our bodies as temples of the Holy Spirit. We reverence the bodies of our dead for what they were and for what we believe they will become at the last day, when we will be raised up in our bodies. Orthodox Christianity is thus much more interested in matter and bodies than people outside our traditions imagine.

Yet at the same time there is a tension among us, because we also sin in and through our bodies. We are fallen beings, innately weakened by the primal fall and its inheritance. The body thus bears within itself a dramatic ambiguity, what the Second Vatican Council in *Gaudium et spes* 13 describes as "man divided in himself," the divisive effects of original sin.

Therefore, while we believe that the Word became flesh in Jesus the Christ, we also distrust our own flesh. When we welcome the Body of Christ in the Eucharist, we also know that we are unworthy of this sublime divine self-giving. Before Communion, we say, "Lord, I am not worthy that you should enter under my roof . . ." We know that human sexuality raises many issues of sin and grace, of joy and suffering, desire and frustration, fulfillment and despair. This applies not only to Christians but, in varying degrees, to everyone, married or unmarried.

ST. PAUL

Drawing on his own experience, St. Paul described the perennial spiritual and moral struggle as the flesh versus the spirit. Did that mean he believed that in each of us an evil body is struggling against a good soul? Not necessarily, because when Paul uses "flesh" he is speaking of the weakness that St. Augustine later described as concupiscence. This term includes the disordered desires of our fallen human nature, and that encompasses everything from gluttony to lust. Yet the same Paul can say bluntly in his letter to the Ephesians that "no man hates his own body."

In the context of his teaching about Christian married life and love, Paul wrote within a Hebrew understanding of the person. He presented a "great Mystery," Jesus the Bridegroom cherishing his bride the Church as a husband cherishes his own body, and this great Mystery is the archetype for the sacrament of marriage (cf. Eph 5:22–33).

The Hebrew religious tradition valued the body and understood persons as living bodies. Strangely, from our point of view, while the Hebrews respected the human body, they had no developed understanding of the soul. Jewish eschatology is still largely vague and disparate as to what happens after death. But Paul already inherited the best form of that eschatology from his Pharisee background. The Pharisees believed in immortality (understood as resurrection), and in spirits and angels, the nonmaterial dimension of creation. Paul was well versed in Greek thought which emphasized the soul, but to him the central reality was the bodily Resurrection of Jesus Christ, that is, the triumph and glorification of the body of the crucified Lord. Through baptism the justifying work of Christ extends to our bodies, which Paul describes as temples of the Holy Spirit.

Nevertheless, the integration of Hebrew reverence for the body and a Greek understanding of the soul that we find in Saint Paul did not always prevail. From the earliest times, Christians have been prone to influences that play upon the moral or physical weakness of our bodies. In particular we have been influenced in various eras by ideas drawn mainly from Greek philosophical sources, exaggerated by mystery religions and promoted in the cults of Gnosticism that flourished in the early centuries of Christianity.

DUALISM

The problem is dualism. In this bodily context this means a sharp, even absolute separation between two realities, matter and spirit, the body and the soul. The John Paul II Institute provides a trenchant critique of dualism, evident in this book and relevant to our times.

At its worst dualism taught that there is an endless struggle between matter and spirit, proposing two gods: the good god of the spirit and the bad god of matter. The spirit or soul is good, created by the good god, but it is imprisoned in the creation of the bad god, the material body, in a material world. The followers of Manes, the Manichaeans, were dualists with this cast of mind.

However, this raises another problem. Dualism can go in two directions, leading to two extreme and opposing attitudes to the body—either ascetical body hating or indulgent immorality. On the one hand the body is despised or beaten down like some animal that needs to be tamed, so that the pure soul may triumph over it. On the other hand, the soul spurns the life of the body and claims an independence and autonomy of its own, so that sins committed by my body are not really my sins because my soul does not consent to them!

The society in which such ideas developed gives us further paradoxes about the body. Greco-Roman civilization emphasized a kind of adoration of the human form, which was inspired by sport and military exploits and expressed in art, as well as in unbridled eroticism and even perversions. At the same time, poetry and literature revealed a pessimism about the body, much meditation on its mortality, its passing nature, understandable in an age of poor health and a short life span. Contempt for the body and belief that we are essentially, or even only, imprisoned souls easily emerged in such a world.

ST. AUGUSTINE AND ST. THOMAS AQUINAS

The Fathers of the first Christian centuries and especially St. Augustine reacted against the pagan adoration of the body and associated immorality. At the same time they had to fight off the dualism of mystery religions and Gnostics. Augustine was a Manichaean with an immoral lifestyle for some time before his conversion. Once he became a Christian he embraced a strict celibate life, a form of monastic life, as did other great Fathers of the Church, and this put a stamp on his writing and teaching about sexuality and marriage. Influenced by Plato, he tended to exalt the soul over the body, but he never suggested that the body was evil and it is unfair to exaggerate his views.

After Augustine, the dominant monastic traditions of the medieval world, West and East, tended to downgrade the human body, treating it as the enemy or as an agent of Satan in the struggle to be chaste and pure. The Celtic Christian tradition is marked with this ascetical attitude. This, combined with Augustinian theology, delayed the recognition of marriage as a full sacrament, a means of grace. Because marriage involved sexual union, it was seen as always tainted with disordered desire, concupiscence. A negative attitude to female sexuality was part of this problem.

In the thirteenth century, St. Thomas Aquinas broke the impasse on marriage by going so far as to suggest that sexual union itself in marriage was a grace-giving activity. He had recovered what was best in classical philosophical thought. Influenced by Aristotle, he sought to integrate the soul and body in a unity of the person in a concept known as hylomorphism. The soul is inseparable from the body in this life, and it is meant to direct and govern the body, but a body remains essential in what constitutes a living human being, or person as we would say today. The body is to be respected in life, in terms of nourishment, health, and procreation, and after death it ought to be reverenced for what it was and what it will become.

St. Thomas was also very conscious of a dangerous revival of dualism in his own times. St. Dominic had fought this pestilence, in the form of the beliefs and practices of the Cathars or Albigensians, whose contempt for sexuality was only matched by their disgust at the processes of human procreation.

CHRISTIAN ATTITUDES TO THE BODY

In the late Middle Ages in Europe, the revival of Greco-Roman culture promoted a recovery of reverence for the human body. This was reflected in later Renaissance art and the gradual acceptance of nudity in art. Vivid examples are the frescoes of Signorelli at Orvieto Cathedral and Michelangelo's triumphant work in the Sistine Chapel. Both artists present the body as beautiful and noble, in particular in the perfect nude figures that have been raised up at the general resurrection of the dead.

Yet soon there was a sharp reaction to the Renaissance, another swing to dualism, first among reforming Protestants with their pessimism about sinful human nature. Luther's thought is marked by dualism, which also runs as a deeper current within Calvinism and its puritan heritage. Reforming Catholics were not immune to that trend, which is understandable in light of the scandals of a worldly papacy that was partly responsible for the Protestant revolt. Michelangelo's nude figures in his *Last Judgement* were modestly draped by a reformer pope.

The trend toward severity developed further in the mid-seventeenth century, in the Low Countries and France, when an extreme Augustinianism emerged among some devout Catholics, who claimed to be the true interpreters of the reforming Council of Trent. Known as Jansenism, after its major theological guide, Bishop Cornelius Jansen, this puritanical Catholicism has had a lingering influence even into our own time, that is, long after its errors had been formally condemned by the popes.

Again the historical context is interesting. Many seventeenth-century Christians slid into Greek dualism, separating the soul from the body. The influential French philosopher René Descartes was a dualist, and he was favored by the Jansenists. Descartes has been described as conceiving of the body as a machine, hence the expression describing a human being as "the ghost in the machine," a dualistic and mechanistic understanding of the person. He also regarded animals as living machines that lack a soul or spirit.

A dualistic attitude toward the soul and body lingered among Catholics, even if it was never officially favored by the Church, which firmly rejected Jansenism. I believe it was maintained over recent centuries in some spiritualities, prayers, and devotions that spoke of the soul as some kind of female component inhabiting a body. "She," the soul, is always yearning to be free of the corrupt body and its passions, aches, and weaknesses. Many devout Christians regarded themselves primarily as souls, detained for a time in a body. A sense of disgust with the body, of prudery and shame, of guilt and scruples, easily developed in such a context. This is far from the teaching of St. Thomas Aquinas on the unity of soul and body, or that of St. Paul on the risen glory destined for the temple of the Spirit. Saint Augustine would have paled at its dualistic implications, for which he is often blamed.

As secularization penetrated the Catholic community in the nineteenth and twentieth centuries, the body-soul dilemma was not clearly resolved, at least in popular Catholicism. This is why some people who abandon Catholicism for unbelief, or an ideology or sexual lifestyle, often cite body-hating spirituality or guilt about the body as reasons prompting their departure. We find this theme again and again in fashionable anti-Catholic literature and films, snickering references to convent school prudery or cruel confessional incidents. While self-justification is obvious, perhaps laced with some hypocrisy, the problem is real. It calls for a remedy, especially because the sexual revolution has unleashed a new kind of dualism, a secular one, that is confusing and corrupting Christians, especially young people. Here John Paul II has offered us a way forward that guides the Institute and is an important component in the curriculum.

THE THEOLOGY OF THE BODY

Karol Wojtyła was an athletic and healthy young man, of strong intellect and body. His early ministry as a Polish priest and university chaplain set the course for his later work. He was involved in the family apostolates, working closely with married couples, mainly with his friends at the university, and then he worked with marriage experts. He made this a key Catholic pastoral strategy alongside the sociopolitical need to help men and women maintain the faith in a communist society where sexuality was degraded and the family was being deliberately undermined. His book on married love, sexuality, and procreation, *Love and Responsibility* (1960), appeared eight years before Pope Paul VI's encyclical *Humanae vitae* (1968).

That famous encyclical reiterated the teaching of the Church against contraception, sterilization, and abortion. What most people do not know is that this was presented in the context of a rich and realistic theology of the body, of total self-giving love in married life. We can only make sense of the negative principles in *Humanae vitae* if we grasp the positive principles first.

Cardinal Karol Wojtyła had a marked influence on Pope Paul VI, especially through his *Love and Responsibility*. "Responsibility" in terms of parenthood equally applies to responsible sexual behavior. But to whom is a couple responsible? To God, source and author not only of human life and its transmission, but source and author of love, including erotic love. This is the assumption throughout *Humanae vitae*. To have a baby is not just a decision made by two individuals, even if they are close as a couple.

It is a decision made in communion with the life-giving, love-giving God. In that context responsibilities to one another, to the rest of the family, to society can be worked out wisely and well.

When we reflect carefully on the central principle of *Humanae vitae*, we also see that it is a contradiction of dualism. What must always be kept together in God's plan is the physical gift of life, fertility, and the spiritual love giving of sexual union. Once we tear these complementary dimensions of married love apart, we have serious ethical and practical problems. The whole person, a union of body and soul, is called to give the self totally, without withholding either fertility or sexuality. Therefore, it is morally wrong to say, "Well, now we cannot manage to achieve pregnancy ourselves, so we will separate the bodily expression of our love by contributing sperm and eggs so that someone else can take over and become the technological parent of our child, dominating the biological production process in his or her origins and treating our child as an object and subject to quality control and selective destruction," just as it is morally wrong to say, "Well, now I am being a loving spiritual person, but we make love using contraception to keep it separate from the bodily reality of the possibility of a baby . . ."

Modern society is riddled with this sexual dualism. Made-to-order babies produced as products and thus without the equal respect for their personhood because the life is generated outside of sexual union are one side of the problem. The other side is the incomplete sexuality, so often undermining the creative dimension of love that has the couple reach out beyond themselves to share in the divine work of creation. They deliberately sterilize the sexual union, temporarily or permanently robbing it of its meaning, and that is what misleads so many young people in a condom culture. Their love, by not being creative, loses the focus on others that is characteristic of divine love.

If people make love while eliminating either the fertile life-giving dimension or the tender self-giving of male-female sexuality, then they are telling lies in and through their bodies. They deny the truth and meaning of human sexuality as a vocation to participate in and give witness to divine love, the truth of who they are as persons made in the image and likeness of God.

THE PASTORAL VISION OF ST. JOHN PAUL II

The Church response to issues in her specific moral teachings places major responsibilities and burdens on men and women. Therefore, people need pastoral and practical support from the Church to help them put the teachings into practice. This pastoral support helps them discover the richness and joy of married life open to God's plan. Cardinal Wojtyła knew this only too well from his work with couples. So he supported family institutes for the formation of experts and pastoral agents and above all to promote the use of natural birth-spacing, or as it is usually called, "natural family planning."

Therefore, not long after he became pope, he established the John Paul II Institute for Studies on Marriage and Family at the Lateran University, with which the Melbourne session is associated. He made the Vatican Committee for the Family into a full Vatican department, the Pontifical Council for the Family. These acts coincided with the fateful day of the attempt on his life, May 13, 1981.

Much of his teaching as pope focused on marriage, sexuality, and the family. Reading the "signs of the times," he continued what was set out in *Gaudium et spes*, at the Second Vatican Council, where he was an influential father. He saw the key battleground of our time as the home, in particular marriage, because the family based on marriage is the source and basic living cell of human society. But at the same time he was well aware of lingering Jansenist influences within European Catholicism, hence the need to re-value human sexuality in the Catholic tradition by eliminating "anti-body" attitudes or pious prudery posing as modesty. We need to propose something better, maintaining chastity, purity, and the virtuous life, but not rejecting the body.

Understanding the body rightly, in terms of the complementary sexual difference between male and female, was a way through a fear of the body within the Church. But it also countered the more dangerous threat of materialistic body worship that was promoted both by Communism and Nazism and in our era by Western secularism through a sexual revolution marked by a sinister dualism of its own.

John Paul II saw that Western secularists misunderstand the body because they do not understand what a person really is. By "person" they really mean a personality, that is, an aggregate of qualities, skills, and experiences—basically, a developed mind: "She's a nice person . . ." Then they fall into dualism, treating the body as something separate from the person or mind: "He has a nice body . . ." The body that houses this mind thus becomes an object, a useful instrument. In the light of liberal individualism and the cult of total freedom, my body is something I can use as I will, because the real "me" is my mind.

Secularists do not believe in the soul in a spiritual sense, even if they might use the word from time to time with a loosely subjective or New Age meaning. For them a person is a mind using a body. A man or woman uses the body for his or her pleasure, fulfillment, recreation, and control. This instrument can be idolized and glamorized, or it can be pummelled around in a kind of mock asceticism in the name of sport, exercise, or diet. The body is even idolized by being reshaped, undergoing a "total makeover" according to some imagined ideal. Then, once the body becomes a heavy burden, it can be cast aside by the act of suicide or removed by euthanasia. This mentality is permeated by the selfish individualism that dominates our liberal permissive societies, an individualism criticized by John Paul II, Pope Benedict XVI, and Pope Francis. This mentality is pervasive among young people, who absorb it through the mass media and in their own peer groups who use social media.

Once one misunderstands one's own body by dissociating it from the "real person," serious consequences emerge, particularly in interpersonal relationships. Other people can easily be regarded as just bodies, then used as instruments or things, no longer treated as persons. Recreational sex is an example of abusing others, and oneself, by splitting the body from the person. My body becomes a possession, a thing I own or something I have—a plaything, a toy. This attitude is then projected onto other people. Their bodies can be exploited for my pleasure, or reduced to entertaining toys through pornography in cyberspace. In cases of child sex abuse, the bodies of weaker persons are used to gain power and control. But young people can be led to recognize these issues by reflecting on what a person really is, on "who I really am."

The concern of John Paul II to tackle the basic issue of the modern misunderstanding of the person was reflected in his Wednesday Catechesis on Marriage, which ran through the first years of his pontificate. The timing indicated the priority he gave to these issues. His method was the complex and focused approach of European phenomenology, a philosophy of being and experience that he integrates with the realism of St. Thomas Aquinas. In phenomenology, one reflects deeply, persistently, on the acting person both as he or she really is, and on how the person thinks, reflects, reacts, and responds.

However, there is a scriptural foundation for the pope's reflections, because he is guided by Divine Revelation. Therefore, following Christ in the Gospels, he goes back to "the beginning," to the book of Genesis and the two creation stories, to find the principles of marriage, and the capacity of the body and human sexuality in terms of the "nuptial meaning of the body." Understanding who we are can be derived from God's plan for man and woman, persons created in the image and likeness of God in their bodily reality. This doctrine of creation in the divine image is always a source of Christian Personalism in theology and bioethics. That return to Genesis, to "the beginning," led John Paul II to present the human person in terms of a theology of the body. These themes are reflected in this book, the fruit of an Institute that joyfully bears his name and humbly seeks to carry out his mission.

chapter 2

The Culture Wars: Saint John Paul II—
Pope of the Civilization of Love[1]

TRACEY ROWLAND

INTRODUCTION

THE INTERNATIONAL JOHN PAUL II Institute, which has its center at the Pontifical Lateran University in Rome and some eight extra-urban sessions around the world, was personally founded by the late pontiff. He was on his way to formally open the Institute on the 13th of May in 1981 when the Turkish terrorist Mehmet Ali Ağca attempted to assassinate him. Since that time the Institute has operated under the patronage of Our Lady of Fatima whose Feast is the 13th of May.

The idea of an Institute for Marriage and Family Studies arose as a result of the young Bishop Karol Wojtyła's pastoral experiences in Kraków during the Communist era. When people are oppressed, and there is not enough food and medicine and housing, and when bureaucrats are running the country in their own self-interest, there is so much tension being exerted from outside the family that couples need to be heroic to

1. This paper is a redaction of two addresses. One was delivered at the Pontifical Lateran University in Rome, published in Italian as "Una Fragile Icona: L'Amore Tra Uoma e Donna," in *Il logos dell' agape: Amore e ragione come principi dell'agire*, a cura di Juan José Pérez-Soba e Luis Granados (Rome: Cantagalli, 2008). The other was delivered at KUL (Katolicki Uniwersytet Lubelski) in Poland and published in Polish.

merely survive. Cardinal Wojtyła understood that alcoholism and domestic violence are usually symptoms of other underlying problems, and thus it was futile to simply remind married couples of their duties and to deliver homilies against bad behavior. If the family was to survive and indeed flourish as a social organism it needed infrastructural support. The Church's pastors needed to understand the pressure being exerted by the culture in which people worked and lived.

Cardinal Wojtyła also understood that the Church needed to develop a theology of marriage that went beyond the formulae of the neoscholastic marriage manuals which were widely used before the Second Vatican Council. He wanted to inject some of the insights from personalist philosophy into the Church's teaching in this area. In other words, he wanted to draw into the Church's theology of marriage ideas that are now presented to the world under the label of "Lublin Thomism."

Lublin Thomism was a development of the Thomist tradition with reference to themes in early twentieth-century existentialist philosophy which so appealed to the generations who experienced the First and Second World Wars and the Depression of the 1930s. For these generations it was important to offer an account of the human person that affirmed the reality of human freedom against the various deterministic ideologies that were powerful at that time—above all, the Marxist, Fascist, and Freudian varieties.

CARDINAL WOJTYŁA AND *HUMANAE VITAE*

One of the fundamental insights of St. Thomas Aquinas that was taken up by Karol Wojtyła in his work *The Acting Person* (first published in 1969) is that action is the self-revelation of being. Applying this to his defense of *Humanae vitae*, Pope Paul VI's encyclical on human life, which famously upheld the Church's centuries-long teaching against contraception, the young Karol Wojtyła spoke of love as a gift of the self, of spousal love as the paradigmatic gift of the self, and of the Trinity as the archetype of such a gift.

In a paper presented on the 11th of April in 1969 to celebrate the fiftieth anniversary of the establishment of the Catholic University of Lublin, Cardinal Wojtyła was critical of the way in which various persons had sought to defend *Humanae vitae* by reference to notions of natural law which were in no way consistent with the ecclesial understanding of natural law. He emphasized that in the ecclesial understanding, natural law is the "participation of the eternal law in a rational creature," not "merely the biological regularity we find in people in the area of sexual actualization."[2] In the twentieth century there was quite a bit of confusion about precisely what the Catholic understanding of natural law is. In some countries the idiom of natural law was adopted by Catholic elites as a way of making arguments to defend the moral teaching of the Church without any reference to God. Russell Hittinger has described this practice as a presentation of natural law for "Cartesian minds somehow under Church discipline."[3] Cardinal Wojtyła, however, was clear that natural law made no sense outside of an order of nature created by God. In his speech delivered at Katolicki Uniwersytet Lubelski, Wojtyła emphasized that

> the affinity between the person and natural law is possible only if we accept a certain metaphysics of the human person, which also entails a certain subordination of the human person in relation to God, a subordination that is, after all, very honorable. On the other hand, if we do not accept such a view of the human being, then a conflict is unavoidable, and this is a real conflict.[4]

A similar point was made by Ernest Fortin when he argued that "natural law becomes intelligible only within the framework of a providential order in which the words and deeds of individual human beings are known to God and duly rewarded and punished by Him."[5]

A year earlier at a theological conference in Kraków, Cardinal Wojtyła had drawn attention to paragraph 8 of *Humanae vitae*. It holds that conjugal love most fully reveals its true nature and dignity when we consider that it takes its origin from God, who "is love" and the Father from whom all fatherhood in heaven and on earth gets its name. As a consequence in paragraph 13 one finds the statement that "to make use of the gift of conjugal love while respecting the laws of the transmission of life is to acknowledge that one is not the master of the sources of life, but rather a servant of the plan established by the Creator." The Creator's plan is, of course, a plan of love in which we are created in the image and likeness of God, loved by him, and designed to love God and neighbor.

At a conference to mark the beatification of John Paul II, Cardinal Carlo Caffarra observed that God understood as the master of life is one

---

2. Wojtyła, "Human Person and the Natural Law," 183.
3. Hittinger, *First Grace*, 21.
4. Wojtyła, "Human Person and the Natural Law," 185.
5. Fortin, *Classical Christianity and Political Order*, 213.

of the principles that the opponents of *Humanae vitae* find so difficult to accept. The so-called modern mind finds it difficult to believe that the Creator is actually involved in each and every human conception. The difficulty is occasioned by the loss of a sacramental view of reality, which is itself the consequence of centuries of secularizing moves on the chessboard of the European intelligentsia, dating all the way back to the rise of nominalism in the fourteenth century. The history of these moves has been well documented in the works of Louis Dupré, Hans Boersma, and Jean Borella, among others. The end result is an eclipse of a sacramental ontology. The reality of having been created and existing in a filial relationship with a Creator is something that many people no longer see. Their metaphysical horizons have been lowered by their immersion in an intensely materialistic culture that is toxic to a sacramental imagination.

In a speech delivered to the scholars of Katolicki Uniwersytet Lubelski in 1987, St. John Paul II described the spiritual problematic in the following terms:

> The human person must in the name of the truth about himself stave off a double temptation: the temptation to make the truth about himself subordinate to his freedom and the temptation to subordinate himself to the world of objects; he has to refuse to succumb to the temptation of both self-idolatry and of self-subjectification: *Positus est in medio homo: nec bestia—nec deus.*[6]

A popular novel at the end of the Communist era was Milan Kundera's *The Unbearable Lightness of Being*. It was in part a reflection on sex and love in a materialist universe. In contrast to Kundera's lightness of being in late Communist Prague, in the plays and poetry of Cardinal Wojtyła there is a sense of the very heaviness of being which is a consequence of his understanding of life as a theo-drama. In Wojtyła's works the human person is faced with a choice between God and various idols, the purveyors of a fake freedom. These idols lure people into traps with the promise of an effortless freedom free of any spiritual demands. They encourage practices that are simultaneously self-idolatrous and self-destroying. These traps turn lives that were destined for sanctification and intimacy with God into narrative wrecks. The high cost of freedom, coupled with the notion that it is precisely this high cost that makes life exhilarating, is a theme pervading almost everything Wojtyła wrote.

---

6. John Paul II, "Address to the Scholars of Lublin University," 51.

NUPTIAL MYSTICISM

As pope, Karol Wojtyła followed through the logic of his earlier essays in the defense of *Humanae vitae* with his *Catechesis on Human Love*[7] based on the two accounts of creation in Genesis and on the theological anthropology of paragraph 22 of the conciliar document *Gaudium et spes*. According to this paragraph it is only in the mystery of the Incarnation of Christ, the Second Person of the Trinity, that the mystery of the human person is made manifest. This was the most frequently cited paragraph from the documents of the Second Vatican Council in the homilies of John Paul II. One might say that it was *the* emblematic text of the whole pontificate. Its theology was echoed in the very first lines of *Redemptor hominis*, the very first encyclical of the pontificate: "Jesus Christ, the Redeemer of Man, is the center and purpose of human history."

Significantly, the account of the *imago Dei* offered in this paragraph was explicitly Trinitarian, not merely "theistically colored." One of the criticisms of the first part of *Gaudium et spes* was that it sought to offer an analysis of "the world" apart from any explicit sense that the analysis had to be carried out in the light of Christ, rather than simply according to a generalized, natural religious perspective. With paragraph 22, something different emerges: it is only in the mystery of the Word incarnate that light is shed on the mystery of humankind. Cardinal Walter Kasper, among others, has argued that it makes an enormous difference to one's interpretation of *Gaudium et spes* whether one emphasizes the first section of this document which is merely "theistically colored" or whether one gives priority to the explicitly Trinitarian anthropology of paragraph 22. Every student of the theology of John Paul II has this particular paragraph etched in their memory as the hermeneutical key to *Gaudium et spes* and indeed to his entire pontificate.

Therefore in John Paul II's *Catechesis on Human Love*, delivered as a series of Wednesday audience addresses in the early years of his pontificate, anthropology was linked to Trinitarian theology, and sexuality was situated within this framework of God's offer of divine filiation. Within this *katological* framework (working downwards from the Trinity to the person), the married couple is raised to the exalted position of being a "radiant icon of Trinitarian love" and the seal of their marital holiness is viewed as nothing less than a "supernatural work of art." To quote Cardinal Marc Ouellet, who is a former Professor of the John Paul II Institute

---

7. Now known popularly as the "Theology of the Body."

at the Lateran University, "The hour of conjugal and family spirituality is therefore the hour of the transcendence of the self into the image of the Trinity, the hour of becoming a house of God, a home of the Most High, an icon of the Trinity, memory and prophecy of the wonders of salvation history."[8]

In his book *Divine Likeness: Toward a Trinitarian Anthropology of the Family*, Cardinal Ouellet explains that this means that the sacramental mission of the couple and their family is not an additional *ad libitum* for those who have time to help out in the parish or diocesan organization. It is not primarily a job or list of social responsibilities. Rather, more fundamentally, the mission is inscribed in the very being of the couple as a *communio personarum* sealed by the Holy Spirit. As a consequence,

> The doctrine of the *Imago Dei* should be reconsidered in a radically Trinitarian perspective. . . . The gifts of creation, the gift of life, the gift of *fides* and of the sacrament signify, in the final analysis, the gifts of the Father to the Son and of the Son to the Father in the Holy Spirit. Created gifts express and signify the uncreated love between the divine persons. Thus human love in its beauty and fragility allows us to see, like a living icon, the Glory within God. The Holy Spirit prolongs in marriage what he does in the relationship of Christ and the Church; he makes of it the nuptial incarnation of the "Nuptial Mystery" par excellence.[9]

Cardinal Ouellet also notes that this perspective is "not simply intended to overcome a certain classical formulation that overlooked the particular gift the divine Persons make to the couple."[10] Rather, "its aim is to understand the sacrament of marriage and therefore the exchange of love between man and woman within the horizon of the *imago Dei*, as the couple's participation in the exchange of 'gifts' between the divine Persons." Thus he concludes, "Assumed within the kenotic-paschal drama of Trinitarian Love, conjugal love is therefore inserted into the missionary dynamism of the Church, sacrament of salvation. Natural *eros* and the personal love of the spouses, blessed by God the Creator and sanctified by Christ the Redeemer, belong to the sacramental order of the Incarnation."[11]

---

8. Ouellet, *Divine Likeness*, 100.
9. Ibid., 234.
10. Ibid., 80.
11. Ibid., 171.

In treating sexuality in this context John Paul II brought to an end the reign of neo-scholastic marriage manuals with their emphasis on rights and duties, and in their place he forged a new theological path in the Catholic understanding of the meaning and purpose of human sexuality. This path or approach is now described by theologians as "nuptial mysticism." It is all a million miles from the idea that marriage is a mere remedy for concupiscence and the many unhelpful ideas that entered into the mainstream of Catholic attitudes toward sexuality via the Jansenist heresy. While Poland may have been spared this heresy, it did an enormous amount of damage in countries where it spread, including countries of the New World. One might say that the papacy of John Paul II not only destroyed European Communism but also struck a death blow to the lingering influence of Jansenism on the Church's teaching in the area of sexuality.

The most extensive account of this theological development can be found in the book *The Nuptial Mystery* (2005) by Cardinal Angelo Scola. It has been published in both Italian and English. Cardinal Scola was for a time the International President of the network of John Paul II Institutes for Marriage and Family Studies before his appointment as the Patriarch of Venice, and now the Cardinal Archbishop of Milan.

In *The Nuptial Mystery* Cardinal Scola explains that the term "nuptial" highlights the relational character of love, and he argues that nuptiality is a fundamental human experience intertwining three factors: (1) sexual difference, (2) love in its proper sense as a gift to another, and (3) fruitfulness.[12] He also acknowledges that as a consequence of the possibilities revealed by science and technology it is now a common practice to separate these three factors from each other. In the 1960s it became fashionable to separate sexual intimacy from love, and then in the 1980s it became a common practice to separate procreation from sexual intimacy.

The general social orientation is toward a kind of mechanization of human relationships and the reduction of the human person to the status of a machine. As Cardinal Ouellet has observed,

> The *homo technicus* that Goethe already proclaimed two centuries ago seems to have taken the place of the *homo sapiens* of Christianized Greco-Roman civilization. He is in the process of reinventing himself and re-creating himself without God, dismissing the fundamental givens of human reproduction. This *homunculus* which has emerged from Faust's laboratory no

12. Scola, *Nuptial Mystery*, xxiv.

longer wishes to love on the basis of the gift that has been made to him and that he receives; instead, he wishes to reproduce himself in an autonomous and narcissistic fashion.[13]

THE MARRIED COUPLE AS A "FRAGILE ICON OF THE TRINITY"

In his *Explorations in Metaphysics*, the late William Norris Clarke SJ described the metaphysical link between anthropology and Trinitarian theology in the following words:

> If every being turns out to include a natural dynamism toward self-communication through action [as Wojtyła argued], we can say truly, in more than a metaphorical sense, that every being is naturally a self-symbolizer, an icon or image-maker, in some analogous way like an artist, expressing itself symbolically, whether consciously or unconsciously. . . . [This] self-symbolizing tendency in all finite beings we know turns out to be an imperfect participation or imitation of the inner being of God himself, revealed to be supremely and perfectly self-symbolizing in its eternal interior procession of the Son from the Father and the Holy Spirit from both.[14]

However, Norris Clarke also observed that there is a significant difference between humans and creatures lower in the order of creation in that those below are limited to an endlessly repetitive self-imaging according to the already determined nature, whereas humans have the freedom to make images not only of themselves but of the whole universe in relation to them in endlessly creative new perspectives and angles of insight.[15] It is for this reason that one can speak of the "fragility" of human love as an icon for the relations of truth and love at work within the Trinity. Unlike God's other creatures, the human couple is free to write the icon in the image of the Trinity which their love urges, but this is not compelled. The iconic mission of the Christian family is therefore far from an automatic side effect of entering into a marriage. Just as in the Eastern Orthodox tradition one finds that there is a particular spirituality associated with the work of painting an icon, for the love between man and woman to

---

13. Ouellet, "Theological Perspectives on Marriage," 419–20.
14. Clarke, *Explorations in Metaphysics*, 52.
15. Ibid.

be iconic of Trinitarian relations, there needs to be a spiritualty or praxis, based on what John Paul II and Benedict XVI call "relations of truth and love." This means in turn that there needs to be an understanding of the dynamics of the relationship between intellectual judgment and affectivity.

BEYOND MORALISM: REUNITING THE AFFECTIVE AND COGNITIVE DIMENSIONS

In order for Catholic morality to move beyond mere moralism or "duty parade behavior" there needs to be an integration of the affective and cognitive dimensions of the human person. In his *Journey of the Mind to God*, St. Bonaventure wrote of the faculties of the soul (the memory, understanding, and will) being consubstantial, coequal, and coeval and interpenetrating one another in a mode analogous to the relations within the Trinitarian processions. The notion of relations of truth and love being central to the spirituality of the married couple and of all faculties of the soul working together in unison are key concerns of contemporary theological anthropology. In particular there is a concern among theologians that not only has there been a severance of the *circumincessive* relations identified in the previous quotation by St. Bonaventure, such that the individual faculties are no longer working together in the pursuit of truth, beauty, and goodness, but the understanding of the operation of each faculty of the soul has become truncated. In the popular, non-theological imagination, the intellect has steadily been reduced to a faculty of instrumental reason, the memory has been reduced to little more than a databank severed from any association with tradition and sapiential experience, and the will has become a faculty of choice severed from any association with beauty, truth, and goodness. For many philosophers the will has been reduced to mere brute instinct or some kind of Nietzschean "drive."

SMUGGLING STOIC AND PELAGIAN COSMOLOGY INTO CHRISTIAN THOUGHT

Following Etienne Gilson, among others, Michael Hanby, a professor of the John Paul II Institute in Washington DC, has argued that the modern notion of the will is a Pelagian fiction. For Augustine, acts of the will always entailed the work of memory and intellect, and while delight/desire is integral to the intelligibility of our actions, "choice" is not. The contemporary emphasis upon the so-called autonomy of the individual's will as the basis of human dignity, and the related notion of rationality as thought severed from all affective sensibilities, cannot be traced back to Augustine but has a much more recent pedigree. According to Hanby the modern detachment of the two sources of human motivation from one another (truth and love) represents the undoing of the unity of knowledge and love in creatures created in the image of the Trinity. It represents nothing less than a rupture in the Trinitarian economy, creating possibilities for human nature "outside" the Trinity and the mediation of Christ. Hanby further demonstrates how this was due largely to an account of volition that the Pelagians imported from Stoicism. For this reason he defines the Pelagian tendency as "philosophizing without a mediator" and an attempt to smuggle Stoic cosmology into Western Christian thought. He summarizes the alternative Stoic and Christian accounts of the will in the following manner:

> In the one [the Christian], *voluntas* is the site of our erotic participation in an anterior gift, and it is at once self-moved and moved by the beauty of that gift. Here will, whether human or divine, is constituted in a relation of love for the beloved and its freedom is established as dispossession. In the other [the Stoic], will names an inviolable power and freedom consists in demonstrating this inviolability, through the double negation both of itself and of created beauty.[16]

Hanby concludes that at issue within contemporary Western culture is the Trinity itself and specifically whether the meaning of human nature and of human agency is understood to occur within Christ's mediation of the love and delight shared as *donum* between the Father and the Son, or beyond it. For John Paul II there could be no true understanding of human nature or human agency outside of an understanding of the Trinity and the ways in which the various Persons of the Trinity relate to the human person. The foundations for this work were set out in his Trinitarian encyclicals *Redemptor hominis*, which dealt with the human relationship to Christ; *Dives in misericordia*, which covered the human relationship to God the Father; and *Dominum et vivificantem*, which offered a study of the human relationship to the Holy Spirit. The alternative idea, that it is

---

16. Hanby, *Augustine and Modernity*, 135.

possible "to construct a rational picture of the human person, intelligible to all, upon which all persons of good will might agree, and to which could be added the Christian doctrines as a kind of crowning conclusion" was described by Professor Ratzinger, as he was in 1969, as a "fiction."[17] Both pontiffs, John Paul II and Benedict XVI, read the documents of the Second Vatican Council, and especially *Gaudium et spes*, with a strong christocentric accent. Applying this theological anthropology to the territory of moral theology, Monsignor Livio Melina, the current international President of the John Paul II Institutes for Marriage and Family, has drawn the conclusion (*pace* the philosopher Immanuel Kant) that Christian virtuous practices do not obey a self-sufficient moral ideal but proceed from a spiritual transformation of judgment: "Practical reason is not to be understood as a mere application of speculative knowledge, but as a specific mode of knowing the good, which arises from within the dynamism in which the subject is attracted to the good."[18]

Contemporary moral theology, working in the tradition of John Paul II, is therefore interested in a retrieval of a pre-Cartesian account of the will situated within an explicitly Trinitarian account of the *imago Dei*, a retrieval of a pre-Kantian account of the intellect as a faculty receptive to divine illumination and transformation, and a retrieval of the premodern (especially Augustinian and Albertine) understanding of the faculty of the memory as a site of divine tuition. Central to all these projects is an interest in the interaction of the human person with the three Persons of the Trinity.

As a logical consequence the contemporary defense of *Humanae vitae* is situated within the framework of this explicitly Trinitarian theological anthropology and the contemporary focus is on the spiritual dispositions that foster receptivity to the nuptial mystery theology. Approaching the issue from another angle, there is an interest in the way in which neo-Stoic and neo-Pelagian attitudes work against the spirituality of *Humanae vitae* and other magisterial teachings in the area of sexual morality.

---

17. Ratzinger, "Dignity of the Human Person," 120.
18. Melina, "Christ and the Dynamism of Action," 131.

THE FEAR OF THE GIFT

In this context Cardinal Ouellet has described original sin as "a refusal of the gift of divine filiation in a futile preference for divinity itself." In the language of John Paul II, original sin is the consequence of the temptation to self-idolatry. In his exegesis of the book of Genesis, Hans Urs von Balthasar described the essence of the temptation as a desire for knowledge without love. Similarly, with illustrations drawn from Shakespeare's *The Winter's Tale*, John Milbank has suggested that the cause of the fall was a "mistrusting of the joyfully confident 'risk'" in the Providence of God, a disposition of fear or mistrust toward one's Creator, rather than a recognition of the Creator as the source of all potential and gift.[19] In other words there is a general scholarly agreement that the temptation to Stoic/Pelagian self-reliance goes all the way back to the garden of Eden.

Arguably it is a kind of neo-Stoicism that is at the root of much that is wrong with contemporary practices in the mission of the family. For example, couples do not normally opt for mere cohabitation because they regard fidelity as something undesirable. Fidelity is still regarded as a good, but people are fearful of commitment because they are fearful of being betrayed, or fearful that they might one day have such a different range of interests that they will no longer be in harmony with their partner. A common variation on this is a fear that their partner's chosen professional interests may not always dovetail with or otherwise complement their own. Many have no idea of the sacramental dimensions of marriage and their iconic significance. Their view of marriage may be contractual, in which case they may live in fear of being the victim of an unfair deal, of having to pay too much and getting a low return. Cohabitation might therefore be a social experiment to see if the risk is worth taking, while contraception is often fostered by a real and not unreasonable fear of poverty. On the other hand, some couples may reject marriage because it is perceived as a public event and they see their relationship as an essentially private relationship, sacred unto themselves, because they lack a sacramental idea of marriage and do not see their relationship as a vocation to participate in Divine love. The motives for the privatization of *de facto* relationships may be complex and the partners might not even share the same reasons why, or even agree on not marrying. The need for marriage may also be seen by a partner as a matter of the other partner wishing to be possessive or dominant, a kind of entrapment. In

---

19. Milbank, *Being Reconciled*, 150.

many ways the privatization of marriage reflects the disunity of the fall, disunity between the partners, and also between themselves and God.

MODMAN NIHILIST AND MODMAN PHILISTINE

The contemporary Catholic family, faithful to the magisterial teaching and struggling to survive within a culture whose fundamental dynamism is rooted in *laissez-faire* economics, is not only an icon of the Trinity but an outpost of Christian civilization. This is well illustrated by Alexander Boot in his *How the West Was Lost*.[20] Boot traces the emergence of modern man, whom he calls "Modman," to the Reformation with its anti-hierarchical forces and contrasts "Modman" with the Catholic "Westman." According to Boot, Modman, an evolutionary development from Reformation man, today comes in two species: "Modman Philistine" and "Modman Nihilist." The central message of Boot's book is that the only resistance to philistinism and nihilism within contemporary Western culture is coming from the Catholic Church and those of her intellectuals who understand that the main weapon of Modman is the "slow imposition of philistine values on society," accompanied by a gradual imposition of political and economic power that can force Westman into compliance. Included within the strategy is the replacement of the historic role of the father by the state bureaucracy and the eventual abolition of the family itself. Significantly, Boot argues that the philistine and the nihilist exist in a symbiotic relationship. The nihilist operates at the level of the cultural, especially intellectual, elite, the philistine at the level of the less well educated. Together they create a kind of anti-culture in which there are no standards, no gradations of excellence in any sphere of human activity outside of economic performance. Even sexual intimacy has become democratized.

The pastoral conclusion to be drawn from Boot's largely sociological analysis is that Church leaders need to put as much effort into resisting philistinism as they do into engaging with explicitly, militantly secularist intellectuals. Catholic youth need access to a high Catholic culture that is sufficiently attractive to compete with the philistine alternatives.

At the root of the philistine outlook is a rejection of the proposition that some modes of being and self-expression, especially artistic self-expression, are actually superior to others. In some Western countries

20. Boot, *How the West Was Lost*.

where liberation theology has been popular, those who seek to promote a high Catholic culture or what Benedict XVI calls "the humanism of the Incarnation" are often criticized for their bourgeois attitudes. Their defense of beauty in the cultural realm is construed by the liberation theologians and those who have imbibed their basic attitudes as a symptom of having received an upper-class education. From the point of view of John Paul II or Benedict XVI, however, beauty is a transcendental property of being, and it deserves to be defended no less than truth and goodness. For a reflection on the importance of beauty in the thought of John Paul II one can refer to his essay on "The Constitution of Culture through Human Praxis"[21] and to his *Letter to Artists*. In his essay on culture he quoted extensively from the Polish poet Cyprian Norwid's reflections on the significance of beauty and concluded that not only is culture constituted through praxis, but human praxis in its authentically human character is also constituted through culture.[22] In this paper, which was delivered at the Sacred Heart University in Milan in 1977, one year before his election to the papacy, Cardinal Wojtyła referenced a point made by M. J. M Domenach, who said that "the ultimate danger of the new European culture is that a culture without clear values and well-defined forms can very easily become a consumer good."[23] This, in a nutshell, is the problem with Modman Philistine. His philistine culture has been disconnected from beauty, truth, and goodness and this anti-culture has become a consumer good. Parallel criticisms of contemporary consumer "junk culture" can also be found in the works of many non-Catholic authors, including the British writers Theodore Dalrymple and Roger Scruton.

Scruton is well known for his heroism in the 1980s in helping Czech anti-Communist intellectuals get their work published in English. In 1985, the Czech government put him on the official list of "Undesirable Persons." He was later honored in the post-Communist period by the award of the Czech Republic's Medal of Merit. His most significant works include *An Intelligent Person's Guide to Culture* (1998) and *Culture Counts: Faith and Feeling in a World Besieged* (2007). In 2010 he delivered the prestigious Scottish Gifford Lectures on the topic "The Face of God."

Theodore Dalrymple is the pen name of Anthony Daniels, a British writer and psychiatrist who claims to be an atheist but who is critical of

---

21. Wojtyła, "The Problem of the Constitution of Culture."

22. Ibid., 269.

23. Quoted in ibid., 274 n. 15. The source of the quotation is given there as M. J. M. Domenach, "Sytuacja kultury europejskiej," *Ateneum Kaplanskie* 69 (1976) 286.

anti-theism. He is the author of *The New Vichy Syndrome: Why European Intellectuals Surrender to Barbarism* (2010). In that work he argues that many intellectuals have contempt for their past history and believe in nothing but personal economic security, an increased standard of living, shorter working hours, and a long vacation in exotic locations. Both Scruton and Dalrymple believe that philistinism in one form or another is a serious problem for Western civilization.

CULTURE AS ESCHATOLOGY SITUATED

A more deeply theological analysis of the problem of anti-culture can be found in paragraph 56 of John Paul II's third Trinitarian encyclical, *Dominum et vivificantem*. Here John Paul II observed that the resistance to the Holy Spirit which St. Paul emphasizes in the interior and subjective dimension as tension, struggle, and rebellion taking place in the human heart finds in every period of history, and especially in the modern era, its external dimension, which takes concrete form as the content of culture and civilization, as a philosophical system, an ideology, a program for action and for shaping human behavior. Thus while cultures have the potential to be epiphanies of God's glory, the philosophical and theological principles that give cultures form can make them inept or even hostile to any attempt of the Church to mediate the grace of the Incarnation to the world.

An International Theological Commission document drafted when Cardinal Ratzinger was the ITC chairman expressed the idea in the following way:

> In the last times inaugurated at Pentecost, the risen Christ, Alpha and Omega, enters into the history of peoples: from that moment, the sense of history and thus of culture is unsealed and the Holy Spirit reveals it by actualising and communicating it to all. The Church is the sacrament of this revelation and its communication. It recenters every culture into which Christ is received, placing it in the axis of the "world which is coming," and restores the union broken by the "Prince of this world." Culture is thus eschatologically situated; it tends towards its completion in Christ, but it cannot be saved except by associating itself with the repudiation of evil.[24]

---

24. International Theological Commission, "Faith and Inculturation," ch. 2, no. 28.

John Paul II described the two alternative cultures, based on the two alternative axes—that is, the axis of the Risen Christ and the axis of the Prince of this world—as a civilization of love and a culture of death. The culture of death is one whose foundational principles resist being centered on Christ and the world that is to come. Its characteristic features are that it treats human life as a commodity or mere biological product; it acknowledges no absolute truth, goodness, or beauty, and in the absence of such absolutes, power becomes the only legitimate political currency.

Proponents of these principles that undergird the culture of death usually agree with Friedrich Nietzsche that Christianity is a crime against life itself. They regard Christianity as a religion built upon the resentment of the weak, who nurture their resentment by fettering the freedoms, especially the sexual freedom, of the strong and talented. In his *Genealogy of Morals*, written in the late 1880s, Nietzsche argued that blindness to the fact that the foundations of Christian morality lie in the resentments of the weak and uncompetitive is the crime *par excellence*, the crime against life itself. According to Nietzsche Christian morality has nothing to do with human dignity or integrity but everything to do with the destruction of *eros* by weak and unattractive people who resent the virility and sexual allure of the strong.

THE GENERATION OF 1968

Some eight decades later the notion that Christian ethics are "a crime against life itself" was widely promoted by the intellectual elite of the generation of 1968 in countries of the Western world outside of the Soviet bloc. The social influence of this elite has been of such a magnitude that French sociologists have coined the expression the *soixante-huitards* to refer to them. Many of the encyclicals of the pontificate of John Paul II, but particularly *Veritatis splendor* (1993) and *Evangelium vitae* (1995), offered critiques of the alternative moral frameworks of the generation of '68. These frameworks included "economism," the idea of subordinating all ethical decisions to the tribunal of economic growth and efficiency; "consequentialism," the denial that human actions have any inherent moral qualities aside from their possible consequences or secondary effects; "utilitarianism," the notion that the best moral actions are those that have the most favorable total or average outcome even though minorities may be much worse off; "proportionalism," an idea related to utilitarianism, but involving an acceptance of the intrinsic but premoral assessment of the evil of the object of an act provided that it is overcome by an assessment of the overall balance of good consequences which would thus mitigate the intrinsic evil; and "fundamental option," a view that trusted that divine grace and forgiveness renders the intrinsic evil of our actions trivial in our relationship to God and Divine love for us. The preferred cocktail of the generation of '68 thus included rather liberal dashings of Freud and Nietzsche (in the area of sexual morality) and either Adam Smith or Karl Marx (depending on political taste) in the field of economics.

The Church in the developed Western countries is now suffering a full-frontal assault from elites formed in the *soixante-huitard* mold. In the United States the Obama government is currently engaged in a political battle against the Church over the issue of "birth control insurance." The government wants Catholic organizations such as hospitals, schools, and universities to make a contribution toward the health insurance of employees which will include insurance to cover the cost of contraceptives. At the time of Obama's election, Cardinal James Stafford gave an address in Washington in which he said that, with the election of Obama, American Catholics had entered the Garden of Gethsemane. Recent political events in the United States and the United Kingdom have also led Cardinal Pell of Australia to argue that "modern liberalism has strong totalitarian tendencies." This is evident in medicine in relation to the loss in some jurisdictions of the legal and ethical right of a health professional to conscientiously object to cooperation in abortion, sterilization, or reproductive technology, and the developing ethical view that it is irresponsible for a woman at risk of having a child with an abnormality not to undergo the invasive tests that are done early enough to facilitate selective abortion, or not to have an abortion in the event of a positive result. As American theologian William T. Cavanaugh has argued, modern liberalism has a tendency to parody Christian soteriology by presenting the State as a savior, that is, as the solution to all human problems, which can be resolved by social engineering. Paradoxically, this kind of attitude is not unlike the mentality of the Communists. In both cases, political leaders use the power of the state machinery to implement social policies against the will of individual persons and in particular against Christian values.

Totalitarian ideologies were a lifelong problem for John Paul II. In his work *The Acting Person* he was especially critical of two attitudes toward action he believed fostered the success of totalitarian ideologies in the twentieth century. The first he described as servile conformism, the second as noninvolvement. He acknowledged that the term "conformism" denotes a tendency to comply with accepted social customs and that this in itself is often a good thing. There is no particular virtue in being a social misfit. Nonetheless, when this normal and healthy social tendency to "fit in" begins to sway toward servility, it becomes highly negative. The servile conformist "fails to accept his share in constructing the community and allows himself to be carried with and by the anonymous majority."[25]

Whereas servile conformists tend not to make judgments, those who take a stance of noninvolvement are fully conscious of the wrong that is being done. There is nothing lacking in their judgment; they simply do not want to take on responsibilities for the wider society in which they live. This may be seen in some forms of Christian fundamentalism which see no need to be involved in opposing the development of cultural evils, as long as their group can operate freely with its own values and culture as a kind of cultural ghetto. Thus, for instance, they would be unconcerned if marriage were legally redefined to include commitments between people of the same sex, as long as they could continue to recognize marriage as they understood it between a man and a woman. The noninvolvement problem is a defect of the will rather than the intellect. Much of what happened in the twentieth century could have been avoided if these two dispositions were not so widely held.

In poetic form John Paul II expressed the price of opposition to totalitarian ideologies in the following words:

> Freedom—a continuing conquest cannot simply be possessed!
> It comes as a gift, but keeping it is a struggle;
> Gift and struggle are inscribed on pages, hidden yet open.
> For freedom you pay with all your being, therefore call that your freedom
> Which allows you, in paying the price,
> To possess yourself anew.
> At such a price do we enter history and touch her epochs.
> Where is the dividing-line between those generations who paid too little
> And those who paid too much?
> On which side of that line are we?[26]

25. Wojtyła, *Acting Person*, 289.
26. Wojtyła, "Thinking My Country," 84.

CONCLUSION

Immanuel Kant famously wrote that the doctrine of the Trinity has no practical relevance.[27] Whether we believe that there are three persons or ten in the deity makes no difference to the conduct of human life. John Paul II, however, thought very differently. For him, all of creation was marked by the form of the Trinity, and the human person, as the crown of creation, was created for nothing less than eternal intimacy with this three-person Godhead. Within this theo-dramatic horizon even human sexual intimacy is potentially and ideally a participation in the creative love of the Trinity. The battle over *Humanae vitae* is therefore at the heart of the battle for a civilization of love. Once one accepts that sexual intimacy can be separated from love and procreation can be separated from sexual intimacy, one is on the road to the culture of death. This was an absolutely central teaching of the pope throughout his quarter-century pontificate and one that continues to be upheld by his successors.

Having spent so much of his life trying to draw people to Christ, whom he understood to be the revelation of God the Father to humanity, John Paul II's dying words were "let me go to the Father's house." To the many youth who loved him and who had traveled to Rome in their thousands to maintain a prayer vigil, he paternally said, "I have searched for you, and now you have come to me, and I thank you." He had reached out to the youth of the world over and against the opposition of the generation of '68 and many came to regard him as their moral compass. His battle for the civilization of love is now their battle, but he left them with his *Catechesis on Human Love* and the theology of the Nuptial Mystery as the foundation stones for what is potentially a new "humanism of the Incarnation."

---

27. Kant, *Conflict of the Faculties*, 65–67.

chapter 3

The *Theology of the Body* in Outline

ADAM G. COOPER

INTRODUCTION

This chapter provides a basic overview of Pope John Paul II's theology of human love in the divine plan, better known as his "theology of the body."[1] John Paul developed this lengthy theological work over the course of a five-year series of catechetical lectures given in Rome from September 1979 to November 1984. The lectures—around 130 altogether—were addressed to the large weekly gatherings of pilgrims assembled at the Vatican on Wednesdays for prayer, teaching, and the blessing of their universal pastor. From their initial delivery right through to their collated and published versions, the lectures captured worldwide attention. One commentator called them a "theological time bomb" waiting to go off.[2]

But making sense of them all is not easy. First, they comprise a massive work: the English edition is more than six hundred pages long! Second, the style is dense: John Paul coined many of his own terms and ideas

---

1. There have been numerous English editions. The best and most up to date is the translation by Michael Waldstein, based on a thorough critical evaluation of the original texts, titled *Man and Woman He Created Them: A Theology of the Body* (hereafter cited as TOB). References below will follow the catechesis and paragraph numbers of Waldstein's text.

2. Weigel, *Witness to Hope*, 343.

and expresses them in a style that demands patient and attentive study. Third, it is wide-ranging, covering almost the whole of the Scriptures and drawing freely on insights from experience, philosophy, Church teaching, and the human sciences. Fourth, despite John Paul's insistence on their limited scope and his speculative and sometimes even hesitant tone, the catecheses enunciate "with extraordinary fullness" what Orthodox theologian David B. Hart described as "a complete vision of the spiritual and corporeal life of the human being."[3] Which means that the often well-meaning attempts to popularize the theology of the body and make it more accessible easily end up misrepresenting the teaching or reducing it to a quirky Catholic obsession with the body and sex.

With all this in mind, the Institute has made it one of its central concerns to teach the theology of the body by directly engaging with the text of the catecheses and by interpreting them within the wider context of Catholic theological anthropology. Their central message can be summed up by saying that the human body, precisely in its sexual differentiation, speaks a language that originates not in itself, nor just in evolution and culture, but in God. This is what John Paul means by one of his central phrases: "the spousal meaning of the body." Our maleness and femaleness signal a divinely inscribed intention which has meaning not only for morality but for our ultimate identity as persons called to deifying communion with the Trinity. The basis for this vision lies of course in God's becoming a flesh-and-blood human being, by which "the body entered theology . . . through the main door."[4] But its outline was already heralded in God's original words and deeds in creating man and woman in his image, word-acts that Jesus refers to as "the beginning" (Matt 19:3–8). Taking this "beginning" as its launching pad, the theology of the body unfolds as a mainly biblical study illuminating the role of human love, the body, and sexuality in the divine plan. For many students who have only encountered more popular versions of the teaching, this approach serves to open up new horizons as they discover its profound subtlety and range of applicability. They come to appreciate its deep roots in the history of salvation and Christian tradition, its convergence with human experience, the way it overtly appropriates the redemptive action of Jesus Christ and invokes the efficacy of the sanctifying power of his Holy Spirit.

3. Hart, "The Anti-Theology of the Body."
4. TOB 23:4.

THE OCCASION FOR A THEOLOGY OF THE BODY

The decision to embark upon a sustained study of marriage, sexuality, and bodily life was occasioned by numerous factors, not least of all the pope's own personal penchant for the subject. Interestingly, the entire text of the catecheses was written while he was archbishop of Kraków, before his election to the papacy. Right from his early days as a graduate student in philosophy, particularly of the phenomenological school, Karol Wojtyła exhibited the marked influence of what has been called the "corporeal turn" in philosophy, with its renewed interest in the physical and concrete.[5] At the same time, Wojtyła was critical of certain Kantian elements in philosophy, especially its individualistic and dualistic accents according to which the body and our affective inclinations, especially toward pleasure, are regarded as an obstacle to moral fulfillment. His early work *Love and Responsibility* (1960) represents a fundamental affirmation of the way our being persons in relation depends on our somatic and emotional dynamisms and their transforming integration within interpersonal projects marked by responsible, self-giving love. To be human is to have and to be a body. If we want to address questions about human morality, what it means to be a person, what it means to be a man or woman, a son or daughter, a father or mother, how to order our lives and behavior, how to love and be loved, then we must attend to the body in its sexed duality.

But duality is not dualism. In the catecheses John Paul points out that ever since New Testament times the truth and power of Christian revelation concerning the person have been threatened by dualistic heresies (such as Gnosticism and Manichaeism) which suspiciously regard matter, the body, and especially sexuality as a principle of evil. This kind of dualism is alive and well today not only in religion but also in secular contexts. "Cartesianism" refers to the modern philosophical view that identifies the person with mind or consciousness or intention and relegates the body to a kind of purely physical entity, an impersonal or biological machine. The effect of these dualisms becomes all the more insidious when coupled with biological reductionism, a fruit of radical Darwinian evolutionism mixed with scientific empiricism and Marxist materialism. Something similar is found in Freudian theory according to

---

5. See Schmitz, *At the Center of the Human Drama*; Kupczak, *Destined for Liberty*. Schmitz refers to Wojtyła's "new sense of the concrete" (140). On the ever-increasing use of the term "the corporeal turn," see Sheets-Johnstone, *The Corporeal Turn*.

which all human behavior is determined by subliminal drives: personal and social problems boil down to the frustration of sexual desire. All these "masters of suspicion," as John Paul characterizes them, in one way or another wrongly turn the experience of concupiscence or disordered desire "into the very nucleus of the hermeneutics of man."[6]

Another factor that occasioned the pope's theology of the body was the tidal wave of sexual insanity flooding our contemporary world, which began doing so at least from the 1960s, though probably before. It is no exaggeration to say that people today, like never before, are obsessed with sex and the body. One need only think, for example, of our primary popular cultural forms: music, media, movies. With few exceptions, they appear saturated with more or less explicit pornographic and exploitative themes. The problem with these themes, as John Paul would argue, does not lie in the fact that they are sexual: properly speaking, the ethical and erotic are positively related.[7] The problem lies rather in the perverse and abusive ways these media present sexuality. One may think also about the sports, fashion, and cosmetic industries and the way they feed and respond to our anxieties about the body, its health, its appearance. Like no other era in history, it seems, the sexualized body is being idolized as a god. But when you divinize sex, you destroy it; when you satiate desire, you strangle it. Western societies have reached the point where people habitually turn to technology and technique to try to create for themselves what in the end can only be received as a gift and cultivated through reverence: personal communion. With this confused culture in mind, the pope's teaching on sexuality and the body can be taken as an attempt to reveal that we are more than our sexuality, that our body, with all its anxieties, yearnings, and vulnerabilities, represents a physical-spiritual whole, a personal being created to reflect God's own beauty and to discover true joy in giving and receiving fruitful love.

John Paul's theology of the body catecheses were further occasioned by the need to explain the Church's moral teaching within a more christocentric and scriptural framework. While Christianity has always taught frankly on matters of marriage and sexuality, it has not always offered a winsome and positive rationale for its teaching. Wojtyła was Archbishop of Kraków in 1968 when Pope Paul VI published *Humanae vitae* (HV). Responding to the question whether it is legitimate deliberately to impede

---

6. TOB 46:1.

7. On the relation between *ethos* and *eros*, see TOB 47:1—48:5.

the conception of a child before, in, or after marital intercourse, HV declared such action immoral. Wojtyła had been on the commission that had helped guide Paul VI toward his decision and supported the teaching of HV unreservedly. Yet the encyclical precipitated a massive backlash within the Church, exposing a division of conviction that remains to this day. Reflecting on the reaction in the years following, Wojtyła realized that HV needed a more pastoral and convincing explanation, drawing more deeply on explicit scriptural foundations. The theology of the body catecheses thus grew out of John Paul's desire to explain the Church's moral teaching in HV by providing an in-depth biblical theology of sexuality, marriage, and the body that was Christ-centered, personalistic, realistic, and confirmed in human experience.

Finally, from his early experience as a priest, John Paul demonstrated a heart for the spiritual wellbeing of the young. Being closely involved in preparing many couples for marriage, he wanted to show how the traditional teaching of the Church on moral issues makes good sense, given the kind of bodily beings we are and the kinds of desires we have for pleasure, fulfillment, faithfulness, and love. Knowing how Catholic moral teaching had been experienced by many people as legalistic, burdensome, or simply irrational, he wanted to explore the ways it corresponds to the intrinsic truth of our physical and spiritual makeup. The human body has been created with a special purpose: "to transfer into the visible reality of the world the mystery hidden from eternity in God, and to be a sign of it."[8] John Paul was attentive to the fact that in the Gospels Jesus himself specifically addresses such topics as sexuality and morality and marriage, and does so with special reference to the Creator's original plan for men and women from the beginning. The disciples of Christ cannot but consider their Lord's teaching on these issues in humble faith. Being a Christian does not simply mean giving mental assent to certain ideas, but involves surrender to a calling or vocation in which we participate in Christ's active retrieval of the original dignity of the sexed human body. God's blueprint for the fulfilment of his image in us, the plan he had in mind in creating us, is a nuptial plan, a Christ-Church marriage plan. Our bodies reflect that blueprint.

---

8. TOB 19:4.

METHODOLOGY AND STRUCTURE

John Paul II's theology of the body is precisely a *theology* and not a physiology, psychology, philosophy, or even a phenomenology. Theology, at least according to the traditional meaning of the word, studies things first of all as they stand in relation to God. Theology tries to adopt God's perspective on things, to learn what God has to say about them. Of course, as a human activity, theology draws deeply upon the vast range of human experience and reason. It listens carefully to what can be known about things through other disciplines and avenues of inquiry. Ultimately, however, theology finds its authoritative basis and reference point in God's own word.

Thus it is no surprise to find that the theology of the body is basically a big Bible study. Moreover, it is a Bible study with a distinctly practical aim. According to John Paul II, the contents of the study present not just a theory, but rather an "evangelical, Christian pedagogy of the body." He goes on: "This pedagogic character comes from the character of the Bible and above all of the Gospel as a salvific message revealing *what man's true good is* for the sake of shaping—according to the measure of this good—his life on earth in the perspective of the hope of the future world."[9] The title of the revised translation, *Man and Woman He Created Them*, taken from the biblical account of creation in Genesis 1, serves as a kind of *leitmotif* for the whole study. What we read in the Genesis narrative not only echoes some of the deepest intuitions and anxieties of human experience, but manifests a gratuitous, divine trajectory.

The entire study constituted by the lectures proceeds by way of a careful, meditative reading of certain central biblical passages that deal with marriage, sexuality, and our bodily life. Although there is something of what we might recognize as a critical exegesis of the original texts, it is clear that the pope's exegetical method bears its own unique stamp. Not without scientific and historical rigor, it is at the same time contemplative and creative, moral and mystical, almost in keeping with more traditional modes of Christian engagement with Scripture. It is true, as the pope explicitly acknowledges, that a far-reaching biblical study on the theology of the body would have to touch on matters much wider than sexuality, such as human suffering and death. His focus, however, is inspired by the fact that the redemption of the body has been brought about by a covenantal act on God's part that is at once sacrificial and spousal in character.

---

9. TOB 122:5.

It is for a special sort of marriage that God first created humanity. It is by a special sort of marriage that God has redeemed it. This reveals what John Paul means when he refers to marriage as "a primordial sacrament." He doesn't just mean that marriage was the first of the seven sacraments. Rather, marriage provides the determining logic and structure for all the sacraments. It is paradigm of all the sacraments.

The first half of the study, in three sections, is structured around three "key words" of Jesus in Matthew's Gospel: his teaching on marriage and divorce with its reference to "the beginning" (19:3–9), his teaching on adultery of the heart (5:27–30), and his teaching on marriage in the resurrection (22:23–33). In these passages are indicated three eras or modes of bodily human experience: that of paradise, history, and the eschaton. The entire triptych, John Paul observes,

> contains in itself a rich content of an anthropological as well as ethical nature. Christ speaks to man—and speaks about man, who is a "body" and is created as male and female in the image and likeness of God; he speaks about man, whose heart is subjected to concupiscence; and, finally, about man, before whom the eschatological perspective of the resurrection of the body opens up.[10]

The second half, also in three sections, is based on passages drawn more widely from the New and Old Testaments, especially the letters of Paul, the prophets, Song of Songs, and the lesser-known book of Tobit. Its subject matter revolves closely around the vocation of marriage as mutual submission, especially as expounded in Eph 5:21–33, but not without qualifying its nature and goals in light of the prophetic vocation of celibacy for the sake of the kingdom. All along, John Paul draws in reflections from all over the Scriptures—not to mention the writings of the church fathers, the Church's sacramental practices (especially the rite of marriage), and insights from art, philosophy, and psychology. What emerges is a vision of marriage and conjugal intimacy as a liturgy, an act of worship, lived out bodily within the logic of gift, reverence, and thanksgiving. Of note is the fact that the study ends with a practical exposition of responsible parenthood, entailing a careful rereading of Pope Paul VI's controversial encyclical, *Humanae vitae*. Far from functioning as an appendix or postscript, this final section brings the rich insights of the theology of the body and conjugal spirituality to bear upon pressing

---

10. TOB 86:4.

critical questions. As John Paul acknowledges, the very sharpness of the reaction stirred up by *Humanae vitae* "confirms the importance and difficulty of these questions."[11]

KEY THEMES AND IDEAS

As already mentioned, John Paul II's catecheses contain numerous novel terms that encapsulate themes and concepts crucial to his pedagogical aims. In the next section I shall explain several key ideas which arise throughout the course of the lectures and to which John Paul makes repeated reference. The list is not exhaustive, but with a solid grasp of these themes the reader is well placed to take in the scope and vista of the entire teaching.

The Beginning

We have already referred to the way John Paul uses Jesus's reference to "the beginning" as a launching pad for analyzing the biblical theology of human creation. But the term "beginning" means much more than the beginning of the Bible or some distant, primeval period of human history. According to John Paul, the "beginning" is deeply present in all of us as a kind of principle (*principio*) of being. When Jesus refers his hearers back to the beginning, he is referring them to "the first inheritance of every human being in the world," "the first witness of human identity according to the word of God," "the first source of the certainty of our vocation as persons created in God's image." In other words, these "beginning" chapters of Genesis are not meant to be read like a scientific text or history book, chronologically far removed from us, but are to be engaged as a kind of power-packed dramatic script, composed by God, depicting the defining ontological structures and existential relationships that underlie human meaning in the universe. God's reported words and actions there express a foundation, a plan, a design, a vocation that remains perpetually applicable to all.

There is yet another meaning of the term "beginning." In the Scriptures, Christ calls himself "the Alpha and the Omega, the first and the last, the beginning and the end" (Rev 22:13). John says that "in the beginning was the Word" and that "through him all things were made" (John

---

11. TOB 133:2.

1:1, 3). Christ was there! He is furthermore the principle of the *new* creation, the new beginning: "If anyone is in Christ, there is a new creation" (2 Cor 5:17); "Behold, I am making all things new" (Rev 21:5). Christ's reference back to the beginning is therefore in some ways a self-reference, a reference to the hope made bodily present in him. What happened at the beginning is like a pattern pointing to its author, a shadow pointing to the reality. The shape of the beginning (the one-flesh union of man and woman) mysteriously signals in advance the shape of the end (the marriage of the Lamb and the Bride). The beginning is not just how things *were*, way back in a state of innocence now inaccessible. It also tells how things can and will be, by the power of Christ's redeeming grace, which is establishing a new creation.

Original Experiences

Envisaging the beginning in this way, John Paul proposes a range of primal or "original experiences" that characterize the state of original innocence. These experiences are elaborated by reflection upon the highly phenomenological rendering of the human situation in Genesis 2. From the statement "it is not good for the man to be alone" (Gen 2:18), John Paul elaborates the experience of "original solitude." From the statement "this is now bone of my bones and flesh of my flesh" (2:23), he elaborates the experience of "original unity." And from the statement "the man and his wife were both naked, and felt no shame" (2:25), he elaborates the experience of "original nakedness." These experiences function in the catecheses as analytical windows through which the distinctive features of our present existential situation become clear. Their meanings are complex and in many respects overlap. For instance, original solitude, as one commentator rightly notes, does not indicate "a mere deficit that is subsequently filled out by the creation of the woman." In fact, it extends into and underlies the interpersonal communion of the man-woman pair. Since it expresses our unique filial relation to the Creator and the "non-identification" of our humanity with the world of other nonhuman living beings, solitude is "an essential experience of the human being, both male and female" and thus "remains at the root of every other human experience . . ."[12] Similarly, original nakedness has nothing to do with any ideal way of life or relative state of undress but symbolizes the

---

12. Anderson and Granados, *Called to Love*, 27.

clarity with which God sees the body's goodness, the transparency of the body to the person and personal values. For man and woman to experience "original nakedness" is for them to see each other "with all the peace of the interior gaze," that is, to see each other more fully and clearly than through the physical sense of sight itself.[13]

These experiences of original innocence lie at the very boundary of our historic human experience, and so appear to stand somehow beyond our reach. Yet they depict the bodily human person in three fundamental relational dimensions which, despite our fallen situation, remain constitutive for our true self-understanding: the vertical, filial relation with God (solitude), the horizontal, spousal relation between man and woman (unity), and the interior relation with one's own heart in the presence of others (nakedness). There is something of these three "originals" that lingers on, like a vague memory, in the fundamental yearnings we experience as simultaneously bodily and spiritual beings. Reflecting a celebrated Augustinian and Thomistic perception, John Paul knows that we are creatures of desire, and that this desire is necessary to inspire passionate, intentional, deliberate action. We are made to love. All we need is for our loves to be—somehow—rightly oriented. By reflecting on these three original relations in the light of our true identity and calling made known in Christ, John Paul believes it is possible to discern the dynamic vocation God originally planned for us but from which human beings have subsequently become estranged by breaking trust with their covenant Father.

The Logic of the Gift

This notion of breaking trust leads to another key theme: "the logic of the gift." It is a common tendency for many Christians to approach moral problems with the logic of command and obligation, somewhat like the Pharisees who question Jesus about divorce (Matt 19:3). John Paul affirms that Jesus's answer concerning the indissolubility of marriage constitutes an abiding moral norm, and so in no way dispenses with the logic of command and obligation. However, following Christ's reference to the beginning, he is concerned to place this logic under a wider and more determinative logic: the logic of gift and thanksgiving.[14] Man before God

13. TOB 13:1.
14. TOB 17:1–6.

exists as a gift given to himself. His body, his life, his consciousness are all fruits of an infinite divine generosity that precedes and supports him. Something analogous obtains with man and woman before each other. The mystery of original innocence consists in accepting or welcoming the other, in his or her bodily otherness, as a divine gift, willed by the Creator not as a means to an end but as "someone unique and unrepeatable, someone chosen by eternal love."[15] The realization of interpersonal communion, by which the image of God becomes most manifest and tangible among us, depends upon this mutually enriching, thankful exchange of self-gift.[16] As John Paul writes, "While in the mystery of creation the woman is the one who is 'given' to the man, he on his part, in receiving her as a gift in the full truth of her person and femininity, enriches her by this very reception, and, at the same time, he too is enriched in this reciprocal relationship."[17]

In this context, the dilemma of sin consists not so much in breaking a command, which would merely result in guilt, but in breaking trust, which results in shame. Sin arises in the heart when "doubt is cast on the Gift." Man turns his back on "God-Love, on the 'Father.' He in some sense casts him from his heart."[18] The logic of gift and thanksgiving is overturned in both the vertical (God-human) and horizontal (man-woman) dimensions, being replaced by suspicion and shame. Fearing how I appear in the other's perception, I am unable to entrust myself in love. Herein lies the true meaning of concupiscence, which "is to be explained as a lack." The body, no longer transparent to the person and interiorly resistant to the spirit, becomes the site of contesting and divisive forces. Instead of regarding the other as a gift, I approach him or her as a possible object of possession or use, and the path to communion is short-circuited. In this way concupiscence poses "a specific threat to the structure of self-possession and self-dominion, through which the human person forms itself."[19]

---

15. TOB 15:4.

16. Cf. TOB 9:3: "Man became the image of God not only through his own humanity, but also through the communion of persons. . . . Man becomes an image of God not so much in the moment of solitude as in the moment of communion."

17. TOB 17:6.

18. TOB 26:4.

19. TOB 28:3.

Ethos of the Heart

Another key concept, arising especially in John Paul's analysis of Jesus's teaching on adultery, is "ethos of the heart." Matthew's Gospel in particular makes much of the contrast between exterior and interior righteousness. Christ directs us to examine the heart because it represents our inner core, the seat of our willing and desiring. Sin has its deepest roots not in the body but in the heart or will, which has become a battlefield where love and lust contend. Our liberation and healing from sin, and the sanctification of our bodies and outward actions, must likewise begin in the heart. Does this mean we should always be suspicious of the heart? "No! It is only to say that we must remain in control of it," John Paul answers. "The spousal meaning of the body has not become totally foreign to that heart: it has not been totally suffocated in it by concupiscence, but only habitually threatened." The heart—the inner person—must not be suppressed or crushed, but set free.[20] John Paul is convinced that Christ's words about the heart appeal to us to rediscover "the meaning of the whole of existence, of the meaning of life, which includes also the meaning of the body . . ."[21] Together with the whole Sermon on the Mount they outline an ethos, a way of living, that is "totally different" from the body-despising attitudes found in Manichaeism. Why? Because they spring from "the ethos of redemption."

Paradoxically, this ethos of redemption, this new way of interiorly purifying the heart, is set into motion by "the redemption of the body." Against all interpretations of Christ's atoning activity which reduce it to an object lesson in divine love or a mere explicitation of what is implicitly already the case, John Paul emphasizes again and again that in Christ redemption has become "a truth, a reality," the "effective" and "definitive realization" of the great mystery God planned before the world was created.[22] Only by understanding Jesus's death as an effective reality—that is, as a performative act that actualizes a new creation, so bringing into concrete being a radically new state of affairs between God and humanity—does John Paul go on to outline the implications of his death at the moral or ethical level. Christ does not simply offer a model or extrinsic example for us to copy. He dramatically enacts and makes possible our

---

20. TOB 32:1–6.
21. TOB 46:6.
22. TOB 46:4; 97:3–5.

full incorporation into the dynamism of his twofold self-offering to the Father and to the world.

It is vital not to overlook the centrality of this theme for John Paul's entire theology of the body and of sanctifying grace. It captures his sense that the human person is essentially redeemable, historically transformable, and that the domination of sin can be overcome and vanquished not only in principle but also in practice. This teaching stands in explicit contrast with every "ethos" that would envision men or women as hopelessly enslaved and determined by genetics, instinct, concupiscence, or subliminal sexual drives. The phrase "the ethos of the body" means that the human situation is not one in which the heart is irrevocably given over to concupiscence. Rather, Christ's redemptive action results in an "effective" call and appeal to the heart—effective, because it actually is capable of changing us from the inside:

> On the foundation of that mystery [of redemption], which St. Paul defines as "the redemption of the body" (Rom 8:23), on the foundation of the reality called "redemption," and, as a consequence, on the foundation of the ethos of the redemption of the body, we cannot stop at the mere accusation of the human heart on the basis of desire and the concupiscence of the flesh. *Man cannot stop at casting the heart into a state of* continual and irreversible *suspicion* due to the manifestations of the concupiscence of the flesh and of the *libido* uncovered, among other things, by a psychoanalyst through analysis of the unconscious. Redemption is a truth, a reality, in the name of which man must feel himself called, and "called with effectiveness." He must become aware of this call also through Christ's words according to Matthew 5:27–28 [on adultery of the heart], reread in the full context of the revelation of the body. Man *must feel himself called to rediscover*, or even better, to realize, the spousal meaning of the body and to express in this way the interior freedom of the gift, that is, the freedom of that spiritual state and power that derive from mastery over the concupiscence of the flesh.[23]

---

23. TOB 46:4. These sentiments echo thoughts expressed elsewhere in John Paul II's writings. In a 1984 address to those taking part in a course on responsible parenthood, in a passage re-quoted again in *Veritatis splendor* 103, the pontiff says the following: "It would be a very serious error to conclude ... that the Church's teaching [on morality] is essentially only an 'ideal' which must then be adapted, proportioned, graduated to the so-called concrete possibilities of man, according to a 'balancing of the goods in question.' But what are the 'concrete possibilities of man'? And of *which* man are we speaking? Of man *dominated* by lust or of man *redeemed by Christ*? This is what is at stake: the *reality* of Christ's redemption. *Christ has redeemed us!* This means

In short, the new shape of human living proposed by Christ is not just an abstract ideal. "Christ's words are *realistic*," says John Paul. They point out to man frustrated by his failings "*the path toward a purity of heart* that is *possible and accessible* for him even in the state of hereditary sinfulness."[24]

Life in the Spirit

It is well known among biblical scholars that the Pauline and Johannine contrast between Spirit (*pneuma*) and flesh (*sarx*) does not equate to a contrast between spirit and body. Nevertheless, John Paul takes great pains to emphasize that the fully human life does not entail any opposition between body and soul, matter and spirit. The New Testament words "flesh" and "spirit" instead commonly signify certain contesting powers at work within the human person as a whole being. Certainly the body is deeply implicated in this contest: sin establishes a disharmony between man's physical and spiritual faculties, so that his spiritual faculties (mind, will, heart) become dominated by sensual impulses. Yet the "sins of the flesh" include ambition and discord as much as they do drunkenness and fornication. The fact that the acts or virtues that stand in opposition to these—love, joy, peace, patience, and so on—are called the "fruit" of the Spirit in Gal 5:22 says something important about their origin and mode of operation in our lives. While they presuppose deliberate choice, an effort of human will, they are above all generated by the life-giving action of the Holy Spirit. Before they are virtues enacted by the human spirit, they are more properly fruits effected by the Holy Spirit.[25]

This also indicates that progression toward purity of the heart and self-mastery consists not just in shunning sin (a negative movement) but also in embracing holiness (a positive movement). Abstinence from disordered attachments is powerless without the positive impulse of reverence and love for what is good. "The *reverence* born in man for everything bodily and sexual, both in himself and in every other human being,

---

that he has given us the possibility of realizing *the entire* truth of our being; he has set our freedom free from the *domination* of concupiscence. And if redeemed man still sins, this is not due to an imperfection of Christ's redemptive act, but to man's will not to avail himself of the grace which flows from that act."

24. TOB 58:5.
25. TOB 51:6.

male and female, turns out to be the most essential power for keeping the body 'with holiness.'"[26]

The ultimate goal of this Holy Spirit–animated, reverential, and joyful regard for the things given special honour by God is "divinization" or personal participation in the intimacy of Trinitarian communion (2 Pet 1:4).[27] This horizon relativizes certain realities that belong to "the present form of this world which is passing away." Jesus's teaching on the resurrection of the body in Matt 22:23–33 confirms that these realities include marriage and procreation, which "belong exclusively to this world" and "do not constitute man's eschatological future. In the resurrection they lose, so to speak, their *raison d'etre*."[28] Although our bodies will retain their specific masculine and feminine characteristics, "*the meaning of being male or female in the body* will be *constituted and understood differently* in the other world than it had been 'from the beginning' and then in its whole earthly dimension."[29]

The special witness of celibacy embraced for the sake of the kingdom prophetically embodies this heavenly mode of existence. Yet John Paul insists on the essentially spousal structure and therefore truly human and interpersonal character of celibacy. The joy of human fulfillment that is found in the sincere gift of self and the communion of persons is not peculiar or exclusive to the married state of life, as though lifelong virginity represented some kind of abnormal, truncated form of human existence. Nor is celibacy opposed to marriage in some kind of holier-than-thou vocational competition. Jesus's words to the Sadducees, "When they rise from the dead, they will take neither wife nor husband," indicate "that there is a condition of life without marriage, in which man, male and female, finds at one and the same time the fullness of personal giving and of the intersubjective communion of persons, thanks to the glorification of his whole psychosomatic being in the eternal union with God."[30] When, in the time before the resurrection, certain persons hear and respond in faith, hope, and love to the call to continence for the sake of the kingdom, which can only be accepted as a gift, the rest of us are enabled to encounter in them a lively, bodily, and animated anticipation

---

26. TOB 54:4.
27. TOB 67:3—69:8.
28. TOB 66:2.
29. TOB 66:4.
30. TOB 73:1.

of that communal fullness in which we all hope to share in the future state of resurrection. In fact, the spousal meaning of the human body will only completely be manifested when it is fulfilled in the virginal state of all bodies of believers in the eschaton.[31]

Language of the Body

Throughout the catecheses John Paul relies on the idea that the spousal structure of human sexuality manifests a language inscribed into the human body by God. We are familiar with the notion of "body language" from popular psychology: we speak about someone giving us "the cold shoulder," or the "silent treatment," or "turning his nose up at us." Maybe we have come across books that try to interpret various bodily movements or postures as so many symbols of a person's interior world. Yet it is not just by what we *do* that our bodies "speak." Rather, our bodies themselves, just by *being*, and specifically by the fact of their maleness or femaleness, signify something, stand for something, say something. Inscribed deep within our physical constitution as males and females is a mysterious spiritual grammar or language.

But if the body speaks a language, then, just like any language, it can be falsified.[32] It can be "enacted" or "embodied" in or out of harmony with the truth. Just as you can tell lies with words, so you can tell lies with the body. The language inscribed in our bodies can be "spoken" or lived in a way that is more or less true or false, eloquent or banal, depending on the degree to which our actions harmonize with the way things really are with us as sexually specific, bodily human beings.

In the area of sexuality moral theologians call such bodily falsehoods "sexual lies." One of the most obvious and common forms of sexual lying involves sexual relationships outside of the special conditions of marriage, that is, the conditions of exclusivity, reciprocity, totality, and permanence. To try to speak the language of marriage with your body, either by yourself or with another person, outside of the true conditions of marriage involves you in a falsified body language of love—involves you, in other words, in a sexual lie.

Being married does not make a person immune to the temptation to commit sexual lies too. There are many different forms of sexual lies

---

31. TOB 68:3.
32. See TOB 103:1–107:6.

to which both single and married people are vulnerable. In all cases, the body's native language is essentially spousal. In marriage, the body language expressed in its consummating act, sexual intercourse, is "true" in so far as it corresponds to the language expressed in the exchange of vows, the vows that express exclusivity, reciprocity, totality, and permanence. The truthfulness of the body language that speaks "one-flesh union" depends upon its correspondence with the language of the vows by which marriage is initially contracted.

Responsible Parenthood

How does what John Paul says about body language and its falsification translate into the sphere of responsible parenthood? In the opening words of the final section of the catecheses, John Paul states that all that he has said so far "would remain in some way incomplete if we did not try to see their concrete application in the area of conjugal and familial morality."[33] For this reason he sets out to reread *Humanae vitae* with a view to offering practical moral guidance.

John Paul first asks us to consider the radical ethical difference between a couple having recourse to infertile periods in order to plan and space children, and using contraception. A married couple's conjugal life unfolds as a continual bodily "affirmation" and "re-proposal" of the pledge they first spoke in words. Those words constitute the "truth" against which their entire conjugal life, in all its individual acts, must be measured.[34] What kind of practical ethical behavior do they lead to in the vocation to parenthood?

At one level the answer is self-mastery. Self-mastery corresponds with the fundamental constitution of the person, whereas the adoption of a purely technical solution places the body under the mastery of a technique or external force. In this way contraception "*breaks* the constitutive dimension of the person, deprives man of the subjectivity proper to him, and turns him into an *object of manipulation*."[35]

It is of course quite possible for couples who use natural regulation to be motivated by the wrong reasons, to have a kind of "contraceptive mentality" at work. "The use of 'infertile periods' in conjugal shared life

---

33. TOB 118:1.
34. TOB 118:4.
35. TOB 123:1.

can become a source of abuses if the couple thereby attempt to evade procreation without just reasons . . ."[36]

But there is another level at which contraception appears as problematic, namely, at the level of body language, and it is with this connection that John Paul seems most concerned:

> As ministers of the sacrament that is constituted through consent and perfected by conjugal union, man and woman are called *to express* the mysterious *"language" of their bodies in all the truth that properly belongs to it.* Through gestures and reactions, through the whole reciprocally conditioned dynamism of tension and enjoyment—whose direct source is the body in its masculinity and femininity, the body in its action and interaction—through all this *man, the person,* "speaks."[37]

The relationship between the language of the vows and the language of the body here comes into play. The marriage vows basically enact four intentions characterized by exclusivity, reciprocity, totality, and permanence. Any deliberate intention not to keep those intentions expressed in the marriage vows would be tantamount to lying, to dishonoring the other, to making the promises with fingers crossed.

The Church teaches that openness to children belongs to marriage by nature.[38] In many rites this is made explicit in the language of the vows: "Are you ready to accept children lovingly from God and bring them up according to the law of Christ and his Church?" But even if this question were not explicitly asked, it is effectively included under all that is involved in reciprocity, the mutual giving of self. When you say, "I take" or "I receive" this man or this woman, you are laying yourself open to the blessing of children. Because with this man and with this woman, with his or her body in its created integrity, goes the capacity to impregnate, the capacity to conceive. The intention that this marriage be

---

36. TOB 125:3.

37. TOB 123:4.

38. Cf. TOB 127:3: "Although, in approaching the issue, neither the conciliar constitution nor the encyclical uses the traditional language (defining the hierarchy of ends: 'procreation,' 'mutual aid,' and 'remedy of concupiscence'), they nevertheless speak about that to which the traditional expressions refer." "[L]ove involves a right *coordination* of the ends . . ." "In this renewed orientation, the traditional teaching on the ends of marriage (and on their hierarchy) is confirmed and at the same time deepened from the point of view of the interior life of the spouses, of conjugal and familial spirituality."

a relationship in "the service of life" is contained within the covenantal content of the marriage vows.

And so, argues John Paul, to the extent that contraception deprives the conjugal act of its procreative capacity, it deprives it of its truth. There is "a real bodily union, but it does not correspond to the inner truth and dignity of personal communion. . . . If this truth is lacking, one can speak neither of the truth of the reciprocal gift of self nor of the reciprocal acceptance of oneself by the person."[39]

Any hope of realizing so great a goal as personal communion calls for the powerful aid of divine grace. John Paul stresses the need for the Holy Spirit's gift of piety or reverence (*donum pietatis*). This reverence manifests itself in a twofold manner. First, as "salvific" fear: "the fear of violating or degrading what bears in itself the sign of the divine mystery of creation and redemption." And second, as "a sensibility full of veneration," a "gift of reverence for the work of God."[40]

CONCLUSION

In the years since John Paul's delivery of his catecheses on human love in the divine plan, some have wondered whether they have taken enough account of the very real complexities and failures in the realm of bodily and sexual experience, of the very common experience of an incapacity, sometimes despite best intentions, to realize the full contours of our calling to personal communion with God and with one another. Others have explicitly criticized his teaching for being too abstract, for lacking any connection with actual experience.

Many of the people who make such criticisms have not in fact read the full text of the catecheses. If they had, they would see that the category of "experience" is absolutely central. According to John Paul, the human experience of love—in all its dynamic complexity—is a legitimate means of interpreting divine love. God's love and human love, even human sexual and erotic love, are not opposed, but are somehow alike. In interpreting the divine revelation of love, John Paul says we must "appeal to experience." Revelation and experience present us with "a surprising convergence."[41] Those who think there is a line of "total antithesis" or "radical antinomy" between them are explicitly criticized for remaining

---

39. TOB 123:7.
40. TOB 131:1–6.
41. TOB 4:4–5.

at the level of the abstract rather than considering the human person in his or her living subjectivity. In most cases revelation is not opposed to human experience, but simply exposes "the extraordinary nature of what is ordinary."[42]

Having said that, John Paul knows with theological tradition that human experience is not always a reliable criterion by which to make judgments about right and wrong, true and false. Human experience is marred by sin and prejudice, by pain and suffering, by unresolved guilt and shame. Through their experiences whole cultures or societies can become insensitive and blind to moral truth. But these problems do not render experience utterly untrustworthy. By reading—or "rereading"—human experience in the light of the "redemption of the body" by Christ, we are able to discern the contours of redeemed experience, an experience that is not just an abstract ideal but a real possibility, a real hope, a way of living and relating that through grace and the power of the Holy Spirit can be realized right in the midst of broken human existence.

Another concern that has been raised is that John Paul's theology of the body poses many more questions than it answers directly. Virtually nothing is said, for example, about homosexuality and same-sex attraction, or on questions concerning people with ambiguous or polymorphic gender identities. How are persons who experience sexuality in ways other than the male and female paradigm presupposed by John Paul to appropriate his theology and teaching? The theology of the body does not offer a completely comprehensive response to all our questions. Indeed, many comments indicate that John Paul never meant it to be the last word on the subject, but a catalyst for further discussion. However, it does offer a rich resource by which to consider and weigh such questions with theological integrity and pastoral intelligence.

Overall, the burden of John Paul's teaching is to outline a moral and spiritual pedagogy illumined by christological truth. Inasmuch as Christ unveils the mystery of what it means to be human, his body—and the bodily life he lives among us—has become a place of healing, a place of recovery and restitution. One is reminded in this connection of George Herbert's beautiful lines:

> Christ hath took in this piece of ground,
> And made a garden there for those
> Who want herbs for their wound.[43]

42. TOB 11:1.
43. Herbert, "The Church," lines 40–42.

Christianity holds that where Christ's body is, there is all of God: Father, Son, and Spirit. The Church teaches that in the man Jesus of Nazareth the fullness of divine life became physically present and permanently available in space and time. It believes that God's love for humanity is essentially ecstatic, such that he goes out of himself and actually becomes the object of his love, willingly suffering in his body the same kind of abuse, torture, and violent treatment that have plagued human history since the dawn of time. But it also believes that this love was not exhausted by his death, but that he physically rose from the state of death, overcoming the final barrier that borders personal human existence and threatens us all with final extinction. These are the basic lineaments of an incarnational theology.

And if all that is true, then the truth is that even the human body, with all the contradictions it has suffered or been involved in, can through the body of Jesus Christ be healed from evil, delivered from death, spiritually revitalized, and united to God. For in his cross, Christ has not just exemplified loving with one's body, but has realized it, decisively fulfilled it, for the world. Christ speaks the language of love not just with words, but through the body-language of sacrificial self-gift and life-giving resurrection. And so now his body, which is encountered mysteriously in the communion of persons that constitutes his Church, has become for all who come to him in trust and hope the source and sign and sacrament of a new life, a fully physical life, but a fully holy life too, in which that original, nuptial meaning of our bodies, inscribed by way of a sort of blueprint at the beginning of creation, finds its proper fulfillment and goal in us. For Saint John Paul II, the redemption of the body in Christ reveals not just an ethical truth, but an anthropological truth as well, or rather, *the* anthropological truth.[44] In fleshing out this truth in studied dialogue with the Church's scriptures and tradition, the great pontiff has done two things. He has joined redemption with creation, salvation with ethics, bringing together again two spheres that the perennial spirit of Gnosticism will always try to keep apart. And he has spoken the gospel with peculiar profundity and clarity, enabling salvation in Christ to be

---

44. TOB 58:5. Cf. Vatican II's *Pastoral Constitution on the Church in the Modern World* (*Gaudium et Spes*) and its famous passages habitually quoted by John Paul II (§22): "The truth is that only in the mystery of the incarnate Word does the mystery of man take on light. . . . Christ, the final Adam, by the revelation of the mystery of the Father and His love, fully reveals man to man himself and makes his supreme calling clear."

encountered in a new way—and perhaps for many of his readers, even for the first time—as sheer and total gift.

chapter 4

Communion with God: Marriage as Metaphor in the Old Testament

ANNA SILVAS

INTRODUCTION

Our Lord Jesus Christ, when engaged on the topic of divorce by the Pharisees, replied to them, "for your hardness of heart Moses allowed you to divorce your wives, but it was not so from the beginning" (Matt 19:8). Hence we need to seek the truth about God's original plan for man and woman and children and family, by going to the book of "the Beginning," the book of Genesis. "The sacrament of Matrimony," declares Pope John Paul II, is distinguished from all the other sacraments, in that "it is the sacrament of something that was part of the very economy of creation" (*Familiaris consortio*, 68).

There are, of course, two distinct narratives of the creation of man in Genesis. The first is Gen 1:26–28, while the second, more folkloric account is in Gen 2, which tells of the creation of Adam and Eve. These texts are the primary sources, the premises or first principles one might say, of scriptural anthropology, that is, an account of the essential constitution of man by the Creator at the beginning. As such they form the prelude to the entire subsequent drama of sin and salvation. What essential truths about man and woman can be elucidated from them?

The first and most profound truth we learn about our human nature is its original, innate orientation to God. Unlike the animals, we human beings were made with a mysterious, inalienable connection to God. As Pope Benedict XVI puts it, "By nature, man is related to the Infinite."[1] For human beings to live in a way that ignores God is not to be "only human," it is to be *sub*human.

So much of theology, doctrine, and catechesis hovers around the phrase "image and likeness of God." According to one very well-founded exegetical tradition, the image of God in which we were created was revealed in the fullness of time to be Christ himself, of whom the Apostle Paul says, "he is the image of the invisible God" (Col 1:15; cf. 2 Cor 4:4). In speaking of Christ we speak of "one of the Trinity," and all which that entails of His relations to the Father and of our adoptive sonship with Him into which his saving work draws us.

There is a related line of exposition, accessible only in the light of the Christian revelation. The grammatically plural form of the Hebrew word for God, *Elohim*, together with the "divine *we*" that occurs in these texts did not escape the attention of the Fathers. They understood it as a providential intimation of the Trinity. If we use this as a key to read the text "in the image of God he created him; male and female he created them," it suggests a meaning something like this: Not only man as an individual, but man precisely as created in the twofold form of male and female reflects something of the nature of God, and that *something* is that the Divine nature is personal and relational, and self-giving in love. This Trinitarian interpretation of being created in God's image is presented in the *Catechism*: "The divine image ... shines forth in the communion of persons, in the likeness of the unity of the divine persons among themselves" (CCC, 1702); "God is love and in himself he lives a mystery of personal loving communion. Creating the human race in his own image ... God inscribed in the humanity of man and woman the *vocation*, and thus the capacity and responsibility, of *love* and communion" (CCC, 2331).

The second creation account also teaches this call to communion, though from a different angle. After God creates Eve from the side of Adam, the text says, "he brought her to the man." Eve is presented to Adam as his wife *by the Lord God*. It is He who brings the two together. The cleaving of man to woman is then described as making them "two in one flesh." These texts show, first, that the union of husband and wife

---

1. Pope Benedict XVI, "Dependence on God," 5.

is constituted by God; and secondly, the *one-flesh union* has no coherence except in terms of one man and one woman, that is, monogamy; thirdly, the *two in one flesh* points not only to the physical, moral, and social union of the couple but also to the "one flesh" of their child, the concrete, physical offspring born of their union. Our Lord Jesus Christ takes up this second creation account and personally ratifies it, using it to teach the indissoluble bond of the spouses: "Have you not read that from the beginning He who made them, made them male and female?" And He said, "For this reason a man shall leave his father and mother and be joined to his wife and the two shall become one flesh. So they are no longer two but one. What therefore God has joined together let no man put asunder" (Matt 19:4–6; cf. 1 Cor 6:12–17).

Returning to the first account (Gen 1:28) we find that God does something for this creation of man as male and female that he does not do in the case of the animals. He expressly *blesses* or "hallows" this primordial human relationship of man and woman. So then, for human beings marriage does not come from below, merely as a matter of the couple itself, but is endowed and commissioned from above. God is profoundly implicated!

Again, unlike the case of the animals, God addresses the man and woman *personally,* God-to-Adam and God-to-Eve and to both together, and gives them a solemn charge: "Be fruitful and multiply." This is the so-called creation mandate. Hence all that the union of man and woman is called to be, is accomplished not by unreflective instinct in the manner of animals, but by a *personal, rational obedience to a divine calling*. Only this gracious response to His blessing and His commission, a freely given response to the God who calls us into being, accords with the dignity of human beings made in His image and likeness.

Moreover, God's charge, His trust and His privileged summons is that the marital union of man and woman "be fruitful." If St. Thomas Aquinas's phrase "goodness is diffusive of itself"[2]—that is, "pours itself out"—applies supremely to God as Creator, then this *fruitfulness* of marital union can be clearly seen as an echo of the superabundant, creative love of the triune God who brings forth creation, who brings forth *life*. From the divine "fountain of life" (Ps 36:9), creative, life-giving love cascades into human spouses who are open to God's purposes and cascades in turn from them into new life. Husband and wife become the

---

2. Bonum est diffusivum sui. *Summa Theologica* III, Q. 1, A. 1.

collaborators of the triune God by bringing forth children made in the divine image into this world, by nurturing them, by building up the communion of family life. Here, in the first commandment given to man, is the core of what Scripture will have to say to the issue of contraception, or deliberately procuring the sterility of marital union.

This creation mandate is honored in the Catholic marriage ceremony. Before proceeding to the mutual consent, the couple are asked, "Will you accept children lovingly from God and bring them up according to the law of Christ and his Church?" Without an intention of openness to the gift and the responsibility of children the ceremony cannot proceed to the vows; if this intention was not present from the outset, the marriage can be declared null and void. So a godly marriage is not about setting up a self-serving twosome on our own or the world's terms—which seems very much the secular image of marriage today—but about a man and a woman growing responsibly into a family on God's terms—a serious moral and spiritual enterprise that will call on all the capacity of the spouses for love and commitment.

After God has finished the creation of man as male and female and has given them His first commands, Scripture says, "And God saw everything that he had made, and behold, it was very good" (Gen 1:31). The whole mystery of man and woman, of human sexuality and procreation is *very good*. God is the inventor of human sexuality and parenthood. God is the author of marriage. The mysterious allure that a woman exercises over a man and a man over a woman is something that is appointed to our nature. Men and women were *meant* to be attractive to each other; each was meant to answer to something in the other—but with this all-important proviso: that these powers do not rule us, but serve our good and God's purpose, which they do when we strive to bring them under the sway of rational obedience to God's plan for their use, as we observed above.

ENTER THE SERPENT

That is the way it was, then, *in the beginning*. Genesis, however, has more to say about human sexuality. In the account of Gen 3, the Serpent, master of subtlety and deceit, insinuates *questions* into Eve's mind about what God *really* meant by saying they were not to eat from the tree in the midst of the garden, the tree of the knowledge of good and evil. Sounding eerily like a master of "higher consciousness," he nudges her to seek "likeness to God" (3:5), but to seek it by self-assertion and secession from obedience. The Serpent did not tempt Eve to manifest *evil*, but rather to the sublime prospect of *likeness to God* instead.

Notice that throughout the elegant theological discussion between the Serpent and Eve, Adam, Scripture says, is "with her" (3:6). But he said and did nothing, and promptly became his wife's accomplice. There are occasions when it is a sin to remain silent, to refuse to intervene, and there is hardly a more calamitous example than this.

God loves our freedom. He does not seek a following of subhuman robots. But the corollary of our freedom is that we are responsible for our own choices, and God will not override that responsibility. Often, our reward or our punishment, in this life and in the next, is to get simply what we wanted—along with all that follows in its train. Adam and Eve's resolve on an act of disobedience, their grasping for autonomy from God, brought catastrophe in its train to them and their offspring: suffering and labor, death, exile from Paradise, and the loss of what the Church's doctors have called *original innocence* or *integrity*, that is, the sweet good order of the human person, in which all our powers—reason, will, imagination, the vital passions and bodily senses—are in right accord with each other, and disposed innately to God's will and God's grace. In the fall, man lost that ready self-command and spontaneous Godward disposition. He contracted an internal disorder. Something became warped in the human condition; it is the wound of our fallen nature.

According to the scriptural account the first consequence of Adam and Eve's sin is that their sexuality was affected: "Then the eyes of both were opened and they knew that they were naked and they sewed fig leaves together and made themselves aprons" (Gen 3:7). A new element of shame, of untoward self-consciousness, of furtiveness and of calculation has now entered into their capacity to be naked to one another, naked to themselves, and, the gravest case of all, naked to God: "and the man and his wife hid from the presence of the LORD God among the trees of the Garden" (Gen 3:8).[3]

Other consequences for human sexuality follow, which we learn especially from the words of the Lord God to Eve: "I will greatly multiply

---

3. In his *Love and Responsibility*, and expanded later in his catecheses on the Theology of the Body, John Paul II explored at great depth the symbolism of Adam and Eve's original nakedness, and of their shame after the fall, and the physical nakedness of husband and wife in each other's presence.

your pain in childbearing; in pain shall you bring forth children, yet your desire shall be for your husband, and he shall rule over you" (Gen 3:16). This last phrase, in particular "your desire shall be for your husband, and he shall rule over you," is especially noteworthy. It means that a disturbance has entered into God's original plan for the relations between man and woman. Instead of the equality and the mutuality of their being *two in one flesh*, an alien element of inequity of power has entered into the relationship, and it is the woman who is especially vulnerable to it and disadvantaged by it. Thus, a greater or lesser degree of man's domination of woman, and even some emotional weakness in woman that leads her to collude with her own intimidation, whether in marriage or in the general relations of the sexes, is historically all too characteristic of the human race. Unfortunately, it has often become entwined in our religious traditions. But we need to grasp very clearly from the scriptural teaching that any historic domineering of woman by man is a mark of our human condition *after the fall*. Something of the Creator's original purpose has broken down because of sin, and this too needs to be redeemed.[4]

So it seems as if it is a dire lookout for woman in particular. Yet a seed of hope and glory for her is given in the words of the so-called proto-evangelium. It comes in the sentence pronounced by the Lord on the Serpent: "I shall put enmity between you and the woman, and between your seed and her seed; he shall bruise your head and you shall bruise his heel" (Gen 3:15). This is the antiphon, the *leitmotif*, to the entire drama of salvation to follow. All human history henceforth is cast as a dramatic *struggle* with evil, a struggle that somehow especially concerns the woman, yet with a mysterious promise of victory to come.[5]

---

4. I rely upon Pope John Paul for this exegesis (*Mulieris dignitatem*, 10 and 24). Following him I add the caveat: the parity of man and woman envisaged in the original creation has to do with their complementarity, their mutuality, the communion they are capable of sharing in their distinctive manly and womanly characters and roles. Equality does *not* mean a kind of moral equivalence or a kind of functional interchangeability. What I am saying here and what Pope John Paul says, provides no argument for a social masculinization of women—or an emasculation of men. These trends in contemporary Western society are symptoms of a retreat from God's own anthropology.

5. Cf. John Paul II, *Mulieris dignitatem*, 9 and 30.

DISORDER IN THE FAMILY

After the fall, Scripture depicts the ever-widening and tragic consequences of human sin. They are manifested first in Adam and Eve's firstborn son, Cain. "And when they were in the field, Cain rose up against his brother Abel and killed him.... And the Lord said, 'What have you done? The voice of your brother's blood is crying out to me from the ground'" (Gen 4:8, 10).

Envy and fratricidal strife have entered the human family. This is a theme that the Old Testament is going to replay again and again. It soon extends to disorder in the "families" of individual nations or peoples, and in the family of the entire human race. God's original plan for the family is shattered. The book of Genesis relentlessly depicts the destructive consequences for the family of violating God's order. Every one of Israel's foes, each of the hostile nations or tribes, is traced back to some sexual sin leading to a rupture in the family and to social ruin. The sins of parents in the sexual realm affect the lives of their children, and their children's children, and so on. In fact, there is scarcely a major figure in Genesis untouched by sexual sin. As a result, even the great patriarchal families are all in one way or another "dysfunctional." What is depicted in Genesis continues throughout the Old Testament. Scarcely a hero of salvation history is uncompromised in his own behavior and that of his own family.

Yet, as the Spirit of God once hovered over the primordial chaos for creation, he now hovers over man for his moral and spiritual regeneration, if he will find any to respond to him. And he does find them.

This is seen first of all in Adam and Eve's progeny through Seth, rather than through Cain. "To Seth also a son was born, and he called his name Enosh. At that time men began to call upon the name of the LORD" (Gen 4:26). A little later it is famously said of one of Seth's descendants, "Enoch walked with God; and he was not, for God took him" (Gen 5:24). One of Enoch's descendants is Noah, and so, through Seth's line, we reach the covenant bearers.

THE METAPHOR OF FAMILY AND MARRIAGE

The experience of the family, positively and negatively, ran so deep in Israel and resonated so much with the inspired authors that they extended family imagery to the nations of Israel and Judah, and to Israel in her covenant relationship with God. When the prophets turn from excoriation to hope, they often portray the coming salvation of the Lord beyond catastrophe and exile in terms of family language. The day of the Lord's salvation will mean the renewal of families, the rapprochement of parents and children, the restored fidelity of husband and wife. Each of these salutary family images is then applied to the relationship of Israel and the Lord. In the very chapter of Jeremiah which sees the announcement of the coming new covenant, the prophet speaks of the God of all the families of Israel: "At that time, says the LORD, I will be the God of all the families of Israel [*mishpehot yisrael*], and they shall be my people" (Jer 31:1).

A few verses later, the prophet invokes the image of father and son for God and Israel: "for I am a father to Israel and Ephraim is my firstborn . . . therefore my heart yearns for him; I will surely have mercy on him, says the LORD" (Jer 31:9, 20). Finally, in the promise of a new covenant, the Lord is referred to as Israel's husband: "Behold the days are coming, says the LORD, when I will make a new covenant with the house of Israel and the house of Judah, not like the covenant which I made with their fathers when I took them by the hand to bring them out of the land of Egypt, my covenant which they broke, though I was their husband, says the LORD" (Jer 31:31–32).

Thus we arrive at the use of marriage as an image of the relationship between God and Israel. At this point, a pithy comment by Jeffrey Satinover offers us a key to understanding all that the Old Testament says concerning human sexuality, marital union, and sexual sin: "From the Judeo-Christian perspective, sexuality—an aspect of nature—cannot itself be 'sacramental.' It partakes of sacramental reality and is thereby elevated (sanctified) only in the context of the 'sacrament of marriage.' Sacramental sexuality, on the other hand, is the very essence of pagan worship."[6]

In short, the Creator's only plan for the fulfillment of human sexuality is marital union. He provided for no other plan. This highlights why on the one hand the prophets had a hard and failing task of it to pull Israel back from succumbing to the ecstatic, orgiastic forms of nature worship of the Canaanites, and on the other hand, why the prophets did

---

6. Satinover, *Homosexuality and the Politics of Truth*, 241. When Satinover (who is Orthodox Jewish) uses "nature" and "natural," he means human nature as it is after the fall.

not choose clinical human "sexuality" per se, but the *marriage covenant* as a suitable analogy for God's relationship with Israel.

IDOLATRY AND SEXUAL SIN

In the pagan religions surrounding Israel, licentiousness became, in the most literal and physical sense, coterminous with religious worship. Cultic prostitution had an ancient history in the Mesopotamian cultures, going back perhaps as far as the Sumerians. In Israel its most prevalent form was the cult of the Canaanite god of the storm and the weather, Ba'al, and his consort, Asherah, frequently conflated with Ashtarte (=the Babylonian Ishtar), goddess of fertility. For the product of such unions, there was always the god Moloch, to whom to make a propitious sacrifice of children "through the fire." The idea was imitative magic: cultic forms of sexual intercourse were practiced in order to secure agricultural fertility. It was the burden of the prophets to recall Israel and Judah from this seductive brew of religious and sexual promiscuity. They had a hard and failing battle of it; it was not eradicated till destruction and exile came down first on the northern kingdom and then on the southern.

Already there is a seminal idea here: idolatry is implicated quite literally in sexual sin, and conversely sexual sin is idolatry. What Israel had to learn all over anew was that the God of Abraham and Isaac and Jacob is not one of these sexualized, orgiastic pagan gods and the cultic life of Israel can have nothing to do with such practices. It was a critical juncture in the life of Israel, and communicating the truths that God's all-holy nature is not sexual and that the natures of the Creator and of the creature are utterly incommensurate—in short, that God transcends all human analogies—was a major burden of the prophetic message.

A TURNING POINT: THE PROPHET HOSEA

The prophet Hosea, in eighth-century northern Israel, was a genius. Taking the association of harlotry and idolatry, he lifted it onto a new plane, full of significance for the future. He initiated the imagery of Israel as the unfaithful bride of the Lord, and, its positive corollary, that Israel was called by covenant as the spouse of one "husband," the Lord. It seems that Hosea developed these ideas around his own painful marriage to Gomer, a wife who turned to rampant adultery (Hos 1:2). Hosea interpreted his own marriage as a prophetic sign, a living parable of the spiritual state of Israel vis-à-vis the Lord. Infidelity to God he likened to the rupture of the most intimate of human bonds, that of husband and wife—only more so. His divorce of Gomer is like Israel's chastisement by destruction and exile. He then turns from using spousal imagery negatively to using it *positively*. Ignoring the prohibition in the Mosaic law of remarrying a divorced wife who has remarried elsewhere (Deut 24:1–4), he will take back Gomer, despite her many adulteries. This becomes an image of the Lord's "re-betrothal" of faithless Israel in a future day of hope, bearing all the hallmarks of a new covenant:

> Therefore, behold, I will allure her,
>   and bring her into the wilderness,
>   and speak tenderly to her.
> And there I will give her her vineyards
>   and make the Valley of Achor a door of hope.
> And there she shall answer me as in the days of her youth,
>   as at the time when she came out of the land of Egypt.
>
> And in that day, declares the LORD, you will call me "My Husband," and no longer call me "My Baal." For I will remove the names of the Baals from her mouth, and they shall be remembered by name no more. . . . I will betroth you to me in righteousness and in justice, in steadfast love and in mercy. I will betroth you to me in faithfulness. And you shall know the LORD. (Hos 2:14–20)

The major prophets—Jeremiah, Isaiah, and Ezekiel—all take their lead from Hosea, by using spousal imagery for the relationship between the Lord and Israel. The prophet Isaiah speaks explicitly of the Lord as the husband: "For your Maker is your husband, the LORD of Hosts is his name; and the Holy One of Israel is your redeemer, the God of the whole earth he is called" (Isa 54:5). The prophet Ezekiel makes extensive use of spousal imagery, and we have already seen how the prophet Jeremiah announces a "new covenant," indeed a marriage covenant, in which the Lord is "husband" (Jer 31:31–34).

THE SONG OF SONGS

The relationship of the Lord and Israel in terms of spousal imagery culminates in a book unique in the entire canon of Scripture: the Song of

Songs. There is no mistaking the literal meaning of the book: it is a series of passionate appeals between bride and bridegroom, glowing with ardor and sensuousness, the highest affirmation of spousal erotic love in the Scriptures. At various times and places the literal meaning of the Song of Songs has been a source of puzzlement, if not scandal. What is this book doing in the canon? However, already in ancient Jewish tradition, as later in the Christian, these love-songs were read as a great poetic metaphor of the love between the Lord and his people Israel. This may even have been the intention of the inspired final redactor and/or those responsible for including it in the Jewish canon in the postexilic period. They accepted it in the prophetic tradition of spousal imagery. Perhaps the Song is best understood religiously as the presentation of a hoped-for consummation in the future when Israel will no longer be unfaithful to the Lord. Her faithfulness will be proved even when the Lord seems to have vanished and she cannot find him. For then her dispositions will have become so purified and steadfast that she will turn aside to another no more. The very experience of absence will then only lead her to a redoubling of her fidelity. Without doubt these mysterious passages about the Bridegroom's *absence* that have so inspired the apophatic[7] theologians, virgins, and mystics over the centuries are the key to the *religious* meaning of the Song of Songs. As can be seen, we pass from earthly marriage to metaphor to the mystical heights.

FROM METAPHOR BACK TO PRACTICE

There is no doubt that the prophetic promotion of spousal imagery for the relationship of the Lord and Israel cast a reflective glow on the understanding and practice of marriage itself. To begin with, it showed what God thought of human sexuality as elevated and consecrated in marital union: this was something so worthy he might use it to intimate truths of an entirely nonsexual nature, sublime truths about the relationship between God and man.

---

7. "Apophatic," from *apophasis,* denial or negation, is used in mystical theology to characterize the "negative" experience of God on the part of those who are *faithful,* that is, the painful experience of seeming absence and of darkness, understood as a paradoxical but very real note of progress toward the God who is *semper maior,* "always greater," whose nature, as the Cappadocian Fathers say, is "incomprehensible," that is, "ungraspable."

Secondly, and most importantly, it renewed the understanding of marriage as covenant, but not covenant as a legal transaction between families, but rather as a deeply religious bond calling for all the personal qualities of loyal love.

Thirdly, the metaphor of marriage as used by the prophets had no cogency whatever except in terms of monogamy, that is, the exclusive relationship of one husband and one wife. "You shall not play the harlot, or belong to another man; so will I also be to you" (Hos 3:3), says Hosea to his wife, Gomer, expressing the exclusive fidelity not only of the wife but also of the husband, which was a rather new emphasis. Accordingly, the same period that saw prophetic exploration of this spousal imagery, from the later pre-exilic prophets onwards, also saw the vanishing of polygyny in Israel. The metaphor had led to a rediscovery of a truth about marriage itself which in turn led to a remedying of defects in its practice.

It is a pity that the deepening understanding of marriage brought about by the prophets did not also realize itself in the eschewing of divorce in Judaism. It almost got there, for a current of thought was certainly moving in this direction. The prophets Hosea and Isaiah had ignored the prohibition of Torah against remarrying a divorced woman, when they spoke of the Lord as *remarrying* Israel after she had been divorced and had prostituted herself with many lovers. The redemptive love of the Lord is so great it would prevail over divorce and harlotry. This was suggestive. One of the last postexilic prophets, Malachi, has some wonderful passages that are well worth quoting. He is alarmed at the growth of marital infidelity and divorce even among the priests serving the temple after the return from exile; their practice of adultery and divorce profanes the covenant with Levi. He explicitly connects the covenant between the Lord and Israel with the marriage covenant between husband and wife. So many themes, of divine fatherhood, of mutual fidelity between spouses and of fruitfulness, of family bonds and covenant, all converge in the preaching of the prophet Malachi:

> The LORD was witness to the covenant between you and the wife of your youth, to whom you have been faithless, though she is your companion and your wife by covenant. Has not the one God made and sustained us for the spirit of life? And what does he desire? Godly offspring. So take heed to yourselves, and let none be faithless to the wife of his youth. For I hate divorce, says the Lord the God of Israel . . . (Mal 2:14–16)

There are other themes in the later Old Testament writings that lead organically like a segue into the New. There are the prophetic sayings, for example, that confer a feminine persona on Israel and Jerusalem, such as "virgin," the "betrothed of the Lord," and "Mother," indeed the fruitful "mother of many" in the eschatological day of salvation. The idea of eschatological virginity, beginning with Jeremiah, picks up swell in late Judaism and is adopted by, for example, the Therapeutae and the Essenes. In those who are sensitive to the progressive revelation and the anagogical drift of the Old Testament—particularly to the ways the prophets are ever anguishing over the enigmas of Israel's covenant with the Lord, and rethinking its terms and deepening the understanding of it and hinting at something new and more splendid to come—this surely prepares in us a strong sense of expectancy.

chapter 5

God and Communion:
Marriage as Sacrament in the New Testament

ANNA SILVAS

INTRODUCTION

The last chapter ended its survey of marriage and family in the Old Testament in the company of the prophets of Israel. It is they who through their use of marriage as metaphor for the covenant relationship between the Lord and Israel deepened the appreciation of marriage itself.

Now we arrive at the great moment of expectancy, the dawn of the promised new and everlasting covenant. While we must affirm the profound continuity of God's purpose between the series of covenants in the Old Testament, and their culmination in the covenant of the New Testament, we must also affirm a new beginning. As St. Paul asserts, "If anyone is in Christ, there is a *new* creation" (2 Cor 5:17). The first words of the Fourth Gospel are intentionally identical to those with which the Septuagint Bible opens the book of Genesis: ἐν ἀρχῇ, "in the beginning." But St. John also declares a *new* beginning and a *new* creation in Christ, the *re*-generation of the human race, when he speaks of the Word who "became flesh and dwelt among us . . . full of grace and truth," enabling all who receive him "to become children of God, born not of blood, nor of the will of the flesh, nor the will of man, but of God" (John 1:14, 12–13).

THE THRESHOLD CROSSED: THE ANNUNCIATION AND VISITATION

When we turn to the manner in which the Divine Word assumed our nature, we find immediately two women and two men: the two women are the barren woman Elizabeth and the virgin Mary of Nazareth, and the two men are Zechariah, priest of Jerusalem, and Joseph, of the house of David.

The Gospel of Luke sets the Annunciation squarely in a context: "in the sixth month"—that is, of Elizabeth's conceiving the child who will one day be as the Elijah who was to return, "turning the hearts of the fathers to their children and the disobedient to the wisdom of the just, to make ready for the Lord a people prepared" (Luke 1:17). Elizabeth is the classic scriptural barren woman made fruitful only through the Lord's miraculous intervention.

Mary, however, really is something truly new: she is both the virgin daughter of Israel, and the Zion who as soon as she travailed brought forth; before her pain came upon her, she was delivered of a son (cf. Isa 66:8). But she is both these, together in one person, and this time not in metaphor only but in living flesh-and-blood reality.

When we ponder the dialogue between Mary and the angel Gabriel, we see all the lineaments of Eve's act of disobedience being undone by her response of obedience: "Be it done unto me according to your word." Mary is, then, *the woman* of the protoevangelium, whose "seed" will crush the head of the serpent. Elizabeth's prophetic acclaim of Mary— "blessed is the fruit of your womb" (Luke 1:42)—is the tribute offered by the scriptural *barren woman made fruitful*, to the still more wonderful instance of the Lord's grace: the *virgin made mother*. At Elizabeth's greeting, a surge of joy wells up in Mary, and just as Eve, the *mother of all the living*, once exclaimed, "I have gotten a man with the help of the LORD" (Gen 4:1), so now the new Eve exclaims, "The Almighty has done great things for me" (Luke 1:49).

However, it is not as if what had transpired was between Mary and God alone, with the figure of Joseph coming in later as a decorative afterthought. *Before* the Annunciation, Mary is described as "betrothed to a man whose name was Joseph, of the house of David" (cf. Luke 2:4–5). God had already "factored in" Joseph, of set purpose.

THE HOLY FAMILY

This brings us to the holy family of Nazareth. As the Old Testament, and indeed the human race, had begun with a family, Adam and Eve and their offspring, so the New Testament revelation also begins with a family: Joseph, Mary, and the child Jesus. Beginning with Mary's undoing of Eve's disobedience, we see in this family *at last* the undoing of all the ills that have tended to afflict even the best of families throughout salvation history, the cessation of the curse that continued to work itself out from generation to generation. In this family, with Jesus at its center, God undid all the effects of sin that ever came upon human families, before or since. If you consider the Holy Family as the first cell of the Church, which is itself the family household of God, in this family lies the remedy of all the ills between man and woman and between parents and children.

We sometimes hear the Holy Family brusquely dismissed as a worthwhile model for the family, or at least for husband and wife, "because," it will be said, "Mary and Joseph didn't have sex." Yet Mary and Joseph did not abstain from sexual relations because there was something inherently unworthy of such between husband and wife. In their case, it is helpful to recall the teachings of the mystical theologians, that those who attain to the maturity of holiness even in *this* life approach the state of original integrity; they go some way to recovering the lost innocence of our first creation. This means that within the person, all the passions, especially the vital passions, are not *annihilated*—far from it—but put in right order, at the disposal of reason and will, the whole person being disposed radically toward God. In the matter of sexuality, this means that our capacity for sexual desire does not run on wildly ahead of us, so to speak, but is ordered to what is entirely appropriate and fitting for the moment. And that might be marital union, as was envisaged in the commission of Adam and Eve before the fall, and certainly is so for most of the married saints.

Both Joseph and Mary were wholly sensitive to the Holy Spirit. Mary, as we know from dogma, was spared in advance the inherited wound of original sin. But Joseph, too, is described as "the just man" (cf. Matt 1:19). The Gospel of Matthew, in particular, shows the promptitude and filial quality of his obedience to God. Joseph was a very holy man who was entrusted as the vicar of God the Father for his divine Son during his life in a human family.

In their betrothal and marriage, Joseph made the gift of his manhood to Mary and Mary of her womanhood to Joseph, as is the part of all spouses to do. But what to do with this womanhood entrusted to him, of one so signally touched by God as to be with child while innocent of sexual intercourse, and a child of such extraordinary election it made one shudder to dwell on it? This was something much more than the divinely favored mothers of prophets in olden times. And we do not know the effect of the confidences that Mary shared with Joseph in the privacy of their home, and of their prayer to God together, but it must have been very, very great. In the case of this marriage, therefore, the only fitting and sensitive response to Mary that Joseph could make was not to think of seeking bodily consummation with her, not until she had given birth, not *ever*. That Joseph should and could act in this way flowed from his obedient acceptance of the intervention of God in his nascent marriage (Matt 1:20), and a profound reverence for the divine seal that had been set upon his wife. And he had all the response to grace and all the self-possession to be able to respect that mystery all his life, even while living a close domestic life with one who, in the words of the Song of Songs, would be forever for him in a very specific way: "my sister, my bride" (Song 4:9).

But if Joseph and Mary relinquished the use of the marriage bed, they did not renounce their complementarity as a man and a woman. As remarked above, God had already "factored in" Joseph before the Annunciation. He sought a true *man*, the *just man*, as the counterpart of Mary, the *woman*, to take the child and his mother into his house, confer on them his name and his protection, and carry out a task for Mary's son that Mary herself could not do: be for him a human model of manhood and fatherhood. God needed Mary to be fully a woman, and Joseph to be fully a man, and that they fulfill those roles for each other and for the child entrusted to their care. This is what God himself deemed necessary for the human upbringing of his own Son, and we ought to ponder this when we see the effects of the unraveling roles of man and woman, of father and mother, on children in our society today, especially the assault on fathers in the divorce industry, and the severe toll that the absence of a father exacts on the growing young.

Several incidents in the Gospels show the astonishing freedom and respect with which our Lord related to women. His sexuality is in such perfect poise that it heals and liberates women to be their better selves—think of his long solitary dialogue with the Samaritan woman at the well, the sinful woman who covered his feet with kisses as he reclined at table (Luke 7:38), his being left alone with the woman taken in adultery (John 8:9), Mary of Bethany who sat at his feet listening to him, the devoted women who followed him from Galilee and stayed by him even at the cross, and Mary Magdalene clasping him in the garden of the Resurrection in the glorious moment of recognition. He is the Son of God incarnate. Yet he did not spurn to submit himself to his own creatures and learn from them in his human nature. Therefore behind the calm, radiant chastity of our Lord, we can perhaps see the traces of Joseph's own ordered sexuality toward Mary his wife, and the beautiful role model of true manliness he gave to the boy whom he cherished and educated as a father.

THE BOY JESUS IN THE TEMPLE

After the infancy narratives, the only incident from the family life of Joseph, Mary, and Jesus given in the Gospels is that of the losing and the finding of the boy Jesus in Jerusalem, when he was twelve years old. Mary voiced her and Joseph's distress at not having been able to find him: "Behold, your father and I have been looking for you anxiously" (Luke 2:48). To which Jesus rejoins, "How is it that you sought me? Did you not know that I must be in my Father's house?" (Luke 2:49) Literally, the Greek reads, "that I must be in/among the things of my Father," or as another translation puts it, "must be about my Father's affairs." This twelve-year-old Jesus, then, knows very well who his real Father is, and names him in exactly the same way that will be characteristic of him throughout the Gospels: *my Father*. From the sheer juxtaposition of Mary's *your father*, referring to Joseph, and Jesus's *my Father*, referring to God, we surely have a gentle but firm correction of his mother's terms of reference, and a relativizing of human family relationships in light of the ultimate relationship with God.

I hope it is not too much to interpret the scene as follows: Jesus is at the brink of puberty, and—we are speaking of his humanity here—he is well apprised of what it behooves him to know about human sexuality. He knows of his mother's virginity and the circumstances of his conception and has weighed its enormous import for him. He is also at the age when he assumes Jewish religious adult responsibility, enacted through the bar mitzvah ceremony at which Joseph, as his putative father, would be his sponsor. So, the significance of this incident, I suggest, is that now the boy Jesus calmly "owns" his own personal and religious identity and quietly affirms it to his mother and to his foster father, Joseph. All of this underscores the freedom and humility of his returning to Nazareth and "subjecting himself" to them, sharing in their quiet domestic life for the next eighteen years or so. Meanwhile, his mother Mary, as is so characteristic of her, "kept all these words in her heart" (Luke 2:51)—from whom we surely have this precious, well-pondered memory recorded in the Gospel.

THE HOLY FAMILY EXPANDED

There are other "corrections" of his mother during our Lord's public ministry. They are all aimed at expanding the borders of the earthly family life they have known, around his own eternal sonship of the Father. It is just as if Jesus were applying the prophet Isaiah's words to Mary: "Enlarge the space of your tent, and let the curtains of your habitations be stretched out" (Isa 54:2). So he gradually educates her to the widening role of her own motherhood in the new dispensation that he is inaugurating. In this new economy of salvation the Lord is instituting a new order of kinship, and it is not one of racial and physical descent as it was in the Old Testament: "Here are my mother and my brothers! For whoever does the will of my Father in heaven is my brother and sister and mother" (Matt 12:46–50). By his use of family language, the Lord means to include all his disciples into one family with him, a family that acknowledges one father, *his* Father, in which we all share kinship with him as his *brothers* and *sisters*.

What Jesus intended for Mary's motherhood is fully revealed when the eschatological *hour* finally arrives. She had *taken her stand*—in the Greek it is a strong pluperfect verb—by the cross of her son. "When Jesus saw his mother and the disciple whom he loved standing near, he said to his mother, 'Woman, behold your son!' Then he said to the disciple, 'Behold your mother!'" (John 19:25–27). No one who has absorbed the accents of the Fourth Gospel will miss the resonances here. Our Lord addresses her by the eschatological title of "Woman," which references the "Woman" of the protoevangelium, and the "Woman" at the wedding feast of Cana. On one level she, as a widow about to be left childless in this world, is entrusted to a male relative. On another, this one disciple, and with him all the Lord's disciples, are to find in her their mother. God's appointments for his family are now all finally in place: In this family there is one Father, the eternal God and Father; one firstborn son, the Son of God himself, who through his incarnation has made himself the eldest of many brothers and sisters, his disciples; and there is a flesh-and-blood woman, *the* woman, mother of the incarnate Son, now designated as the eschatological *mother of all the living*.

A few weeks later we find Mary assuming her spiritual motherhood of all the disciples. "All these with one accord devoted themselves to prayer, together with the women and with Mary the mother of Jesus" (Acts 1:14). The scene of the Annunciation and that of Pentecost echo each other. Both are theophanies of the Holy Spirit. It is fitting that the disciples should pray with her who had been overshadowed by the power of the Most High (cf. Luke 1:35), the Holy Spirit. She had led the way, and now in her company they were all of them "filled with the Holy Spirit" (Acts 2:4). She was present at the birth of the Church as a mother to the brethren of Jesus, the household of God.

THE CHURCH, THE FAMILY HOUSEHOLD OF GOD

The Church as family household figures prominently in the opening and closing greetings of the Epistles. If you have ever thought that these were tedious and formulaic, think again. They offer precious insight into the internal life and domestic character of the early Church. They reveal a constant reciprocation between the wider Church as the universal household of God, and local family households as cells of the Church—quite literally "house churches," domestic churches, which host the celebration of the Eucharist.[1] It is often hard to know where one begins and the other leaves off.

Just as Martha had regularly welcomed the Lord Jesus into her home at Bethany, so too in the early Church: local households welcomed the apostles and became a base camp for the spread of the Church in that locality. Women notably were "proactive" in ecclesial hospitality and are mentioned by name. Theirs was a role of spiritual motherhood, for in mothering the apostles and church workers, they mothered the early church. In fact, this was how the Church first established a beachhead on European soil. "One who heard us was a woman named Lydia, from the

---

1. See the discussion of the family as a domestic church in chapter 10.

city of Thyatira, a seller of purple goods who was a worshipper of God. The Lord opened her heart to give heed to what was said by Paul. And when she was baptized, with her household, she besought us saying, 'If you have judged me to be faithful to the Lord, come to my house and stay.' And she prevailed upon us" (Acts 16:14–15). And there are other instances in the Acts showing whole households following their master or mistress in receiving the gospel and baptism, and then offering the hospitality of the household for the propagation of the Church in that local area.

The Lord's Day and the Eucharist, of course, could not be celebrated in synagogues. That meant that in these early years Christians frequently came together for the sacraments and catechesis in family households. In the last chapter of Romans Paul salutes old friends, a married couple who were great entrepreneurs in the establishment of the Church: "Greet Prisca and Aquila, my fellow workers in Christ Jesus, who risked their necks for my life, to whom not only I but also all the churches of the Gentiles give thanks; greet also the church in their house" (Rom 16:3–5).

What is obvious here is the great spirit of collaboration between men and women and between what we might call in later terms the "lay" and clerical orders, without the least upset to the apostolic and sacramental constitution of the Church—rather in service of it. The key to understanding this is surely the early Church's consciousness of being a "family," the sense of all being brothers and sisters in the one household of the faith, in which the apostles are warmly and gratefully acknowledged as spiritual fathers and elder brothers in Christ.

FAMILY LANGUAGE AMONG CHRISTIANS

The language of address used among Christians is another window on the domestic sensibility of the early Church. Overwhelmingly, the terms used are those of family relationships: brother, sister, father and mother. Thus Paul instructs Timothy as a new bishop: "Do not rebuke an older man but exhort him as you would a father; treat younger men like brothers, older women like mothers, younger women like sisters" (1 Tim 5:1–2). In the very earliest stratum of the New Testament writings we find the apostles exercising the role of fatherhood in the household of the Church: "Like a father with his children, we exhorted each one of you and encouraged you" (1 Thess 2:11–12). Again and again in the First Letter, St. John tenderly calls his addressees "my little children" (2:1), echoing the Risen Lord on the shore of the lake of Galilee: "Children, have you caught any fish?" (John 21:5). St. Paul even uses quite strongly maternal imagery on occasion, as did our Lord when he likened himself to a hen gathering her brood under her wings. Nobody who reads the farewell of the Church at Ephesus to Paul (Acts 20:36–38) can mistake the spontaneous and tenderly felt paternal and filial bonds between him and the Christians of Ephesus. This is the apostolic origin of the fatherhood of bishops in the Church. Incidentally, in the Patristic era, "Father" was the proper term of address for bishops, not for presbyters.

All these observations convey a familial model of the Church, founded in our Lord's own unique filial relationship to his Father and in the self-communication of the Holy Trinity, actualized in the Holy Family of Nazareth. The nature of the Church has little to do with the secular political constructs of democracy or Marxism—or those tiresome political dichotomies, left and right, progressive and conservative, etc. The image of the Church as God's household dovetails very well, I think, with the model of *communio* promoted by Pope Benedict XVI and others of the *ressourcement* tradition.

CHRIST THE BRIDEGROOM

Thus far in the New Testament, we have sought the truth about marriage and family in the events of the Incarnation, in the holy family of Nazareth and in the gradual expansion of that family as the Church through our adoption in Christ as the children of the Father. Of the various ways that the New Testament continues the family imagery of the Old Testament none is more significant than our Lord's owning of himself as *the Bridegroom*. In Jesus of Nazareth, the Bridegroom of Israel so long proclaimed by the prophets and in the Song of Songs has come, in the flesh.

The theme of Christ the Bridegroom is found in all four Gospels. The first to announce it may have been the austere prophet, John the Baptist. Remembering that the apostle and evangelist John was himself first a disciple of John, we encounter it first in the Gospel of John when the holy forerunner deprecates himself as merely "the friend of the Bridegroom": "You yourselves bear me witness that I said, I am not the Christ, but have been sent before him. He who has the bride is the Bridegroom; the friend of the Bridegroom who stands and hears him rejoices greatly at the Bridegroom's voice; therefore this joy of mine is now full. He must increase, but I must decrease" (John 3:28–30). Fittingly, he who confessed

Christ as the Bridegroom died for no other cause than that of defending the sanctity of marriage (cf. Matt 14:3–12).

Matthew confirms the connection of the Bridegroom theme with John the Baptist. In conversation with John's disciples our Lord identifies himself as the Bridegroom. "Then the disciples of John came to him, saying, 'Why do we and the Pharisees fast, but your disciples do not fast?' And Jesus said to them: 'Can the wedding guests fast while the Bridegroom is with them?'" (Matt 9:14–15). He employs an idiom already known to them from their teacher.

In the parables the Lord himself uses marriage imagery. He likens the kingdom to a wedding feast: "The kingdom of heaven may be compared to a king who made a wedding feast for his son . . ." (Matt 22:2). The king, clearly, is God, and the Son whose wedding feast it is, is Christ himself. Another example is the parable of the ten virgins who await the return of the Bridegroom from the wedding feast to take his bride into his home. "As the bridegroom was delayed, they all slumbered and slept. But at midnight there was a cry, 'Behold the Bridegroom comes, go out to meet him!' . . . The Bridegroom came, and those who were ready went in with him to the marriage feast" (Matt 25:1, 5–6, 10). Just like the prophets of Israel before him, our Lord uses earthly marriage as a dramatic metaphor of a relationship more intimate, profound and demanding than the relationship of husband and wife, something quite transcending the sexual: the covenant of God and Israel of old which is now realized in Christ who comes to espouse His Church.

THE WEDDING AT CANA

This spousal imagery underpins the episode of the Lord's presence at the wedding in Cana, where he worked the first "sign" of his public ministry (John 2:1–11). The episode is presented in the Gospel of John, three days after the Lord's baptism at the hands of John. The Lord attends the wedding feast with his new disciples. His mother Mary was there too. The wine for the feast runs out, and at his mother's quiet insistence, the Lord changes the jars full of water for the Jewish rites of purification into wine, the *good wine*, kept till the last. "This, the first of his signs, Jesus did at Cana in Galilee, and he manifested his glory" (John 2:11). The fact that this wedding scene is dignified by the first of Jesus's signs means that all the elements of the story carry a particular weight in terms of Christ's mission. Every word is fraught with resonances. Here again is the "woman" of the protoevangelium. The Lord addresses her with this title in connection with his eschatological *hour*. The "woman" and the "hour" will come into conjunction again in this Gospel, at the Cross.

Then there is the aureole of the entire wedding event itself. On one level, our Lord hallows the earthly marriage of this husband and this wife through his presence: indeed, the Lord's own phrase, "the Bridegroom is with them," applies in the most literal manner to this particular couple. His blessing is signified by the overflowing generosity of his supply of good wine, which is a double gesture, operating on both the mundane and metaphorical levels because it is called the first of his signs. The sign worked by Jesus is a happy surprise, the transition from the mere water of the Jewish rites which has run out to the superabundant good wine of the Gospel, according to a common interpretation. Applied to marriage itself, it is a promise of raising the water of all that is natural and earthly in marriage to a participation in divine realities through his salvific presence. It also bears eucharistic connotations through the change of the elements and of the "good wine" itself.

With so many resonances running through it, the wedding at Cana adds up to a foreshadowing of the Lord's own espousal of his Church when his "hour" shall come. That will be the hour of his glorification, here hinted at by anticipation, the hour when he shall be lifted up on the cross and the water and blood shall flow from his pierced side, which is memorialized and communicated in the eucharistic banquet. And thus we are brought back again to the "best wine" poured out at the wedding banquet.

Note that if, in this wedding feast of Cana, the "Bridegroom is with them," so too the Bride is with them, in the form of the nascent Church, that is, in Mary his mother and his first disciples, one of whom is the evangelist himself, who only three days earlier had left the side of John the Baptist to follow the "Lamb of God," at the self-abnegating behest of his former teacher. John shall again be with Mary in the forlorn little group representing the Church at the foot of the cross, when the eschatological "hour," the Lord's hour of espousal, has come at last.

CHRIST AND THE CHURCH

The Apostle Paul applies the Gospel imagery of Christ the Bridegroom specifically to Christian marriage in his Letter to the Ephesians. It is a

New Testament passage of huge importance for the understanding of Christian marriage and family. Here, St. Paul identifies Christ's Bride as the Church. Here, marriage in Christ is called *mysterion*, from which we derive "sacrament," when St. Paul describes marriage as "a great mystery, and I mean in reference to Christ and his Church." The text must be heard in full:

> Be subject to one another out of reverence for Christ. Wives, be subject to your husbands, as to the Lord. For the husband is the head of the wife as Christ is the head of the Church his body, and he himself is her Savior. As the Church is subject to Christ, so let wives also be subject in everything to their husbands. Husbands, love your wives, as Christ loved the Church and gave himself up for her, that he might sanctify her, having cleansed her by the washing of water with the word, that he might present the Church to himself in splendor, without spot or wrinkle or any such thing, that she might be holy and without blemish. Even so husbands should love their wives as their own bodies. He who loves his wife loves himself. For no man ever hates his own flesh, but nourishes and cherishes it, as Christ does the Church, because we are members of his body. For this reason a man shall leave his father and mother and be joined to his wife and the two shall become one flesh. This mystery is a profound one, and I am saying that it refers to Christ and his Church (Eph 5:21–32).

In this passage Paul glosses the prophet Ezekiel 16 and cites Gen 2:24, as he transposes the traditional spousal imagery of the Old Testament into a Christian key. The Lord God as the Bridegroom and Israel as the Bride is fulfilled in the New Testament in Christ Jesus as the Bridegroom and the Church as the Bride. He then "rereads" the relationship of husband and wife in Christ in the light of the spousal metaphor already owned by our Lord himself. He sees marriage in Christ invested with a tremendous richness of meaning. How profound and indissoluble is the union of Christ and His Church! And if this is the case, then how profound and indissoluble is the union of a husband and wife whose marriage is *in Christ*, for they are imitating the marriage of Christ and his Church! Throughout this passage Paul weaves so closely between human marriage and the metaphor of the Christ/Church union that at times it is almost difficult to distinguish which dimension he is referencing, and that is as it should be.

SACRAMENTAL SYMBOLISM

Before probing the symbolism of marriage in the Ephesians text, we need to pause over the terminology Paul uses. The Greek word translated into English as "mystery" is μυστήριον. The English word is a little pallid and uncertain: suggesting something baffling, unknown, or puzzling. In the ancient Greek culture, μυστήριον and its cognates had a concrete, liturgical register, meaning an initiation into sacred rites, or *leitourgia*. Later, it came to be used of the secrets of God and the sublime truths that were held to be revealed to the initiate through participation in these rites. Still later, among the Greek Fathers, a *mystagogue* is not a speaker who obfuscates his topic, or perhaps someone who introduces you to mysticism, but someone who is expounding the meaning of the sacramental rites. Its ambience is thoroughly liturgical.

This ritual register of the Greek word was understood by the ancient Latin translators when they chose to render it as *sacramentum*. Originally, a *sacramentum* was the oath of allegiance taken by a new soldier at his enlistment. Eventually, *sacramentum* came to mean something that was meant to be kept sacred. The common element between the Greek and the Latin terms was the idea of witnessed ritual initiation. So then, marriage in Christ is a *sacramentum*, a kind of solemn oath-taking over which God Himself yearns, a *mysterion*, a liturgical initiation, a "sacred sign" that reveals to its participants and in its participants something of the secrets of God, which Paul declares is the relationship of Christ and His Bride the Church.

There are two aspects of the Ephesians sacramental symbolism I wish to highlight here. The first concerns the *weakness* of the Church. Saint Paul borrows from Ezekiel the imagery of Israel found by the Lord God prostrate in helplessness and gradually transformed and prepared for marriage solely through his merciful, redemptive love. So also in the Christian dispensation, Jesus Christ finds the Church in weakness and cleanses her by the washing of water with the word and prepares her to be presented to himself in splendor. The love Christ bestows on his church is wholly unmerited by her; it is only his redemptive love that makes her lovely. Christ Jesus will never withdraw his love from the Church, never abandon her, no matter how compromised she may appear to be in the eyes of the world, due to the sins of her children. I think there is a very important truth here. Christ Jesus went to his Passion, suffering not only the rejection of the leaders of Israel but also knowing fully the weakness and cowardice of his own disciples at that hour, and that this was how it would be in the future with not a few who would be called by his name. Yet he still chose her and called her and loved her. Therefore, a deep, inalienable mystical love of the Church, perhaps all the more in her apparent weakness and debility, is one of the strongest marks of a truly Catholic mind, and, I submit, one of the surest criteria of true holiness. For such a love has taken on the nature of Christ's own redemptive spousal love for his Bride. This is truly to put on the mind of Christ.

This aspect of Ephesians' marriage symbolism has a very important bearing on the practice of Christian marriage itself, and that concerns the fact that bride and bridegroom espouse each other in weakness. Each is marrying a fallible and sinful human being and must be very clear-eyed about doing so. By pledging themselves to each other for life and clothing themselves in the grace of Christ, they are undertaking to grow together to human and spiritual maturity. "All husbands and wives are called in marriage to holiness," Pope John Paul II says in *Familiaris consortio*, meaning that marriage is set before spouses as a call to moral and spiritual progress, "a progress that demands awareness of sin, a sincere commitment to observe the moral law and the ministry of reconciliation. It must also be kept in mind that conjugal intimacy involves the wills of two persons, who are however called to harmonize their mentality and behavior: this requires much patience, understanding and time" (34).

Another aspect of the Ephesians passage concerns the issue of male headship and female subordination. Is the wife to be "subordinate" to the husband? I am not entirely clear on this issue myself and can only propose a few ideas for your consideration. I have observed in all the teaching of Pope John Paul a conspicuous absence of the language of subordination, and instead the language of complementarity. It seems to me to be quite revolutionary in *Mulieris dignitatem* (cf. especially 6–7, 10, 23–25) that he uses the first account of the creation of man in Genesis, with its absolute parity and complementarity of the sexes, as a hermeneutic key with which to interpret the second creation account, so that all the "help" to man that the woman is meant to be, is held to operate *reciprocally*. In fact, Paul himself prefaces the Ephesians passage with a remarkable statement of *mutual* subordination: "Be subject to one another out of reverence for Christ." I think we would follow Pope John Paul if we take this as a kind of antiphon, a *hermeneutic key* to all that follows, so that the Ephesians text is not understood in a one-sided way, as if the husband provides all the spiritual leadership in the marriage, almost as if he were the principle of his wife's spiritual life. No indeed! In fact, the husband is just as much a child of the Church as is his wife, just as dependent on the ministrations of Christ's saving grace to and through his Church; in short he, like her, participates in the femininity of the Church in relation to God. The same, incidentally, is to be said of every ordained priest. Certainly, in their role as priests, above all at the altar, they stand in the *persona* of Christ the Bridegroom before his Church. But inwardly, they too are the children of their mother the Church and participate in her espousal to the Lord.

That said, I think there is still an issue, not, let us say, of subordination, but of *order*. Is there "subordination" in the Holy Trinity? The results of the third- and fourth-century debates and of Church dogma are clear: there is no subordination but perfect *coequality* of the divine persons. Yet there is an *order* of relation in the Trinity, with the Father as the ἀρχή (source/principle) of the Son and, not without the Son, of the Holy Spirit. So there is meant to be *order* in marriage and the family, as indeed there is in the Church herself. I reflect on my own position as a woman in the Church. Only men are eligible as candidates for priestly orders—for at least one obvious reason: that in the intensely symbolic/participative world of the Liturgy, only *they* can fittingly represent the *Bridegroom* at the eucharistic wedding banquet. I have no problem whatever in looking to bishops as apostolic fathers in the family household of the Church. It is something I freely accord them as part of God's order, and I do not feel in the least diminished by it, but set free to act within Christ's will. Just as fathers exist to make motherhood and the family possible, so when bishops are fulfilling properly their role as spiritual fathers and elder brothers, they will promote the spiritual and natural motherhood of women in the Church—without abdicating their role as fathers. Conversely, spiritual mothers in the Church will rejoice to see spiritual fatherhood exercised in the Church, *in full*. So let us say there *is* meant to be order in the family, with the man fulfilling his own distinctive role as husband and father—this is his "headship" of the family—and the woman fulfilling hers as wife and mother, without confusion or equivocation of their roles.

Finally, the Ephesians text patterns the marriage of Christian spouses on Christ's espousal of his Church. Thus, the ground of the indissolubility of Christian marriage is that such a marriage *in the Lord* is assumed into Christ's fidelity to his Church. How utterly right then is the Church to maintain this truth about marriage against the huge swell of cultural forces raging against it. In fact, I would suggest that the epidemic of sexual amorality, the assault on the integrity of the family, and the progressive erosion of all ethical considerations concerning the defense of human life from conception through to death that we see all about us in our liberal Western society may be traced to the civil admittance of a culture of divorce as to the first principle.

THE EUCHARIST AS ESCHATOLOGICAL WEDDING FEAST

The New Testament has much more to tell us of the metaphorical resonances that penetrate Christian marriage. We have kept the best wine till last. So far in this chapter we have seen that our Lord identifies himself as "the Bridegroom" and that he speaks in the parables of the "wedding feast" that the King arranges for his Son. Next we saw Christian marriage described as the *mysterion* of Christ's union with his spouse the Church. But the Church has another sacrament, the Sacrament of sacraments, the Eucharist, which Scripture presents to us in a range of ways as the "wedding feast" of the new covenant and the foretaste of the wedding feast at the end of time in heaven. The Eucharist is the key to understanding the mystery of marriage in the highest spiritual terms: as the marital covenant between God and man.

In the words with which our Lord chose to institute the eucharistic mystery, he gathered up all the themes of covenant, new covenant, eternal covenant, and marital covenant from the Old Testament. The words, "This is the blood of the new and everlasting covenant," echo several scriptural texts: first of all Moses's words over the sacrifice that ratified the Covenant of Sinai: "Behold the blood of the covenant" (Exod 24:8), then the "everlasting covenant" promised in the prophet Isaiah (55:3), and finally the "new covenant" promised in the prophet Jeremiah (31:31). The theme of *marital* covenant is also deeply implicit. In the very passage appropriated by Jesus in which Jeremiah announced the new covenant, God is spoken of as "their husband" (Jer 31:32). So our Lord Jesus came to his hour knowingly as the Bridegroom of the New Covenant foretold by the prophets: "With desire I have desired to eat this Passover with you before I suffer; for I tell you I shall not eat of it until it is fulfilled in the kingdom of God" (Luke 22:15–16).

Other resonances of marital imagery can be detected. Compare Adam's declaration of Eve, "this is bone of my bones and flesh of my flesh" (Gen 2:23), and the words "unless you eat of the flesh of the Son of Man" (John 6:53). As marriage is the *one-flesh* union of husband and wife, so the sacrificial feast of the new covenant is a kind of *one-flesh* union between Christ and his faithful. One can begin to sense why the Church guards carefully both the sanctity of marriage and the sanctity of the Eucharist and sees the sanctity of both sacraments as profoundly coordinate.

Yet even in the institution of the Eucharist there is a provisional quality. It is an advance made to us now of a fulfillment that will only come at the end of time. In the Synoptic Gospels, the Eucharist is presented as the new covenant partly realized, but partly-not-yet. It is an *earnest* of what is to come when *all is made new* (2 Cor 5:17; cf. Rev 21:5). Thus, when our Lord institutes the eucharistic mystery, he leaves it to his Church as a viaticum for the long pilgrimage of history until the consummation of the age. He invests it with a forward yearning for its eschatological fulfillment, using the image of a banquet: "I assign to you, as my Father assigned to me, a kingdom, that you may eat and drink at my table in my kingdom" (Luke 22:29–30).

So, there is a covenant banquet *here* in space and time, and a covenant banquet *there* in the *eschaton*, the end time. Likewise, we have a progression from earthly marriage to marriage as metaphor, then from metaphor to sacrament, and then from the sacrament to the eschatological consummation when all sacraments will pass away before communion with God in eternity.

In the Gospel of John we have something a little different: a mysterious *convergence* of the sacramental and the eschatological, in what has been called an "interiorized eschatology." Here is the deepest meaning of the Eucharist: to partake of the Lord's flesh and blood *here* is to participate even *now* in that union with God that we shall enjoy in eternity: "He who eats my flesh and drinks my blood *has* eternal life, and I will raise him up on the last day. For my flesh is food indeed, and my blood is drink indeed. He who eats my flesh and drinks my blood abides in me and I in him" (John 6:54-56).

Finally we come to the last book of the scriptural canon, the Apocalypse, dealing with the *eschaton*, or the last time. Here, the consummation of sacred history is presented as a marriage and as a marriage feast. In the apocalyptic visions Christ appears under the figure of "the Lamb," the lamb of Lord pointed out by John the Baptist, the Passover lamb, the sacrificial victim of the new and eternal Covenant.

The age-long war with evil announced at our banishment from the garden of Eden is finally over. After the immense tribulations of human history and through rivers of blood and slaughter, we find that we have mysteriously arrived again where we first began. "And he who sat upon the throne said, 'Behold *I make all things new*'" (Rev 21:5). Behold, we find ourselves again "eating of the tree of life which is in the paradise of God" (Rev 2:7), and in that paradise we find ourselves present at the celebration of a "marriage." Only it is not a marriage of one man and one woman, but the eternal marriage of Christ and the Redeemed in which the human race is restored and raised up forever: "Alleluia! For the Lord our God the Almighty reigns. Let us rejoice and exult and give him the glory, for the *marriage of the Lamb* has come, and his Bride has made herself ready. . . . And the angel said to me, 'Write this: Blessed are those who are invited to *the marriage supper of the Lamb*'" (Rev 19:6–7, 9).

And what of the family begotten of this union? "I looked and behold, a great multitude which no man could number, from every nation, from all tribes and peoples and tongues, standing before the throne and before the Lamb" (Rev 7:9).

How many are the scriptural themes that converge in this splendid imagery: marriage, covenant, sacrifice, wedding feast, eucharistic mystery, and eschatological fulfillment! And how significant it is that of all the sacraments of the Church, at the end just two are seen to converge: marriage and the Eucharist, the sacraments of "the beginning" and of the consummation, as it were. The last two chapters of the Apocalypse—and indeed, of the entire scriptural canon—are shot through with spousal imagery: "And I saw the holy city, new Jerusalem, coming down out of heaven from God, prepared as a bride adorned for her husband" (Rev 21:2); her spouse is "the Lamb" (Rev 21:9). Finally we come to the very last words in the entire canon of Scripture. Is it any surprise that they are in the idiom of the Song of Songs, expressing a profound spousal longing for consummation? "The Spirit and the Bride say: 'Come!'" (Rev 22:17). And the Bridegroom answers, "Surely I am coming soon." To which the Church responds in earnest, "Amen. Come, Lord Jesus!" (Rev 22:20).

chapter 6

The Story of God and *Eros*

ADAM G. COOPER

How is God related to *eros*? Is not *eros* a human category? Is it appropriate to use erotic language to speak of God? Can we learn anything theologically and spiritually positive from human erotic experience, without it becoming some kind of idolatrous pursuit in its own right? Why is there such confusion today in the sphere of sexual eroticism? How can the long tradition of Christian reflection on *eros* contribute to a pastorally practical theology of marriage and sexuality?

When C. S. Lewis first set out to write his now famous book on love called *The Four Loves*, he thought it would be an easy undertaking. All he had to do, he figured, was to draw a sharp line of distinction between "need-love" and "gift-love." Need-love is selfish, while gift-love is selfless. Need-love arises out of lack or poverty, gift-love out of fullness and wealth. Need-love is characteristically human, gift-love is characteristically divine. In the end, only gift-love truly deserves the name love, because God has no needs, and God is love.

However, Lewis soon discovered that it was not that simple. He realized not only that human beings were often capable of remarkably generous gift-love, but that need-love deserves the name love as well. Although need-love, like any impulse, can be selfishly indulged, not to feel it "is in general the mark of the cold egoist." The refusal to accept one's neediness is symptomatic of a spiritual problem. In fact, our love for

God will almost always be a need-love. "This is obvious when we implore forgiveness for our sins or support in our tribulations. But in the long run it is perhaps more apparent in our growing . . . awareness that our whole being by its very nature is one vast need."[1]

THE ORIGINS OF *EROS*

Long before Christianity appeared on the scene, people recognized this vast neediness that characterizes our human situation and gave it the name "eros."[2] *Eros* was not just a word for sexual erotic passion. It symbolized everything in us that searches for meaning, yearns for fulfilment, cries out for a personal response. *Eros* is what we experience in the presence of beauty: an air of promise, a sense of the eternal, an urge to fly (the gods, recalls Plato in the *Phaedrus*, called Eros not "winged one" but "wing-giver"). It is the motivating impulse behind every human project, from the poetry of lovers to the building of pyramids, from the sensual indulgence of the hedonist to the spiritual contemplation of the philosopher. When Christianity came along, with its good news of a world reconciled to God in the crucified and risen Christ, this idea was not rejected, but overwhelmed by a new focus on the creative and generous *agape*-love of God. This love does more than merely answer to our need, but actually draws us into its infinitely fruitful, inexhaustibly life-giving ambit. By receiving the love of God, our capacity to love as God loves reaches new and unforeseen heights.

But it did not take much reflection for Christians to come to realize that the God whom they worshipped, the God whom they proclaimed in Christ Jesus as creator and redeemer of the world, was not just a God of *agape*-love but a God of *eros*-love as well. Just as Jesus commended an intense and exclusively passionate commitment to himself (Mark 10:21; Luke 7:38–47), just as he eagerly desired to fulfill the divine will, making the completion of his Father's work his "food" (John 4:34), so too he actualized the yearning and "thirst" of the eternal Father for every human being. There is nothing detached, disinterested, or unaffected in the incarnate Son's love for sinners. He searches them out, is moved by their need and desires, and enjoys their company and wants to be loved by them in return. Already in the New Testament Jesus is depicted as the

---

1. Lewis, *Four Loves*, 7–9.
2. See Osborn, *Eros Unveiled*.

prophetically heralded divine bridegroom, now come to usher his bride into the heavenly banquet feast, while his gathered people, "adorned as a bride in her splendor," return his advances with joy-filled and adoring surrender. Enfolded in the gratuitous and unconditional gift-love of Christ is the divine desire to be loved with the kind of unconditional, definitive, mutually reciprocal commitment typical of marriage. Reflecting on the story of Jesus's evocative encounter with the woman at the well and on the way it illumines the dynamics of Christian prayer, the *Catechism* seems to concur:

> Christ comes to meet every human being. It is he who first seeks us and asks for a drink. Jesus thirsts; his asking arises from the depths of God's desire for us. Whether we realize it or not, prayer is the encounter of God's thirst with ours. God thirsts that we may thirst for him. . . . Prayer is the response of faith to the free promise of salvation and also a response of love to the thirst of the only Son of God.[3]

EROS IN CHRISTIAN TRADITION

Taking the scriptural witness to incarnate divine love at face value in this way clearly requires us to go beyond a purely philosophical account of God as first cause, pure act, or unmoved mover. While Christian teaching holds to God's transcendent freedom and invulnerability to change, it also affirms—on the basis of the Incarnation—God's capacity for passion, feeling, and a love that seeks to be loved. Scriptural attributions of affectivity to God are not easily accounted for, but it is not appropriate just to explain them away as ancient anthropomorphisms. It has often been assumed by modern scholars that the tendency to interpret the Bible allegorically arose from an embarrassing discomfort with anthropomorphic images for God. Yet according to one of the greatest allegorists of early Christianity, Origen of Alexandria, even God the Father "is not without suffering. If he is asked, he has mercy and takes pity, feeling some love. . . . He undergoes human sufferings for us."[4]

This same Origen of Alexandria was among the first to reflect deeply on the especially nuptial shape of the relational convergence of loves in

---

3. *Catechism of the Catholic Church*, nos. 2560-61. For a good overview of the Fathers' teaching on *eros* and *agape*, see Andia, "Eros and Agape."

4. Origen, *Homilies on Ezekiel* 6.

Christ. In the prologue to his *Commentary on the Song of Songs*, Origen said that there is "no difference whether God is said to be loved with *agape* or loved with *eros*, nor do I think anyone can be blamed if he calls God *eros*, just as John called him *agape*."[5] Origen's theology of divine *eros* was to make a marked impact on the history of spirituality for centuries to come. In the biblical book of the Song of Songs he found the most adequate language to express the profound relationship of the Christian soul to God. Given its highly erotic language and sexually evocative imagery, the Song of Songs appears especially prone to allegorizing or spiritual interpretation. But the fact is that the central influence the Song of Songs exercised throughout the history of Christian exegesis and spirituality was not *in spite of* its eroticism, but precisely *because of* it. If the story of the soul is a love story, and if God is love as he has effectively demonstrated in Jesus Christ, then there is no more suitable vocabulary to express the relationship between the Christian and God—in all its depth and intensity, its power and precariousness, its thrill and promise—than that sanctioned and approved by the Holy Spirit himself in the exuberant erotic poetry of the Song.

Anyone who has read great works from the history of spirituality will instantly recognize the way the Song of Songs has come to shape Christian prayer. Just think of the *Confessions* of Augustine, the sermons of Bernard of Clairvaux, the letters of Catherine of Siena, the poems of John of the Cross. For these authors the love of Christ enchants the soul like music, pierces the heart like an arrow, inspires in the believer the warmest affection and ardent response of prayer. They saw that, in a way most closely akin to erotic experience, spiritual life in Christ is structured within a range of intense emotional dialectics: presence and absence, anticipation and fulfillment, now and not yet, possession and separation, longing and consummation, yearning and rest.[6] All these polarities find their parallel in the more or less fitful progression of salvation history toward its heavenly fulfillment in the kingdom of God. By writing the first Christian commentary on the Song, Origen inaugurated a tradition of spiritual reflection on the Song that was to motivate the imagination and enrich the practice of Christian prayer—especially among celibates—for more than a thousand years.

---

5. See the English translation by Greer, in Origen, *Exhortation to Martyrdom*, 223–31.

6. See especially Turner, *Eros and Allegory*; Kingsmill, *The Song of Songs*.

This erotic way of interpreting and expressing the dramatic and dynamic interaction of divine and human loves in the Christian story has not only been important for Christian spirituality, but for dogmatic theology and Christian metaphysics as well. Dionysius the Areopagite, the pseudonymous Eastern theologian whose writings so profoundly influenced the direction of medieval thought, and who was quoted by Thomas Aquinas more often than any other author next to Augustine and Aristotle, located *eros* right at the heart of his theological and cosmic worldview. Dionysius summarized the meaning of *eros* as "a capacity to effect a unity, an alliance, and a particular commingling in the Beautiful and the Good."[7] In other words, *eros* is the glue that holds together both the universe and the Church. As an innate attraction to beauty and goodness, it draws the individual out of herself into harmonious community with others. If this is true, then we must go on to speak analogously of God the Trinity as the subject of erotic love:

> We must dare add this as being no less true: that the Source of all things himself, in his wonderful and good love for all things, through the excess of his loving goodness, is carried outside himself, in his providential care for all that is, so enchanted is he in goodness and love and longing. Removed from his position above all and beyond all he descends to be in all according to an ecstatic and transcendent power which is yet inseparable from himself.[8]

Wherever this *eros* or mutual communion is to be found, the result is an *ekstasis*: a going out of oneself in order to be possessed by the beloved, as exemplified by St. Paul: "It is no longer I who live, but Christ who lives in me" (Gal 2:20). In this, says Dionysius, "Paul was truly a lover [*erastēs*] and, as he says, was beside himself for God, possessing not his own life but the life of the one for whom he yearned, as beloved above all things."[9] Through the translation of Dionysius's writings into Latin, this erotic, Christ-centered worldview found its way right into the heart of Western theology. Richard of St. Victor's interpersonal Trinitarian theology of love, Bonaventure's doctrine of the spiritual senses and affective knowing, and Aquinas's doctrines of God the creator's self-diffusive

---

7. Pseudo-Dionysius, *Divine Names IV*, 12, in *Pseudo-Dionysius: Complete Works*, 81.

8. Ibid., 10–15, 78–83.

9. Ibid., 13, 82.

goodness and the human person's ecstatic deification are all expressions of this fundamental Christian vision.

THE REJECTION OF *EROS*

Between the metaphysical and cosmic centrality of *eros* in the Catholic theological tradition on the one hand, and the role of its images and language in the spiritual and mystical traditions of Catholic prayer and biblical interpretation on the other, the erotic and ecstatic notion of divine love found a home in Christian culture and imagination. Yet it is peculiar that it did not make its mark more profoundly on the Catholic doctrine of marriage and sexuality. Part of the reason for this may have been due to the overly legal and canonical management of marriage and its mishaps throughout the medieval and Renaissance periods. This was not an era devoid of sound marital theology or of an affirmative view of sensuality, which were both ultimately grounded in a realist and sacramental ontology. But in practice these aspects seemed to be outweighed by an overly codified penitential system, a heavily clericalized ministerial economy, and an inadequately developed doctrine of discipleship that would outline a sociology of the domestic Church and properly situate marriage within the universal vocation to holiness. With the Protestant Reformation came a predictably radical reaction: along with the call to return to the sources, to slough off abuses that had overlaid the simple gospel of forgiveness in Christ's name, and to discover again the biblically sanctioned language for divine grace, came a suspicion of metaphysics, monasticism, mysticism, and spiritual exegesis—all longtime bearers of the erotic worldview. For all its good intentions and resolutions, the Catholic response, too often locked in a polemical frame of mind, was hampered for centuries from revisiting the doctrine of marriage from the nuptial perspective of divine *eros*.

But the late nineteenth and early twentieth centuries ushered in a turn in focus. In 1932 a Swedish Lutheran bishop by the name of Anders Nygren wrote a powerful book called *Agape and Eros*, bringing *eros* back into theological conversation in a new, albeit controversial way. Nygren was a deeply learned theologian and a widely respected ecumenist, but his thesis explicitly challenged the ancient nuptial spirituality of convergent loves. Nygren wanted to identify the distinguishing essence of Christianity, stripped clean of any accretions of history or tradition. He found the answer solely in *agape*, a term strictly reserved for divine love, and utterly distinct from all forms of human love. *Agape*, he argued, is marked by four main features: 1) it is spontaneous and unmotivated, 2) it is indifferent to value, 3) it is creative, and 4) it initiates fellowship with God. Unlike human love, which is always basically a self-centered desire for whatever makes one happy, divine *agape* is entirely unconcerned with the respective level of goodness in its object but is instead creative of the good. "Agape does not recognize value, but creates it. Agape loves, and imparts value by loving. The man who is loved by God has no value in himself; what gives him value is precisely the fact that God loves him. *Agape is a value-creating principle*."[10]

In contrast to *agape*, which is God's action toward human beings, Nygren characterized human love as entirely underwritten by *eros*. Stemming from the pagan mystery religions and Greek philosophy, the *eros* motif denotes an egocentric desire or yearning for completion, a driving, upward motivation to establish oneself as immortal and be like God. As such, *eros* constitutes the "born rival" of *agape*. In fact, they are "diametrically opposed to each other."[11] By *eros*, man seeks to ascend to God in order to have fellowship with God at his level. By *agape*, God descends to the human level and communes with man as a fellow-sinner.

It is hard to exaggerate the influence of Nygren's thesis, whose inspiration he traced back especially to Martin Luther and the Protestant Reformation. Its impact was by no means limited to the Protestant world. Appearing within the context of new philosophies of existentialism and personalism, it echoed a similar emphasis in the thought of Søren Kierkegaard, the father of modern existentialism, who sharply delineated between natural, erotic, and preferential love on the one hand, and supernatural, unconditional, and divine love on the other.[12] It seemed also to dovetail with the increasing and happy shift in Catholic theology away from a moralistic and legalistic understanding of Christian life toward a renewed focus upon the infinite gratuity of divine love, the centrality of Christ in effecting the world's salvation as testified to in the Scriptures, and personal reception of God's forgiveness through sacramental encounter.

---

10. Nygren, *Agape and Eros*, 78.
11. Ibid., 81.
12. See Kierkegaard, *Works of Love*.

Nygren's thesis also had the unwitting effect of forcing Catholic theologians to think again about *eros*, and the propriety of an erotic account of God, the human person, and the universe. In the period following its publication, alongside new currents in philosophical personalism and the widespread recovery of the original biblical and patristic wellsprings of Catholic theology, a critical reading of Nygren's book led to the paradoxical reinstatement of *eros* right back into the heart of the theological story.[13] Among the numerous problematic presuppositions that were found to have tainted Nygren's conclusions and propelled him to forge unwarranted divisions, was his *a priori* opposition to the natural motions of human desire. How could this be reconciled with the clear biblical witness to the created goodness of human love and the deep human thirst for God? A second problem showed up in Nygren's failure to appreciate the positive contribution of doctrinal development, especially in coming to understand better what it means for human beings to be created in the image of God. If *eros* really is egocentric in a moral sense, if it is always shot through with sin, then Nygren is right in opposing it to *agape*. However, if he had appreciated the patristic and medieval understanding of *eros* as created desire, the innate tendency of a spiritual being made by God and for God, he would have recognized how little the purity of *agape* is threatened by it.

This second problem is closely connected to a third. Nygren's thesis lacked a solid doctrine of creation (it is merely mentioned in passing here and there). Its sole concern is with man the sinner, to the virtual exclusion of man the creature. It doesn't attend closely enough to the question, who or what is redeemed? Behind Nygren's thesis lies an anthropology in which there is forced a mutually exclusive opposition between man created and man redeemed. But this prompts the question, is the pre-Christian man crushed and replaced by the Christian man, or is he redeemed and made whole?

Nygren believes there can be no positive correspondence between human desire and divine revelation. He discerns no deep relation between the gift of creation and the gift of redemption. Human love is irredeemable due to its radical egocentricity. Thus when a Christian loves

---

13. For critical appraisals of Nygren's book, see Mascall, *Recovery of Unity*, 75–86; D'Arcy, "Eros and Christian Theology," in *Mind and Heart of Love*, 74–99; Lubac, "Eros and Agape," in *Theological Fragments*, 85–87; Pieper, *Faith, Hope, Love*, 207–81; Werpehowski, "Anders Nygren's *Agape and Eros*," 433–48; Schindler, "The Redemption of Eros."

God or his neighbor, he or she acts not as the real agent and subject of love, but only as "the tube, the channel, through which God's love flows."[14] This echoes early Gnostic interpretations of Mary's motherhood, which denied that the Son took his humanity "from her" and allowed only that he became human "through her." It is basically a dis-incarnational and anti-creational anthropology, since it denies that (*a*) a human being can ever be the proper subject of love, and that (*b*) human nature, as created, is equipped with any tendency toward supernatural finality.

In the end, Nygren's ideal of *agape*-love is unrealistic. It fails to account for the actual conditions of human life and creaturely experience, according to which the "yes" of our response to God is preceded not only by God's "yes" to us in Christ, but by the "yes" of our creaturely and physical being, with all its inherent impulses, vulnerabilities, and tendencies (quite distinct from, even if fully implicated in, the defects of sin). Nygren wants us to love God selflessly, disinterestedly, without motivation, hoping to receive nothing in return. And that may be a fair enough goal. But can human beings not want to be happy? Is it wrong to love God because I have come to believe that only God can make me happy? May we detect in Nygren's thesis Immanuel Kant's distrust for everything done out of natural inclination, that is, "out of joy"?[15] Pope Benedict XVI's criticism of Nygren's thesis in *Deus caritas est* is apt: "Were this antithesis between *eros* and *agape* to be taken to extremes, the essence of Christianity would be detached from the vital relations fundamental to human existence, and would become a world apart, admirable perhaps, but decisively cut off from the complex fabric of human life" (7).

THE RECOVERY OF *EROS*

So far I have told a mainly theological history. But it may well leave the reader asking, what does this have to do with real life now? How does it affect the ordinary person—the child at school, the student at university, the woman and man in the street?

One way of interpreting the cultural and spiritual confusion of our time is in terms of a widespread crisis of *eros*. As a combined effect of Darwinian evolutionism, Nietzschean atheism, and Freudian psychologism, in both theory and experience, *eros* has been reduced to the genetic

---

14. Nygren, *Agape and Eros*, 735.
15. Pieper, *Faith, Hope, Love*, 232.

and genital, the sexual and selfish. Like Nietzsche's universe, it has become "a monster of energy, without beginning or end."[16] But the problem with our hyper-sexualized culture is not that it has become too erotic, but that it has lost the erotic. Sexuality has become divorced from its properly erotic, relational roots in both the human and divine spheres, and so become a law unto itself, a rapacious, consuming appetite, a deterministic material force that must be either obeyed or obliterated. C. S. Lewis gave the name "venus" to this kind of raw genitality stripped of the erotic. The difference between venus and *eros* is far-reaching. Sexual desire, without *eros*, wants *it*, the sheer sensation. *Eros*, by contrast, "wants the Beloved." A lustful man does not "want a woman." "Strictly speaking," explains Lewis, "a woman is just what he does not want. He wants a pleasure for which a woman happens to be the necessary piece of apparatus." There is a sense in which venus is saved, dignified, and ennobled by *eros*, for *eros* is akin to wonder and enchantment. *Eros* leads to a delighting in the mystery of another in his or her attractive power and beauty. In fact, *eros* makes a man really want, not just a woman, but one particular woman. "In some mysterious but quite indisputable fashion the lover desires the Beloved herself, not the pleasure she can give." Thus *eros*, "without diminishing desire, makes abstinence easier."[17]

In the vision of reality outlined by Christianity, the universe is essentially a sign of the *agape-eros* of God. He is the cause of *eros* in all things. It is true that human *eros* is only a feeble imitation of God's. It is true that it can become an idol, that is has its own limits, and that it needs to be disciplined, directed, and surpassed. But by no means is it only a grasping or acquisitive desire. Many understand Christian morality solely in terms of prohibitions in the sphere of *eros*. But how would their outlook change if they understood *eros* first as God reaching out beyond himself to communicate goodness and being to things in the order of creation? In the Christian notion of *eros* we find an active power whose features Nygren would associate exclusively with *agape*: it is divine, creative, and brings about fellowship with God.

The implications of this positive theological and philosophical account of God and *eros* for pastoral ministry are twofold. First, it provides a basis to affirm the essential goodness of bodily sensuality, pleasure, and emotion, notwithstanding the abiding effects of sin and concupiscence. It

---

16. Nietzsche, *Essential Nietzsche*, 151.

17. Lewis, *Four Loves*, 86–90.

has been said that, as a young priest, Karol Wojtyła "fell in love with love." Lovers were of special interest and delight to him. As a priest he walked alongside them, listened to their struggles, and became well acquainted with all the complexities of love and the moral drama. As a young actor and playwright he himself had come very close to becoming engaged. His intimate friendship was only halted from going further because of his deep sense of call to the priesthood. Shaped by these pastoral encounters, Wojtyła beautifully struck the balance when in his book *Love and Responsibility* he acknowledged sensuality, pleasure, and the emotions as providing the crucial "raw material" for the blossoming of mature, interpersonal love. *Eros* in this sense belongs to the vital human experiences of enchantment, wonder, nostalgia, promise, and hope, without which love—and all the great projects of love—would shrivel up and die. Moreover, as he proposed as Pope John Paul II in his *Theology of the Body* catecheses, such common human experiences are a legitimate means of interpreting divine love. God's love and human love, even human sexual and erotic love, are not necessarily opposed. In interpreting the divine revelation of love, John Paul says we must "appeal to experience," for revelation and experience present us with "a surprising convergence." Those who think there is a line of "total antithesis" or "radical antinomy" between them remain at the level of the abstract, instead of considering the human person in his or her concrete, living subjectivity.[18]

On the other hand, and this is the second point, experience is not always a reliable criterion by which to make judgments about true and false, right and wrong. Man, "in his present state of existence in the body, experiences many limits, sufferings, passions, weaknesses, and finally death itself..." On its own, experience cannot grasp the "content" and "reality" given in divine revelation.[19] Thus the human experience of love can never be wholly decisive. It is marred not only by the limitations of time and space, but by sin and prejudice, by hurt and suffering, by unresolved guilt and shame. Even so, these problems do not render experience—not even erotic experience—utterly suspicious and untrustworthy. By "rereading" human experience in the light of God's word, and especially in the light of what John Paul II called Christ's "redemption of the body," we are able to discern the contours of redeemed human experience, an experience that is not a far-off, abstract ideal but a real possibility, a real hope, a way of

---

18. John Paul II, *Man and Woman He Created Them*, 144–46 (catechesis 4:4–5).
19. Ibid., 145–46 n. 8 (catechesis 4:5).

living and relating lovingly that through grace and the power of the Holy Spirit can be realized right in the midst of broken human existence. In this way we are personally able to actualize in our own lives "the mutual relation" between the ethical and erotic.[20]

That is also why in *Deus caritas est* Pope Benedict XVI both acknowledged the limitations of *eros* and at the same time was able to point out the way for the impulses and experiences of erotic love to be integrated and led along a sure "pathway" to fulfillment in *agape*. It is true that God is love. But not all loves are God. This can be especially true of those erotic impulses that have their main sphere of operation in bodily sensuality. As Benedict states,

> The apparent exaltation of the body can quickly turn into a hatred of bodiliness. Christian faith, on the other hand, has always considered man a unity in duality, a reality in which spirit and matter compenetrate, and in which each is brought to a new nobility. True, *eros* tends to rise "in ecstasy" towards the Divine, to lead us beyond ourselves; yet for this very reason it calls for a path of ascent, renunciation, purification and healing. (*Deus caritas est*, 5)

The path that *eros* must tread is the path that any love, if it is to be true, must eventually walk: the path of crucifixion with Christ. In the cross of Jesus, in his pierced side, human *eros* is lifted up to the level of divine *agape* and transformed into a holy, creative, and death-defying oblation. The more we sacrificially unite our loves to Christ, the more we surrender them to his will, his guidance, his truth, the more the full nature of love will be realized in them.[21]

WHERE TO FROM HERE?

In a multitude of ways, this story of God and *eros* informs the entire mission of the John Paul II Institute for Marriage and Family. Any attempt to understand the world—whether natural phenomena, history, metaphysics, human culture, the good of society, the conditions for human flourishing and fulfillment—which does not somehow take into account the fundamentally erotic and ecstatic nature of being will end up being

---

20. On this "mutual relation" and the role of self-mastery, see ibid., 314–21 (catechesis 47:1—48:5).

21. See especially *Deus caritas est*, 7.

somehow short-sighted and diminished. But in one of our subjects we make it a central focus for study, both in the relation of *eros* and *agape* to each other, and in their combined relation to *logos* (reason or truth). The subject brings together a rich range of voices that together bear witness to the fact that the human experience of *eros* manifests a personalistic rationale, since it belongs intrinsically to the human person as a tangible and relational aspect of the *imago Dei*. This image is not just a given, but a goal, a calling, a personal, ecclesial, and cultural task. It is realized in us through a cooperative venture, a shared project in which man and woman discover in their bodily dynamisms a sign saying that they will find their true fulfillment not by living for themselves but by giving themselves away in love, by entering into interpersonal communion, first with one another, but ultimately with God.

This approach offers a unique way of discerning an enhanced level of dignity, enchantment, and sense of sacramental wonder in the dynamics of human erotic love. Just think of what is involved in the normal development of human love. First there is the experience of parental love, of receiving and enjoying the affection of a mother and father and wanting to be loved by them. Gradually through being loved we ourselves learn to love. We learn to delay our own gratification for the sake of some higher value. We learn that we want to be loved unconditionally and for our own sake and not just as a means to an end. Then there are the experiences of friendship, the strangeness of and fascination with persons of the opposite sex, of falling in love, the mysteries and anxieties of sexual arousal and attraction, the pleasures of human company, touch and closeness, the joy and stability that come to our lives through loyal friendship or faithful marriage.

These are the ways God himself has given us so that step by step we can be introduced to his special divine love in a way that corresponds to our humanity and its temporal, physical, and emotional development. On their own, human loves can't completely fulfill us. In and through them, however, we can discover our vocation to love, our inbuilt calling to an interpersonal communion with the God who is himself a triune communion of love.

PART II

APPLYING THE MYSTERY

chapter 7

Bodily Love and the *Imago Trinitatis*

CONOR SWEENEY

INTRODUCTION

Saint Pope John Paul II famously constructed a theology that made the body its central theme.[1] Such a project may no doubt appear strange to us; for how could the body imply a theology? What could corporeality have to do with theology, with the study of God, with love?[2] And further, what could the body have to do with the Trinity? In a culture that tends to treat the body as an object or machine, our capacity to understand the body outside this paradigm tends to be short-circuited before it can even begin.

The former pope gives us a short answer to this question in his *Theology of the Body*, where he proposes that the body enters theology through the "main door" inasmuch as God himself took on a body: "The fact that *theology also includes the body should not* astonish or surprise

---

1. John Paul II's *Theology of the Body* originated as a series of General Audiences given in Rome between September 5, 1979, and November 28, 1984. There have been two English publications of these addresses: John Paul II, *The Theology of the Body: Human Love in the Divine Plan*; John Paul II, *Man and Woman He Created Them: A Theology of the Body*.
2. This is a question treated systematically in chapter 6.

anyone who is conscious of the mystery and reality of the Incarnation."[3] Jesus Christ had a body. This seemingly mundane point is often lost on us. Sometimes we might forget that the divinity of Christ is paired with his humanity. Unconsciously, we perhaps often posit the person of Christ in "alien" terms: we are so blinded by his divine countenance that we forget that, in fact, his divinity is mediated to us via his humanity. But the fact is that in the Old Testament and the New, we see the use of images and metaphors that paint a deeply embodied, deeply interpersonal portrait of the love of God. In the Old Testament, God's relationship with Israel is parsed through nuptial or spousal metaphors, while in the New the love of God in Jesus Christ for his Church is explained in even more precise nuptial terms: we are told that Christ's relationship to His Church is like a marriage, and that He loved his bride to the point of giving up His own life.[4] The significance of this is that the transcendence of God is revealed to be something profoundly intimate and personal—a "one-flesh" union of love. "God is love," as St. John says. When God takes on human flesh through the Son, he therefore reveals an intimate connection between the body and love.

In this chapter, we will explore this connection. For God to take on a body suggests the *sacramental or iconic*[5] *meaning of love* as the deepest reality of existence. By entering the bodily dimension of our existence and enacting our salvation within it (Tertullian called the flesh "the hinge of salvation"), God makes love dramatically concrete. The "nuptial mystery"—referring to a central biblical image of Christ as "spouse" of the Church—expresses the intuition that *what is most real is love*, something perhaps more keenly understood by the poets rather than the philosophers, and even, dare we say, many theologians. Against Descartes, this is to say not "I think, therefore I exist," but rather, "I love and am loved, therefore I exist." This calls into question any insufficiently narrow definition of the human person as a rational animal. The Aristotelian-Thomist tradition (or at least, the caricature of that tradition) has tended to focus

---

3. John Paul II, *Man and Woman He Created Them*, 221.

4. See chapters 3 and 4 for an account of the biblical foundations of the nuptial mystery.

5. The use of "sacramental" here refers not to the technical theological description of a sacrament as "a sacrosanct sign producing grace," but rather to the more general sense that created reality in some sense reflects and participates in God's creative love. To keep this clear, we will hereafter use "iconic" as descriptive of this secondary sense of the word "sacramental."

on the human person's rational intellect, while Martin Heidegger described human being as the only being capable of inquiring about his own existence. While both these affirmations are true, they are not the entire story. For one might argue that the capacity to ask the deeply existential questions—e.g. why is there something rather than nothing?—is preceded by the experience of love, or more precisely, of *being-loved*.[6] This is to say that consciousness, rather than being an actual, self-contained reality from the start, is rather something only brought to itself through being-in-relation. Therefore, one could claim that the *why*—the very capacity and motivation to question in the first place—is given the very reason for its anguished utterance in the experience of already having experienced a "thou," an "other." We only ask *why?* if we care; and we only care, if we have been loved. On this basis, one can thus make the bold claim that God's creation can only be understood adequately through love in a strong sense, not simply as something cosmetic. This is to say that existence in general is formed and irradiated by love, and that human existence in particular, is formed and irradiated by love. In this way, space is cleared to talk about Christological and Trinitarian love having some absolutely fundamental role to play in the bodily dynamic of human love. Space is cleared to assert that *what is most real is Trinitarian love*, and that it is this that is communicated through the Incarnation and participated in through the iconic structure of the body.

Our goal is to work towards a more articulate understanding of the relationship between the body and the Trinity, beginning with an empirical defense of our claim that love is the very engine that drives reality. Our second section attempts to view our claims about the ultimacy of love in the more explicitly incarnate light of Christ and salvation history, and further, in the light of the mystery of the Trinity.

LOVE MAKES THE WORLD GO 'ROUND[7]

The claim that "love makes the world go 'round" perhaps flies in the face of our experience of the world. To say so may appear as little more than

---

6. An education in being human, then, is fundamentally an education in love.

7. Many of us perhaps know this phrase from Dante's *Divine Comedy*—Dante spoke of the "love that moves the sun and the other stars" (*l'amor che move il sole e l'altre stelle*)—but Edward Grant observes Aristotle's much earlier, if somewhat cryptic, notion that ultimately all movement was the result of being loved. Aristotle explained what it is that enabled an unmoved mover to produce motion by saying, "It produces

a romantic, poetic, or idealistic claim that can easily be deconstructed by natural selection, evil, and suffering. In the end, when viewed "from below" love in fact can appear as something only wishful, illusory, or at best temporary. In particular, the body more often than not appears as a site of *violence*, not love: a dis-integrating rather than unifying force.

But it is possible to tell a counterstory. John Paul II claimed that human experience could in fact verify the centrality of love that we are claiming lies at the very heart of human existence.[8] To begin to justify the grand claim that love is the very engine of reality, let us draw on a filial image rooted in human experience from the late Swiss theologian Hans Urs von Balthasar. For him, a central testimony for the claim that "love alone is credible"[9] is the experience of the infant who gazes for the first time into the loving smile of her mother.[10] This child, who is not yet "rational," needs no one to explain the meaning of this smile as iconic of the absolute and unqualified love of her mother. Two points can be made here. First, this smile is for the infant that which is most real, most true, most good, and most beautiful. In this experience of being-loved, there is no Cartesian doubt, no anxiety, no suspicion about the quality of the love that suffuses the entire encounter. This is to say that it is love, not strict knowledge (the paradigm of our analytic Western culture), which first irradiates the existence of the child. What we have in this experience is a kind of primordial knowing—the "knowing" of love—that comes before consciousness, and which therefore precedes all forms of doubt. This is a kind of "background knowing" that shapes the child's self-awareness and sense of value, a deeply mysterious encounter that transmits the context

---

movement by being loved" (*Metaphysics* 12.7.1072b.3–4). No doubt this seems to the modern mind an idiosyncratic mixture of science and myth/religiosity, but it perhaps suggests Aristotle's deeper, if necessarily inchoate, theological conviction that ultimately the answer to the question of why there is something rather than nothing is only approachable at a deeply mysterious level. Cf. Grant, *Foundations of Modern Science*, 67.

8. John Paul II refers to man's "original experiences" before sin and argues that these experiences are in some sense available to us now: "When we speak of original human experiences, we have in mind not so much their distance in time, as rather their foundational significance. The important thing, therefore, is not that these experiences belong to man's prehistory (to his 'theological prehistory'), but that they are always at the root of every human experience." John Paul II, *Man and Woman He Created Them*, 170.

9. Cf. Balthasar, *Love Alone Is Credible*.

10. Cf. ibid., 76; *Glory of the Lord*, 5:616; *Explorations in Theology*, 3:15–16; *My Work*, 114; *Unless You Become Like This Child*, ch. 2.

from which the child can understand herself and the meaning of life. The child for whom this experience is given in full and nurtured throughout the course of her development is the child equipped to perceive love as the very heart of what it means to be.

Second, the interplay provoked by the mother's smile reveals that the "other" is somehow structurally internal and fundamental to the fullest actuality or being of the self. The smile of the mother is the catalyst that awakens the child to consciousness. The "thou" emerges as necessary for the full constitution of the "I." There is a filial intimacy between mother and child that can nowhere else be duplicated.[11] This is therefore a love built upon the body, as the principle of fruitfulness and origin of the profound unity of mother and child. The mother's smile thus represents a principle of profound unity whereby the child intuitively understands that being-in-relation and being-dependent are not imperfections, but the very means through which the self is realized.

The mother's smile tells us, if in an inchoate or intuitive way, that love is what is most important and is something communicated to us at the very dawn of our existence. The one who appreciates the significance of this encounter is also able to appreciate a second important experiential foundation for the notion that "love makes the world go 'round." Connected to the mysterious intimacy of the mother-child relationship is the equally mysterious nuptial bond of husband and wife. The first sections of John Paul II's *Theology of the Body* unpack the anthropological foundations of the man-woman pair, as does the pope's apostolic letter *Mulieris dignitatem* 6–8.[12] In these documents, John Paul II develops conciliar document *Gaudium et spes*' "personalist" analysis of marriage. If the earlier tradition emphasized the so-called Augustinian "ends" of marriage (*proles, fides,* and *sacramentum*[13]) the conciliar personalism emphasized the *meaning* of marriage as an infrastructurally sacramental, personal relationship of love. That is to say, this shift in approach sought to complement, contextualize, and integrate "ends" analysis with a greater

---

11. A study at Bar-Ilan University in Israel made the intriguing discovery that the face-to-face interactions of mothers and their infants had the effect of synchronizing the heartbeats of mother and child to within milliseconds. See Feldman et al., "Mother and Infant Coordinate Heart Rhythms." This helps provide empirical verification of the remarkable bond that exists between mother and child, one that shows the extent to which the identity of each is tied up in the other.

12. Cardinal Angelo Scola observes that in "*Mulieris Dignitatem* we find the most organic expression of the pope's thought on this subject." Scola, *Nuptial Mystery*, 4.

13. Children, mutual help, sacrament.

appreciation of the full sacramental *meaning* of marriage as a whole, from which any "ends" derive their full meaning.

John Paul II pursues this task by studying what he calls our "theological prehistory." By this, he means the original experiences of Adam and Eve prior to their fall into sin and death. A central claim of John Paul II's analysis here is that the "original solitude" experienced prior to the creation of the "other," archetypically represented in Eve, is a cipher for the notion that only in "communion" and "self-giving" can the human person be fulfilled. This is also a development of *Gaudium et spes* 24, which teaches that "man, who is the only creature on earth which God willed for itself, cannot fully find himself except through a sincere gift of himself." Not only does this solitude and desire for self-giving attest to the Augustinian notion that "our hearts are restless until they rest in thee," but it also underscores that any such desire for transcendence is mediated through the human relationships here on earth. *Eros* is the "training ground" for and the place of the transmission of Divine Love, as it were.[14] Specifically, for John Paul II, nuptial love is a privileged paradigm that iconically communicates the kind of Divine Love that we will see in the person of Christ in his relationship with the Church (Eph 5:25).[15]

Thus, at the center of love is the *human* experience of loving; and we have again an experience rooted in and mediated by the body. For it is on the basis of their respective masculine and feminine identities, in the context of a shared human nature, that Adam and Eve discover the means to overcome the "frontier of solitude." A simple way to describe this is to say that our first parents realize that *relationship is as constitutive of their identities as is their individuality*. In other words, through my powerful gendered desire for the opposite sex, through the enrichment I discover in the other way of being human, I come to realize that *being-in-relation* is somehow the fulfillment of what it means to be an embodied, gendered human person. From out of their experience of their original solitude, Adam and Even thus discover an "original unity": an intimate relation made possible by the sexual difference, something revealed through their "original nakedness," at this point in the biblical narrative unscarred by sin. Angelo Scola explains John Paul II's theme of "original unity" in the

---

14. Cf. Pope Benedict XVI's encyclical *Deus caritas est*, and chapter 6 of this volume.

15. The Old Testament's portrayal of the God-Israel relationship in nuptial terms can be read typologically in light of the Christ-Church relationship.

language of "identity" and "difference."[16] Man and woman are "identical," in the sense that each is the image and likeness of God as an individual human person,[17] but within this shared human identity they are also "different": it is their sexual difference that provides the ground for their unique and intimate relation to one another, something that goes beyond the general category of "friendship" (what the ancient Greeks called *philia*), inasmuch as it is a bodily-personal relationship capable of generating new life. The love of husband and wife, then, is another important iconic site that manifests love as the driving force and meaning of existence. If the filial paradigm of love (the mother's smile) is the first precognitive experience of the primacy of love, the nuptial paradigm of love is the fully formed vocation of love that emerges out of that first experience of love. It more concretely represents the call to come out of oneself, to fulfill and be fulfilled by the other, and to become the parent who now transmits the smile of love to the next generation.[18]

Like the mother's smile, the nuptial paradigm also witnesses to what we can call the "otherness" of love, something again disclosed through the body. That is, just as the mother's smile witnesses to the fact that I cannot be myself except through the other, so too does the nuptial encounter witness to our vulnerability and reliance on the other. And further, both filial and nuptial loves are a powerful witness to our need for God's love. Both attest to the fact that love is not in any remote way "secular": love is not something *only* natural or human and closed in on itself, but is rather an opening to an otherness that transcends us. Indeed, we intuitively sense the constitutive *lack* in any experience of human love, even the most fulfilling experience of filial or nuptial love. For such love never truly or ultimately conquers the sting of solitude, never truly conquers death. The contingent and "needy" nature of filial and nuptial love

---

16. Scola, *Nuptial Mystery*, 25–26.

17. "John Paul insists that man and woman are both whole, even though each sex embodies this wholeness in different form." Anderson and Granados, *Called to Love*, 77.

18. Consecrated celibacy, it should be stressed, is not opposed to the this-worldly vocation of marital self-giving but is rather an "eschatological" participation in the kind of ultimate self-giving of the beatific vision, in the coming time where men and women "neither marry nor are given in marriage but are like the angels in heaven" (Matt 22:30). Consecrated celibacy enters into or anticipates this heavenly reality in the here and now of historical existence, and in this, celibates live their vocation to self-giving through prayer and service to others. For more on this, see chapter 12.

thus witnesses to our constitutive need for a far greater otherness. "The 'nuptial meaning' of the body," write Carl Anderson and José Granados,

> is thus an invitation written into our very corporeality, to recognize that everything we have is a gift, beginning with our own selves and our very existence. The "nuptiality" of the body thus establishes a relationship with the Absolute; it reveals God the Father who gives us life and surrounds us with his care.[19]

Through the human experience of love, we become fully aware of our need for God's filial love—for our insertion into the Fatherhood of God, through the Son, in the Spirit. In a certain sense, then, all genuine forms of human love—but in the texts of the New Testament, in a special and important way, nuptial love—can be regarded as iconic indicators or restless signifiers of the Divine Love of the Father; as the preparation for and call to the ultimate Trinitarian communion of God the Father, God the Son, and God the Holy Spirit. The gift of the child in the nuptial relationship further witnesses to the fact that love is something that ultimately transcends us; that is, love always breaks through our efforts to constrain it and blossoms into something richer and more fruitful than we could imagine. The child is the concrete seal that visibly confirms the oath of the couple and witnesses to the way in which love always transcends us. All of this reminds us that love is never simply something natural or human: it is always iconic of our deeper vocation in God's love.

This section has taken us from the mother's smile through to the nuptial relationship of man and woman. In both cases, we have seen how the body transmits the principle of otherness and relationship in created reality; the body is created for relationship, for love, and iconically transmits the fact that our ultimate destination is relationship with God. For John Paul II, it is the qualities of love as self-giving, and as made possible and made visible through the body, that are the primordial features of our capacity for relationship. For this reason, we can view marriage as a whole as a privileged "type" or creational paradigm of the the "nuptial mystery": the marriage relationship of man and woman, in a particularly vivid and profound way, reveals love as the meaning of our humanity and our divine calling and destination. Marriage, without even considering the way it offers sacramental grace to the couple, is both "sacramental" (again, in the sense of an icon, both referring to and embodying divine love) and "eschatological" (that is, as anticipating and pointing toward

---

19. Anderson and Granados, *Called to Love*, 70.

our heavenly destiny). It shows us in a particularly lucid way that human love is both a profound human reality and a divine reality. It shows us that love indeed does make the world go 'round. We now turn to explore what these fundamental anthropological insights look like when viewed concretely from the perspective of salvation history.

THE BODY AND TRINITARIAN LOVE

For the person with some inkling of what the Trinity is all about—especially with an intuition that 1 John 4:8's claim that "God is love" refers to *Trinitarian* love—what we have said thus far roughly coincides with the kinds of things we talk about when we talk about the Trinity. The anthropology sketched above has enabled us to transcend a purely "natural" understanding of the identity of human persons, where the body is more natural than it is personal, more biological than it is symbolic or iconic; that is, it makes visible and attests to the unique network of relations based on love that it makes possible. For all this grandeur, however, we do need to be careful that we do not make the sacramental site of love absolute or automatic: filial and nuptial love are not *in themselves* ultimate, for the sign is never the signified, and neither can they be properly fulfilled outside of an "existential" relationship with Christ that incorporates us into an adoptive, filial relationship with the Father (cf. Gal 4:4–7). Before we get carried to the point that we begin to "worship" love in its transcendental manifestation, so to speak, we have to briefly pause and consider its limitations.

As we have already suggested, we who live in this world soon recognize that there is a fundamental lack at the heart of the experience of the fullness of love. There are three basic observations that can help us prevent the icon from becoming an idol. First, we must recognize how love is plagued and scarred by the curse of sin. St. Paul voices the despair that comes with the experience of our fallen bodies: "For I take delight in the law of God, in my inner self, but I see in my members another principle at war with the law of my mind, taking me captive to the law of sin that dwells in my members. Miserable one that I am! Who will deliver me from this mortal body?" (Rom 7:22–24). Without redemption, we remain incapable of living up to our true grandeur. Second, the temporality of love in a fallen world helps us realize that it is not absolute in and of itself. From this perspective, there is *death* in the mother's smile and death in the nuptial embrace, inasmuch as human love cannot escape the tragic "knowledge-generation" cycle emphasized by Patristic writers. This refers to the endless and closed cycle of union-generation-death necessarily implied by participating in the mortal body's dynamisms. This cycle, viewed in an entirely natural way, is simply one more attestation of our individual mortality, or what Heidegger referred to as our "being-towards-death." Not only do we struggle to make love work and last, but no matter the success of this endeavor, in the end love must, in a temporal world, come to an end. Third, the filial and nuptial structure of love uncovered earlier reveals a structural otherness or difference at the heart of love, as we have said. The love experienced by human persons, if it is to be called love in the fullest sense, can never fully satisfy; it always refers to or signifies a deeper reality. Again, this is why marriage is a sacrament: not only does it communicate grace, but it attests to the deeper reality of the Christ-Church "marriage" and our vocation within this marriage, thereby pulling marriage out of any purely natural or human description. Overall, there is thus a fundamental riddle or paradox at the very heart of the phenomenon of love: while love seems to call us as an ultimate and absolute reality, it cannot on its own achieve the high standard that it sets for itself. These intuitions serve to halt any premature elevation of the grand sentiments spoken of in the first half of this essay outside of the radical newness of salvation history, outside of the specificity of the event of Christ.

It is at this point that we have to enter history to make sense of this paradox of love. For it is in history, in the person of Christ, that we encounter LOVE: a Love that overcomes sin, decay, suffering, and death; a Love that fulfills and *exceeds* the mother's smile by offering to it the absolute and redemptive smile of the Father; a Love that fulfills, exceeds, and redeems the nuptial embrace by offering it *the* paradigmatic filial-nuptial embrace in the relationship of Christ and His Church, the love of God the Father, and the love of the Trinitarian Persons. Here, John Paul II refers to the dramatic reality of the "redemption of the body." We can thus see how, as we said at the beginning of this chapter, Jesus Christ is not an alien who simply cancels out or transcends His creation in the act of redeeming it. Not only does He mediate eternal life, but He tells us that we begin to live that life in the here and now of created existence. Working within the original plan from "the beginning," Christ transforms human love from within, giving it a new standard and a new orientation.

This new standard is set by the Christ-Church relationship, the concrete historical signification of God's Love. Human nuptiality is called to participate in the radical self-giving that Christ shows for his "spouse," the Church. Here we discover the ultimate pattern and calling of love, an offering up of oneself for the other, a free, total, fruitful, and faithful dynamic of self-giving. But this is not all. For we cannot forget that Christ becomes man to impart the Divine Love of the Father, and that the Holy Spirit is the shared gift of the Father and the Son. We are touching an even greater mystery. The implication is that human love, particularly in marriage, raised to the level of a sacrament of God's Love, is not only christological but also *Trinitarian*.

In one sense, as we have suggested, for the person who has loved, there should not be too much difficulty in seeing a basic similarity between human love and Trinitarian love. In Trinitarian love, just as in human love, we can speak of a dynamic of giving and receiving, identity and difference, otherness and relationship, a kind of mutual subordination—in short, of Love. Based on the fundamental intuitions of the Second Vatican Council—in particular, on *Gaudium et spes*' strong christological and personalist emphasis—John Paul II therefore boldly asserts that, in some mysteriously analogous way, the man-woman pair is the image of the *Trinitarian* God:

> The fact that man "created as man and woman" is the image of God means not only that each of them individually is like God, as a rational and free being. It also means that man and woman, created as a "unity of the two" in their common humanity, are called to live in a communion of love, and in this way to mirror in the world the communion of love that is in God, through which the Three Persons love each other in the intimate mystery of the one divine life. The Father, Son and Holy Spirit, one God through the unity of the divinity, exist as persons through the inscrutable divine relationship. Only in this way can we understand the truth that God in himself is love (cf. 1 John 4:16). (*Mulieris dignitatem*, 7)

With this, says Scola, "the pope holds that the *imago Dei* also includes man's communional quality. He discerns an analogy between man's existence in dual unity and God's existence in the relations of the Trinity."[20] And further, affirms Marc Cardinal Ouellet, this makes it legitimate to place "anthropology within the framework of Trinitarian

---

20. Scola, *Nuptial Mystery*, 5.

theocentrism."²¹ The implication of this is thus that the man-woman relationship, based on the archetypical relationship of Christ and His Church, also originates from the Trinitarian relationship.

But, as we have hinted, there is nothing static, objectivist, or automatic about the discovery that we are made in the image of God to be in relationship. Indeed, it is only in and through the real, concrete, and historical act of being in relationship with God, through baptism, through the sacraments, that it becomes possible to live the fullness of a Trinitarian anthropology and to be in relation with the human other. It is only by first being a son or a daughter (filiality) that it becomes possible to become a husband or wife (nuptiality), a father or mother (human filiality within divine filiality). It is in baptism that sin is "immersed" and "crucified" in its waters, where the Christian rises again with Christ and enters the new world of faith as a dramatic, existential reality. It is in the liturgy and the other sacraments that this process of death and rebirth is repeated, continually re-placing us in relation to the Father. Quite literally, then, the world itself changes for the baptized Christian. You enter the reality of the event of the Son; through the Son, you enter the reality of the Father's Love; you discover yourself as *child*. You discover the new reality of the Church as Mother, of brothers and sisters in Christ. Without this baptismal existence, the kind of sacramental belonging that we are talking about here is not possible. It is only by being *in Christ*—existentially, sacramentally, liturgically—that true participation in the *imago Dei*—the *imago Trinitatis*—can be concretely realized.

Taking all of this seriously means that (among other things) we must reconsider the way we construe the relationship of husband and wife, and their collaborative relationship that gives rise to the family. Let us consider three examples. First, to say that the man-woman relationship is modeled on Trinitarian love is to accent the fact that there can be nothing like a simple or purportedly "natural" "ruling" of the husband and an equally simple or purportedly "natural" "subordination" of the wife, understood in the fallen terms of household politics or power.²² Rather, the Trinity shows us the primacy of a self-giving, mutual love, something that John Paul II develops in spousal relations in terms of

---

21. Ouellet, *Divine Likeness*, 16.

22. The perspective of grace overcomes the political implications of the curse of Gen 3:16, where God tells Eve that "your urge shall be for you husband, and he shall be your master."

"mutual subordination" (Eph 5:21) (*Mulieris dignitatem*, 24).[23] Spousal relations are placed "inside" this kind of love. Second, gender differences themselves are rooted in this horizon and thus possess a more basic co-dignity, such that specific feminine and masculine "roles"[24] each flow from this same love and take place within it, and consequently cannot be thought of in "competitive" terms. For in the Trinity, to give is of equal worth as to receive. Further, giving and receiving can only be understood relationally, that is, in relation to each other and the common aim of love. There is no "giving" dimension that can make sense outside of a "receiving" dimension. Husband and wife form a relational whole. This we learn from the Trinity, where there is a genuine sense in which giving and receiving interpenetrate such that giving and receiving no longer make sense in terms of perfect or less perfect. Third, human fruitfulness flows from the total gift of self in the marriage act, which is not itself unlike the kind of total self-giving, fruitful love operative in the Trinity. Again, this raises procreation to a new, theological level, taking it firmly outside the realm of mere animal reproduction, linking it directly with spiritual fruitfulness and making it an objective sign of the created order's transcendent destiny. Thus, both filial and nuptial love share in the Trinitarian dynamic of love.

All of this is to claim that bodily love is intrinsically linked to, and even a sign of, the Trinitarian relations. The body is not *first* biological and material. Rather, it is *first* "love." The biological and material occupy the space within this love and become expressive of it. The only adequate hermeneutic for the body, therefore, is a Trinitarian one. This is not to say that the hermeneutic is perfect or that there is a direct correspondence between human persons and Divine Persons. In *Mulieris dignitatem* 8 John Paul II provides both an important warning as well as principles to prevent the analogy overstepping its limitations.[25] The existential, sacra-

---

23. This is not to deny in advance any enduring place for the biblical teaching that the husband is the head of his wife, but it is to stress the fact that such a teaching needs to be interpreted in a new theological context.

24. "Mission" is perhaps a better, less ideologically loaded choice of word than "role," though perhaps equally ambiguous. At any rate, Scola insists that "sexual difference is not reducible simply to a problem of roles." Scola, *Nuptial Mystery*, 8.

25. "This characteristic of biblical language—its anthropomorphic way of speaking about God—*points* indirectly *to the mystery of the eternal 'generating'* which belongs to the inner life of God. Nevertheless, in itself this 'generating' has neither 'masculine' nor 'feminine' qualities. It is by nature totally divine. It is spiritual in the most perfect way, since 'God is spirit' (Jn 4:24) and possesses no property typical of the body, neither

mental, and liturgical emphasis articulated above is absolutely essential for the safeguarding of the analogy. The key point is to say, not that there is an exact similarity between Divine Persons and human persons *per se*, but rather to say that there is a profound similarity between the *Divine way of loving* and the *human way of loving*, lived and experienced within the sacramental bosom of the Church.

CONCLUSION

In this chapter, we have traveled from an obscure intuition—that love is of the very essence of reality, as implied by the mother's smile—to the uppermost echelons of Trinitarian love as its fulfillment. We have argued that the only fully adequate way to understand the human person is through the lens of this Love. We have articulated the notion that the human body signifies and mediates the presence of Trinitarian love in the here and now of historical man, a signification and mediation that are a foretaste of the fullness to which we are eschatologically destined. Scola and Ouellet, the two "Trinitarian cardinals," have in their respective works gone to some lengths to show how that might look in more detail.[26]

Some of us may be somewhat hesitant or downright scandalized about trying to posit such a grand connection between divine and human love: is it not too grand, too romantic, too idealistic, or perhaps even idolatrous? But we are not reifying or collapsing nature, but showing its true calling and destiny. The twist that we have been suggesting here is that marriage is a Trinitarian relationship before it is a natural reality. The family is called to be a Trinitarian *communio* before it is a natural social unit. In fact, there would seem to be a straight line from thinking of love and marriage as purely natural or human realities to the radical secularization and deconstruction of sexuality, marriage, and love in general. Dwelling for too long on a "natural law" perspective on marriage,

---

'feminine' nor 'masculine.' Thus even *'fatherhood'* in God is completely divine and free of the 'masculine' bodily characteristics proper to human fatherhood. In this sense the Old Testament spoke of God as a Father and turned to him as a Father. Jesus Christ—who called God 'Abba Father' (Mk 14:36), and who as the only-begotten and consubstantial Son placed this truth at the very centre of his Gospel, thus establishing the norm of Christian prayer—referred to fatherhood in this ultra-corporeal, superhuman and completely divine sense. He spoke as the Son, joined to the Father by the eternal mystery of divine generation, and he did so while being at the same time the truly human Son of his Virgin Mother."

26. Cf. Scola, *The Nuptial Mystery*; Ouellet, *Divine Likeness*.

or trying to show how Christian marriage is "rational" according to a supposedly common secular language, has the risk of making us more and more non-receptive to the true grandeur of self-giving. To trap this truly mysterious reality in the realm of "nature," reductively understood, is thus to secularize love itself. And the secularization of human love has the undesirable consequence that our hearts and desires begin to lose their receptivity to divine love. The intuition behind the nuptial mystery is that the human experience of love is actually the primer for ultimate fulfillment in Trinitarian love. Cut out or naturalize the human experience of love, and one begins to lose the radical edge of the New Testament teaching that God is love. Without the human mediation of love—without the intimate closeness of the mother's filial smile or the one-flesh union of man and woman—we render ourselves susceptible to degrading our concept of God to an abstraction or mere concept: the highest Being, the Uncaused Cause, the lawgiver, the rational principle. We lose the intimacy, the filial and nuptial realism of God's passionate love for his people. The risk is that the gift of Revelation becomes unrecognizable or extrinsic to me once human love is evacuated of its iconic significance.

Pastorally speaking, there is great value in affirming that a couple's love for one another is not simply a contractual arrangement, an instrumental or calculative way of fulfilling oneself or "getting to heaven," or the mechanical duty of begetting and raising children in a merely divinely ordained "natural" sphere. Rather, marriage is *first* about an intimate sacramental bond, rooted in the mysterious difference of sex, which incorporates the person into the mysterious bond of love between Christ and His Church and between the Trinitarian Persons. It is precisely this bond—the whole complex of desire, relation, reciprocity, sacrifice, mutuality, and fruitfulness—that uniquely and iconically discloses the "deep" meaning of marital and parental love. And it is therefore precisely this bond so understood that can fire the imagination, capture the heart, and communicate the splendor of the vocation to which spouses are called. Beginning here, rather than from the perspective of duty or morality, for example, can help the spouses see that the moral and ethical demands of married life are not extrinsic burdens (however burdensome or onerous these demands may sometimes feel!) but flow directly and organically from a deeper form of existence. As Ouellet puts it,

> We will not defeat cultural and ideological resistance through a simple repetition of traditional moral instructions. We must develop a positive vision of domestic values, a "personalist" family

spirituality which truly grounds conjugal and familial relationship within the Trinitarian communion incarnated and revealed in Jesus Christ.[27]

Marriage is demanding, yes—as are all vocations of love and gift—but its demanding features originate in the profound fulfillment that comes with the iconic intimacy of nuptial self-giving. For example, the Catholic demand that each act of sexual intercourse be objectively open to life is not one based on biologistic premises, but on the awareness that the gift of new life directly correlates to the total self-giving of the spouses. The child witnesses to the radically spiritual "fruitfulness" of the love of the spouses, the concrete presence of God in this love, and our calling to an ultimate presence and otherness that transcends our earthly existence. For the spouses to see the value of openness to the bearing of children, they need to see both the mysterious fullness of their own love and the deep connection that exists between this love and God-as-Love.

To see the true dignity of marriage and family, we need a spiritual vision strong enough to transcend all forms of reductionism, whether they come from the outside—from a secular culture that no longer knows how to love—or from the inside, from a Christian culture that simply "settles" for the least confrontational or demanding option. We need to foster and promote the kinds of practices and disciplines that communicate the truth of love, not simply by cognitive processes but by the kind of osmosis born of a genuine bond of love of a couple who are receptive to the graces offered in their marriage. The goal of this chapter has been to show how intimate the link is between our bodies and the Trinity, and to suggest that it is this spiritual vision that will be fundamental for an enriched appreciation of marital spirituality as well as a powerful antidote to the culture of death. The task is not easy, but the calling and the rewards are great.

---

27. Ouellet, *Divine Likeness*, 59.

chapter 8

A Constructive Approach to Secularism

COLIN PATTERSON

INTRODUCTION

THE CATHOLIC CHURCH IS losing the battle with secularism. Part of the problem is that she has grown accustomed to working within the rules—the rules, that is, of secularism itself. And those rules are heavily weighted against the mission of the Church. Yet the Bridegroom does not desert his Bride, and one does not have to dig far to discover resources that might be useful for the conflict. Although in itself the work of the Second Vatican Council does not provide any more than indicators and directions, their suggestive power is significant. Part of this essay will consider the impetus given by the council especially as it relates to the question of how Catholics might start afresh in combating the corrosion of secularism.

But talk of battle and conflict is not especially "constructive," so we need to affirm that there is much in secularism from which the Church has learned and can continue to learn. The aim is not the total annihilation of secularism, but rather a serious and sustained engagement with it, one marked by ground rules that allow for such an engagement. We will therefore also give some thought to how this needs to shape our approach to it. I take the term "secularism" in the broad sense as the post-Enlightenment acceptance of the principle that governments are to work for worldly ends, that the public sphere is to operate on the basis of this-worldly rationality, together with the justifying ballast that provides it with such widespread approval.

The task then is to draw upon key conciliar teachings, together with some post-conciliar elaborations and consider where they lead us in our efforts to reconfigure our relationship with secularism.

THE PROBLEM

Let us begin by briefly rehearsing to ourselves the "secularism" problem we as Catholic faithful face. When we view dispassionately the efforts of the Catholic Church, hierarchy and laity, to bring especially the Western world to an acknowledgment of the truth of Christ, we would have to say that things have not gone well. The facts are well enough known and there is no benefit in examining already well-trodden paths. Yet one would have to say that, in the face of decades of failure and religious/moral decay, recent trends continue to surprise. In the space of eight years to 2012, on the question of same-sex marriage, a commonly recognized proxy for attitudes toward religiously based moral beliefs, Australians' support for it rose from 38 percent to 62 percent.[1] Even the United States, that engine of Western culture, the nation whose strong religiosity has to date been the exception that called into question the thesis that social development necessarily leads to loss of religious commitment, even there we are now observing recent sudden and rapid growth in nonreligious conviction. In 2007, 15 percent of the population owned no religious affiliation, and this figure had grown to 19.6 percent in 2012—a mere five years later. Even more telling is the finding that one in three persons under the age of thirty years identifies himself in this manner.[2] Needless to say, the general failure to find a way to constructively engage secularism has left many with a sense of enervation or even defeat.

---

1. 2004 survey results from Newspoll; 2012 Galaxy poll provided the results for the latter figure.

2. Pew Forum on Religion and Public Life, "'Nones' on the Rise." http://www.pew-forum.org/unaffiliated/nones-on-the-rise.aspx.

THE APPROACH TO DATE

Let us also recall how the Church and her members have engaged with the modern world. When an issue arises that calls for a Catholic response, it is typically the case that, out of respect for those of other religions as well as those without any such commitment, a natural law justification is offered for the Catholic claim. The argument is based on the notion that the rules and expectations of a society should work toward the betterment of that society, and that everyone has an inner awareness of at least the basics of how we should go about achieving that betterment. It might take some further rational explanation to help people see some less obvious implications of the natural law, but at least in principle, this whole process should result in broad community support for moral positions that not only Catholic, but other Christian and non-Christian religious groups, generally speaking, are able to affirm. Put briefly, what this approach is grounded upon is a belief in a creator God, some kind of transcendent destiny for mankind, and an awareness of that which is conducive to the good of mankind. Even those with no religious beliefs have been thought to be open to natural law arguments since they were at least seen to have retained the third capacity just mentioned, that is, a responsiveness to justifications of utility or the common good. In Australia, the normal formulation of arguments proposed by Catholics in relation to IVF, euthanasia, the abortifacient medicine RU-486, Victorian abortion law reform, and same-sex marriage has taken this form. For each of these—except euthanasia—the outcomes have been disappointing.[3] In general on these issues, Catholics and other religious groups have lost the public debate. In short, people seem not to be hearing the message. Worse than that, it seems that even those who identify with the Catholic faith are vulnerable to opposing secularist arguments.

---

3. The case of euthanasia has been a little different. The successful arguments have appealed to the lack of safety of abortion law proposals. Usually a majority have opposed change to the law on the grounds of safety while saying that they support euthanasia in principle. In other words we in fact lost the in principle argument while winning the debate on the legislative proposals. The situation is at risk of a proposal that contains very strict safeguards that would weaken the safety argument.

FOUNDATIONS FOR AN ALTERNATIVE APPROACH

A cursory examination of the interventions during the first session of the Second Vatican Council quickly reveals a broad push for conciliar statements to be pastoral, ecumenical, and positive in how they address the nonbelieving world. Yet initially the momentum was in opposition to the scholastically shaped schemas that were first proposed. Only later did the solution of conciliar opinion begin to crystallize into a number of key redirections. One can point to such notions as the fuller recognition of the laity,[4] the affirmation of religious freedom and its related ideas,[5] the strongly personalist language[6] and perhaps most profoundly, the christological turn as it surfaced in *Gaudium et spes* 22—that the mystery of mankind is only fully revealed in Christ. In other contexts, one might easily point to alternative core ideas, but for our purposes, we will stay with these four principles and see where they take us.

The Lordship of the Christ Who Respects Human Freedom

"Almighty, ever-living God, [your] will is to restore all things in your beloved Son, the King of the universe . . ." Thus we pray on the Solemnity of Christ the King, and thus we believe. And surely the prayer speaks not only of the time of Christ's return, but also now in this present age. Certainly, too, Christ's rule is to extend beyond the hearts and minds of individuals so as to encompass all states, all institutions, indeed every social structure that exists within the world.[7] And yet, in some kind of relation to this affirmation, we need to place that of the Second Vatican Council: "If by the autonomy of earthly affairs we mean that created things and societies themselves enjoy their own laws and values which must be gradually deciphered, put to use, and regulated by men, then it

---

4. Cf. *Lumen gentium*, 4, 5; *Apostolicam Actuositatem*; *Gaudium et spes*, 24.

5. *Gaudium et spes*, 36. Religious freedom is, of course, the central theme of the decree *Dignitatis humanae*.

6. Cf. *Gaudium et spes* (passim).

7. The institution of this feast is not without its ambiguities. Pope Pius XI, who inaugurated it in 1925, had hopes that its celebration would work to oppose anticlericalism and remind leaders of the Lordship of Christ even in the political sphere. However, one cannot help wondering to what extent the introduction of the solemnity represents the persistent smarting of the popes at the loss of their temporal powers.

is entirely right to demand that autonomy."[8] A fully independent earthly realm? Not quite, answers *Gaudium et spes*. For

> if the expression, the independence of temporal affairs, is taken to mean that created things do not depend on God, and that man can use them without any reference to their Creator, anyone who acknowledges God will see how false such a meaning is. For without the Creator the creature would disappear. For their part, however, all believers of whatever religion always hear His revealing voice in the discourse of creatures.[9]

As the history of the Church has shown, it is difficult to thread one's way through these constraints. The temptation on the Church's part has been to pursue what one might call a "totalizing" approach that subordinates the State to the Church.[10] Pope Boniface VIII at the beginning of the fourteenth century, for example, was pushed by the uncooperative Philip IV of France to issue his bull *Unam sanctam*, in which he wrote that "one sword ought to be subordinated to the other and temporal authority, subjected to spiritual power."[11] Some centuries later, at the First Vatican Council (1870), the schema *De ecclesia Christi*, prepared and championed by the Roman Curia with the presumed support of Pope Pius IX, contained chapters some of which contain fully totalizing teaching. We read thus: "We teach ... that [this power of the Church] ... is not only linked to the internal forum and to the sacraments, but also operates in the external, public forum, a power absolute and full, truly legal, judicial and coercive." The Fathers of the council, as it turned out, rejected all but Chapter XI of the schema, which eventually became *Pastor aeternus*, the decree on infallibility.[12] Even in our day, one can find well-reasoned arguments enunciating similar notions. Thomas Pink, of Kings College, London, recently penned an article in which he made the case that in Vatican II's *Dignitatis humanae*, the Council Fathers, while making a prudential judgment that in our present era there could be a

---

8. *Gaudium et spes*, 36.

9. Ibid.

10. The term "totalizing" is used here to denominate the attempts to create a monolithic intellectual structure marked by a clearly articulated ordering of inner principles. It stands in contrast to frameworks that, for example, provide for unresolved tensions that must be dealt with by continuing dialogue.

11. Pope Boniface VIII, Bull *Unam sanctam*, DH 873.

12. The Latin text can be found in Leto, *Eight Months at Rome*, 311–20. Chapter XIV of the schema deals specifically with Church-State relations.

"right" to religious freedom, nevertheless deliberately avoided renouncing the "traditional" teaching that the Church could order the State to use its coercive powers in the interests of the Church.[13]

Against this line of argument is the New Testament witness to a concept of two (non-parallel) authorities, Caesar and God. We recall here Jesus's advice on what to render to whom (Matt 22:21; Mark 12:17; Luke 20:25), and also Peter and John affirming that the seemingly overarching authority of the state must be qualified by obedience to God (Acts 4:19; 5:29). Ratzinger, in an essay that first appeared in 1980, wrote of Jesus's saying that

> it is precisely this separation of the authority of the state and sacral authority, the new dualism that this contains, that represents the origin and the permanent foundation of the western idea of freedom. From now on there were two societies related to each other but not identical with each other, neither of which had this character of totality.[14]

Ratzinger elsewhere goes further with this line of thought, presenting the case that without an external source of moral values such as the Church, a state will tend toward the assertion of itself as origin of its moral legitimacy. "In general it is clear in the contemporary world that the faith's claim to public validity should not impair the state's pluralism and religious tolerance. But a complete neutrality with regard to values on the part of the state cannot be deduced from this. The state must recognize that a basic framework of values with a Christian foundation is the precondition for its existence."[15]

What might we conclude from this? Positively it can be argued that in itself there is nothing inherently wrong with the notion of a state that *qua* state identifies with the Christian faith. It might do this in the public symbols by which it defines itself. And such identifications still linger on in pale form in many Western societies. One might think here of Sunday as a publicly differentiated day of the week, the recognition as public holidays of major Christian festivals such as Christmas and Easter, but also as one observes, for example, in Italy, the positioning of a crucifix on the front wall of courtrooms.[16]

---

13. Pink, "Conscience and Coercion."
14. Ratzinger, *Church, Ecumenism and Politics*, 161.
15. Ibid., 219.
16. Ibid., 219–20.

However, in terms of actual public policy, such symbolic affirmations carry little bite. We must go on to raise the possibility that if Christ is truly to be acknowledged as King, then we must call into question a pervasive presupposition that the state must remain a neutral player in the political sphere. Negatively we can say that when a state (as well as civil society) require(s) secular reasons in the exercise of public discourse, when it is blind to the nonsecular goals of its citizens, when it promotes a secular public education system, and more generally acts in a way that is nonreligious, then one can reasonably conclude that, whatever the allegiances of its participants, it is presenting itself as nonreligious. To write in these terms is to call into question the notion of a "neutral" state. Perhaps one of the most corrosive effects of this reality is the power of the state to influence the personal morality and indeed the religious commitments of its citizens.[17]

In theological terms, it seems reasonable to point to two conciliar keys as supportive of the above propositions: the relative autonomy of the secular sphere and its associated idea of religious freedom, on the one hand, and the rethinking of the nature-grace relation that began with de Lubac's *Surnaturel* and found expression in the *Gaudium et spes* 22 principle.[18] This latter conviction carries the implication that the relationship between faith and secular reason is not one of separation and independence but of a messier complexity in which the "relative" part of *relative autonomy* must be taken into full account. Perhaps better than Ratzinger's reference to dualism we might use the term "dialogic," with each of the dialogue partners conceived of as imperfect rather than perfect societies.

A Language of Public Justification?

As we have hinted above, the move from the totalizing approach of some Church documents during the nineteenth century to the framework proposed at Vatican II, especially in *Dignitatis humanae* and *Gaudium et*

17. In fact, one might draw attention to *formal* similarities between the demand of the state in ancient Rome for all its citizens to recognize the supremacy of its cult over their own religious allegiances, and the condition of participation in modern Western societies as the acknowledgment of the neutrality of the state. Psychologically, one would expect similar effects of compliance in both settings.

18. The most accessible account of de Lubac's theology of nature and grace is to be found in his *A Brief Catechesis on Nature and Grace*.

spes, represents a significant—and to some, quite disturbing—turn. But it does not address the so-called problem of public justification. What kind of language is to be used as a kind of conceptual *lingua franca* so that all citizens can fully participate in public discourse? The secularist position, widely accepted, is that what is needed is that which is acceptable to all. As a lowest common denominator, secular language, that which argues from empirical reality and logical coherence, is the only acceptable possibility. A deeper notion of justification based upon a theory of the good (for example, that a religion might propose) cannot apply since individual citizens will not agree upon any such theory. Those who accept this position are commonly referred to as consensus theorists and they mirror the dominant assumptions of those who participate in the public sphere in Western societies.[19]

Two key problems arise here. First, the truth is that in most cases, arguments couched in the language of a religious commitment cannot be easily translated into secular terms. An argument against divorce, for example, that draws upon the authoritative teachings of Jesus loses its core affirmation—divine authority has spoken on this matter—if one attempts to translate it into a statement about how widespread acceptance of divorce will lead to social disruption. Second, the whole notion of translation to secular language fails the fairness test since all religious citizens are required to shed key elements of their argument in the interests of translation into secular terms, while nonreligious persons are not obliged to translate and thereby to gut their argued case.

Increasingly, however, different possibilities are being put forward by those who are called convergence theorists. They hold that different religious and nonreligious reasons might be used to justify a public policy argument and that, as their name suggests, it is the convergence of stances in relation to policy that is the condition for its acceptance. Of course, there must be operative constraints which would define the suitability or appropriateness of confessional justifications. Claims of fact in support of a particular justification would be rejected if they were found

19. Foremost among consensus theorists is John Rawls, who wrote extensively on public justification. In fact, he allowed for the introduction of confessional justification into public discourse, but held that eventually it would need to be "translated" into secular language in order to properly serve its purpose. See especially his book *Political Liberalism*. Also influential as a consensus theorist is the German philosopher Jürgen Habermas, though again the label is not strictly applicable given his more recent comments about the place of religion in the public sphere. Cf. Habermas, "Prepolitical Foundations," 19–52.

to be false. Likewise, claims of value would have to be tested against some criterion of acceptability, perhaps agreed upon by the major confessional groups involved in public conversation.[20]

The difficulty with this latter type of proposal is that it is quite uncertain whether a truly engaging public discourse could even be established. Such discourse is surely more than a mere tossing in of one's opinion on a matter; it requires the genuine testing and weighing of ideas in order for the optimization of decision-making.

Perhaps there is a third alternative that takes advantage of both types of theory. Suppose that a Catholic politician were to argue the case for a matter of moral significance by calling upon Scripture and Tradition (and magisterial teaching, if needed), but also highlighting elements of that argument that represent commonalities with the kinds of arguments that might be proposed by a politician from a non-Christian faith tradition. This is possible because we do not typically provide only proof-texts even within ecclesial discourse, but also include explanations or justifications that derive from other parts of the transmitted word of God. These latter, because of their more general character, often enunciate truths that are relatively transparent to other faith traditions. (e.g., God's love for his creation, His interest in the marriage relationship, etc.). At these points, we are dealing with elements of the natural law as it manifests itself in history and in the real world. In this way, a genuine non-reductive dialogue among people of diverse religious traditions could proceed.[21]

But what about nonreligious citizens? Would they not be excluded from the debate? To answer this question, we need to draw attention to another aspect of "translation" necessary within the current secularist mode of public discourse. Not only do religious arguments drawing upon authoritative sources have to be excluded from secular conversation, but

---

20. Among convergent theorists one would include Jeffrey Stout, Nicholas Wolterstorff, and Paul Weithman.

21. The use of the term "natural law" needs to be nuanced. The notion of "natural law" is a Christian theological concept based upon confessionally particular presuppositions even though it points to a reality "beyond" Christian faith as historically instantiated. Perhaps a better expression is "religious moral law" which would refer to moral commitments as they exist in actual religions rather than what is commonly treated as an idealized, abstracted form derived from a Judeo-Christian framework. What this means is that Christians, within a Christian state, are unable to use the revelatory truth they possess as a trump card in the engagement between themselves and other religious communities. They must settle for a dialogically achieved best option that respects the "relative autonomy" of social groupings within society.

religious notions of the good also have to be reduced to those of a secular nature. Spiritual goods are beyond the scope of such discourse to which only secular goods have a place.[22] And yet, religious arguments typically include notions of secular as well as spiritual good. At this point nonreligious argument becomes relevant, for here there is an area of common ground, certainly more limited than what obtains when diverse religious arguments engage one another, yet still important since, at least on the basis of empirical truth, neither side is seen to have any advantage—the playing ground, at this point, is level.[23]

The theological rationale—as distinct from political considerations—for this approach is that while natural law, at least in part, can serve as a moral foundation for a polity, it never appears in reality divorced from its "incarnation" within a determinate religious context; there is no Platonic form called the natural law. In the practice of politics, Christians must address adherents of other faith communities (both bilaterally and multilaterally) who must be allowed to articulate their own moral convictions. These convictions the Christian dialogue partners will need to interpret as expressive of the natural law, but they will not be able to "correct" or "improve" them by recourse to a superior, non-sin-affected knowledge of natural law as elucidated by revelation.

It must be said that the idea of developing an alternative mode of public discourse participation is daunting. In fact, for many the initial thought would be one of the improbability of it all. Nevertheless, the perspective must be one that takes a long-term view of things. Further, there is an inherently persuasive element in the argument which criticizes the use of secular language as the language of public justification, particularly

---

22. The importance of publicly presenting the case for the centrality of spiritual goods for believers is often overlooked. This perhaps suggests a loss of confidence in this dimension of the Christian life, an overshadowing of the theological virtue of hope. On the side of the state, one might suggest that a state needs to recognize the reality of both secular and spiritual dimensions to the seeking after the good that its citizens pursue, and yet, since it cannot exercise coercive or persuasive power to urge a particular religious orientation upon its people, it is obliged simply to acknowledge the good that is the pursuit of religious and moral truth and to that extent provide appropriate forms of assistance to such associated activities. While the particular aspects of this assistance must be worked out within specific circumstances, at the very least it precludes such notions as the "wall of separation" which has become a kind of quasi-foundational jurisprudential principle in American legal circles.

23. It must be noted, however, that this kind of argument seems to be difficult to sustain in view of ideological, quasireligious commitments to freedom and autonomy. Cf. recent same-sex marriage debates.

among those who have not implicitly adopted secularist commitments in their life and thought.[24]

Considering these notions in terms of our conciliar keys, we argue that taking seriously the principle of personalism so pervasively present in *Gaudium et spes* requires of us, first, to be clear about the identity of persons, individual and corporate, who participate in public discourse, and secondly to relate to them in ways that fully acknowledge their dignity as human beings. The reality is that the "neutral" state is not neutral and thus must not be so treated. The deceit of this claim must be persistently called into question. On the other hand, other religious communities must be viewed as genuine bearers of convictions that express the natural law and the *form* in which they express that truth must be respected. Likewise, nontheistic commitments must also be respected as genuine, and indeed, partly the result of the failures of Christian believers themselves.

Church and State?

In *Gaudium et spes* we find the following acknowledgment by the Council Fathers: "Now many of our contemporaries seem to fear that a closer bond between human activity and religion will work against the independence of men, of societies, or of the sciences" (36). Many would own that the Fathers' observation was fully justified. Although in most Western nations the direct and extensive participation of the Church in political affairs is now a thing of the past, for whatever reason, historical memory is particularly strong in this respect. It was in 1648 that the Peace of Westphalia concluded the extraordinarily destructive hostilities of the so-called Thirty Years' War, and this negotiated settlement is often seen as marking a turning point in the relationship between the Church and the State. We have remarked on how ingrained the thinking arising from those times has become in nations with Christian foundations, and we have suggested an alternative framework with regard to how we are to understand the role of the State.

But what about the Church—how is it to be understood in its relations with the State? One of the unfortunate elements central to the issue

---

24. One Australian public figure who has managed—quite successfully, it would seem—to incorporate confessional language into his public utterances is the former Anglican Archbishop of Sydney, Peter Jensen.

is precisely the phrase "Church and State," for, while the notion of the State is relatively straightforward, that of the Church is quite ambiguous. Given the insistence of Vatican II that, first, the secular sphere is primarily that in which the laity are to be involved, and second, that religious freedom is a fundamental right, the distinction between the Church as hierarchy and as laity becomes crucial to our discussions. In fact, one could make a case for the idea that the problem is better expressed as the relationship between hierarchy, laity, and state. In this case, the laity takes on its full responsibility as the primary representative of Christ and the Church within the secular world, a responsibility that the Church hierarchy is called to support rather than compete with or undermine by a too ready intervention in public policy debate. In that role, the laity serves as a kind of buffer between hierarchy and state, freeing the Church leadership to pursue its calling to preach, teach, and lead and at the same time functioning as a fully legitimate, *Christian* conversation partner in the public sphere and in relation to the state. That is, the laity is the primary means by which the truth of Christ is to find form within society and government.

How is the laity to organize itself to engage in this work? Certainly, such work is and has always been carried out believer by believer, each bringing the truth and joy of the gospel to his or her life context. And yet more is required. To put flesh on the bones of the notion of the laity as a third player in the hierarchy-laity-state constellation, some form of institutionalization is called for. Forms of joint activity by those learned in both theology and the various secular sciences and humanities might be developed and their work could contribute to the public conversation on various matters. To function effectively, such institutions would need to be and to be seen as being at arm's length from the Church hierarchy, and at the same time, faithful to Catholic teaching and publicly identifiable as—and in fact—representative of the legitimate range of positions existing within the Church. Note that multiple rather than single institutions are envisaged since this would underline the truth that on most matters of public policy, the Christian faith by itself is insufficient to specify what should be the content of, for example, a particular piece of legislation.

Admittedly, in terms of our conciliar principles, this last proposal is not easily connected. Nevertheless, the Council's willingness to shine the spotlight on the nature and mission of the lay faithful certainly suggests some confidence in their capacity to truly participate in Christian mission in a secular age. Further, it is not unreasonable to argue that the "tradition" of Church and State as the two principles of authority within society, while certainly ancient, *at least in that form*, is not a foundational tradition. The Catholic faith clearly distinguishes the vocations of ordained and lay ministry, and there is no reason why that truth cannot find expression in our conceptions of how we as Church are to relate to the State.

CONCLUSION

This essay has been an experiment in imagining an alternative, *partly* constructive approach to secularism. On the basis of inspiration from some key themes found in the teaching of Vatican II, it has proposed a dialogic form of the relationship between the State and the Church, a public language embracing confessional and natural law justifications, and a reconceptualization of the Church-State relation as that between hierarchy-laity-state. Together these ideas are intended as a contribution to the Church's ongoing efforts to discover modes of mission that truly communicate the power of the gospel both to individuals *and* to "principalities and powers," both to the religious *and* to the secular.

chapter 9

The Role of Natural Law in Bioethics: Anthropocentrism or Theocentrism

NICHOLAS TONTI-FILIPPINI

INTRODUCTION

The practical problem of how to conduct oneself as a Christian and a philosopher or bioethicist in public debate, or engaged in government agencies or the formation of public policy, is difficult. A solution has been to approach the issues on the grounds of our natural law tradition but understood anthropocentrically with the ultimate end not being communion with God but integral human or communal fulfillment. A common contemporary approach of this kind is called New Natural Law (NNL) and identified principally with John Finnis, Germain Grisez, Robert P. George, and Joseph Boyle. This approach has been pursued as a way of allowing a dialogue with nonbelievers.

This separation of philosophy and theology has had its critics, most notably Pope Benedict XVI and his predecessor, Pope John Paul II. They took a different approach that was essentially christocentric, involving a close partnership between philosophy and theology, but recognizing the autonomy of philosophy, practical reason, and natural law. However, in recognizing the autonomy of natural law epistemology, they rejected granting sovereignty to reason and they espoused a form of natural law that accepted the place of a creator and understood our relationship to the creator as being relevant to understanding human finality.

There have been approaches not only in the secular world but also within the Church that overlook the dependence of human reason on Divine Wisdom and on the need, given the present state of fallen nature, for Divine Revelation as an effective means for understanding moral truths, even those of the natural order. Pope John Paul II referred to those who proposed a *complete sovereignty of reason* in morality, saying, "God could not be considered the Author of such a law. The participation of the natural law in the divine law recognizes the interdependence of faith and reason" (*Veritatis splendor*, 36).

As I shall explain, this is a problem with the project that John Finnis sought to achieve in part II of his *Natural Law and Natural Rights*, discussed below. There is a related problem with a view expressed by Germain Grisez, who rejected the notion that our ultimate end is communion with God, asserting instead an anthropocentric view that our ultimate end is integral communal fulfillment. This approach also permitted a development of natural law that did not need to recognize the existence of a creator and thus afforded dialogue with nonbelievers by, in effect, sharing their premises, at least for the sake of the dialogue.

The proponents of NNL in the 1960s and 1970s sought sincerely and loyally to defend the faith against both a growing tide of secularism without, and the development of proportionalism and the fundamental option within, the Church. No one should underestimate the importance of what they did. But now when one reads, for instance, the defense of Magisterial teaching in the minority opinion of the Papal Commission on Birth Control,[1] one realizes how much of a reform there has been of natural law and the understanding of marriage and sexuality in the Church through the Second Vatican Council and the papacies of Pope Paul VI, Pope John Paul II, and Pope Benedict XVI.

In my own experience in more than thirty years of public involvement in bioethics and public policy formation, I have discovered that the NNL approach has two overwhelming problems. What is offered to the secular dialogue, as an anthropocentric natural law, often sounds false to secular others because we propose something apparently guided by our beliefs, but fail to acknowledge that contribution. However, something that I have discovered latterly in that approach is, in fact, that it is false

---

1. Pontifical Commission on Birth Control, "Minority and Majority Opinions."

by our own Christian standards. By the anthropocentric strictures we impose on our contribution we, in fact, ignore the New Law instituted by Christ, the law of love. The NNL project has proved to be a failure where it has been tried, and was doomed from the outset, because in being anthropocentric it was essentially lacking: the answers that it gave to problems were often unsatisfactory because of a failure to consider the place of love, and the particular demand of our actions needing to be capable of being oriented toward God, the God of love.

The NNL approach tended to produce a casuistry that was too liberal and too lacking in understanding of the essential role that affectivity plays in our lives, created as we are in the *imago Dei*, in the image and likeness of the God of love. Such a morality demands much more than anthropocentric reasoning can achieve. In my experience, the NNL approach usually fails even to convince believers because it is not based in who they are, why they exist, and what their ultimate end is, except anthropocentrically. Its claims to the self-evidence of basic human goods are simply unconvincing because they are given no relationship to our ultimate end in communion with God. Basic human goods are related to human flourishing, and the ultimate end determines what it is to flourish as a human being.

Even the first principle of natural law, defined by the NNL in such a way as to be recognizable as the Pauline principle, that one must not do evil in order to achieve good, is not in fact self-evident because without an ultimate end in communion with God, there seems to be little reason to hold that one cannot destroy a basic human good in order to achieve a greater benefit in terms of other basic human goods—or choosing the lesser evil. Because our ultimate end is communion with God, the authenticity of a human act is related to love of God and neighbor, the latter being made in God's image and likeness.

The most difficult battle against secularism is in establishing absolute moral norms. In my experience, an anthropocentric, atheist, or agnostic natural law seems to be incapable of persuading anyone other than those perhaps who already believe in absolute moral norms. As I will explain, this would seem to have something to do with the theological virtues whose dimension of affectivity has no place in an anthropocentric natural law. In fact, NNL is at least deeply suspicious of affectivity within moral reasoning.

In recognizing these difficulties I propose to illustrate the way they play out in the NNL in the application of double effect reasoning, specifically the case of condoms within marriage for disease prophylaxis, and craniotomy, a classic test case for moral theological principles. NNL has difficulty identifying evil in the object of the act both because of its anatomy of the moral act and because it does not identify the ultimate end theonomically. Then I will draw some wider implications and suggest an alternative approach that reflects a partnership between philosophy and theology as espoused by the Second Vatican Council, and by Popes Benedict XVI and Pope John Paul II, an approach that I have tried with some success in chairing government committees.

THE NEW NATURAL LAW AND ANTHROPOCENTRISM

Among other matters, the International Theological Commission discussed the possibility of a universal ethic that is common to those endowed with reason in relation to the requirements for establishing a just society.[2] In Western society we are witnessing the growth of a secularism that has not only discarded Christianity, but also the balance between God, man, and nature that is at the heart of our tradition, and with it, the teleology that gives meaning and purpose to human activity. With that rejection, secularism has virtually ended the possibility of developing a universal ethic. In its place is an individualism that in this postmodern era rejects absolute moral norms, such as the protection of innocent human life, in favor of life lived as an individual narrative judged only for its autonomy. There is a categorical rejection of the very basis of what is known traditionally as natural law and thus seemingly little scope for discussion between Christianity and secular culture, if we persist in thinking we can engage the culture by adopting its anthropocentric premises and yet still achieve recognition of a universal ethic. The culture rejects both our teleology and moral absolutes because it rejects the notion of objective reason.

The Commission cautions us to "be modest and prudent when invoking the evidentness of the precepts of the natural law," but nonetheless

---

2. International Theological Commission, *The Search for Universal Ethics*. There is no official English version available. However, an English translation by Joseph Bolin is available at www.pathsoflove.com/universal-ethics-natural-law.html. The official French and Italian versions are available at http://www.vatican.va/roman_curia/congregations/cfaith/cti_index.htm.

calls on us to engage in a dialogue with a view to a universal ethic.³ It is difficult to see how this is achievable using anthropocentric ideas of natural law that lack the affectivity of the theological virtues.

However, the Commission refers to the convergence of philosophy and religion in the natural law,⁴ and its view of natural law is not anthropocentric. The Commission maintains that the doctrine of natural law possesses coherence and validity on the philosophical plane of reason common to everyone, acquiring its "full sense within the history of salvation: in fact Jesus Christ, sent by the Father, is, with his Spirit, the fullness of every law."⁵

The Commission also explains the dependence of the natural law on grace:

> Grace does not destroy nature but heals it, strengthens it, and leads it to its full realization. For this reason, even if the natural law is an expression of reason common to all men and can be presented in a coherent and true manner on the philosophical level, it is not external to the order of grace. Its claims are present and operating in the different theological states through which our one humanity has passed in the history of salvation.⁶

The Catholic tradition recognizes the role of faith and reason as complementary: "like two wings on which the human spirit rises to the contemplation of truth" (*Fides et ratio*, introduction). However, the role and nature of practical reason or natural law is a contested subject. There are a number of propositions that indicate the nature of the disagreements.

The dominant view taught in seminaries until the 1960s was largely informed by the philosopher Francisco Suárez (1548–1617).⁷ According to John Finnis, for Suárez the principle questions were what is fitting for human rational nature and what is unfitting for it. Finnis writes that the first principle of natural law for Suárez is "follow nature." This approach is often described as *rationalism* and is to be contrasted with St. Thomas Aquinas, who spoke instead of the basic forms of human well-being and the potentially realizable ends of human conduct. Finnis also associates Suárez with *voluntarism*, the view that obligation is essentially the effect

3. Ibid.
4. Ibid., 11.
5. Ibid.
6. Ibid., 101.
7. Suárez, *De Legibus*, Book II, Ch. 7.

of an act of will by a superior being. That is to say that the natural law has to be attributed to a superior being.[8] To be a law a law must have a lawmaker who is superior to those who are subject to the law. This differs from the view that Finnis would take that the natural law reflects truths about human nature. In that respect the task is to recognize that truth is discovered through reasoning rather than that anyone invents it.

Finnis developed an approach to natural law in which he avoids any need to advert to the question of God's existence or nature or will.[9] He bases his approach, he argues, in Aquinas, claiming that the latter recognized that (1) the existence of God is not self-evident to the human mind, (2) the knowledge that friendship with God is our last end is not available by natural reasoning but only by revelation, (3) achieving that end is not possible by natural means but only by supernatural grace, and (4) the will of God cannot be discovered by reasoning.[10]

The feature that distinguishes natural law approaches is that they reflect a search for truth that tests the soundness of a proposition using human reason. Natural law is thus to be distinguished from faith which accepts a proposition as a teaching by an authority. Thus Christians may understand morality as a matter of reason and they may understand it as a matter of faith in Jesus and the Scriptures, in divine Revelation. It is a matter of different epistemologies. One assesses truth by reason, the other measures truth on the basis of authority. This is basically how it seems to have been understood by Aquinas, who did not overlook the presence of the complementary forms of wisdom—on the one hand *philosophical* wisdom, based upon the capacity of the intellect to explore reality, and on the other hand *theological* wisdom, based upon Revelation and exploring the contents of faith, entering the very mystery of God (*Fides et ratio*, 44).

CONDOMS WITHIN MARRIAGE AS DISEASE PROPHYLAXIS

To give an example of the difficulty in relation to understanding natural law anthropocentrically and understanding it as a theonomy,[11] consider

---

8. Finnis, *Natural Law and Natural Rights*, 45.
9. Ibid., 49.
10. Ibid., 48–49.
11. This is the term used by John Paul II in *Veritatis splendor* 41 and that is discussed later in this chapter.

the vexed contemporary issue of condoms to prevent HIV transmission in marriage from a seropositive person to his non-seropositive spouse. In summary, Archbishop Anthony Fisher explained that condomized sexual intercourse is nonmarital because it is *not apt for generation of new life* and it is not genuine marital union because *it involves deliberately preventing the two-in-one-flesh union that is the type of act that may be capable of generating new life*.[12]

How might Aquinas approach explaining the wrong involved in the latter? In his *Summa contra Gentiles* he explains the wrong of fornication:

> Each and every part of man, and every one of his acts, should attain the proper end.... The male semen is ... necessary in regard to the propagation of the species.... What is sought in the case of semen ... [is] ... to emit it for the purpose of generation, to which purpose the sexual act is directed. But man's generative process would be frustrated unless it were followed by proper nutrition, because the offspring would not survive if proper nutrition were withheld. Therefore, the emission of semen ought to be so ordered that it will result in both the production of the proper offspring and in the upbringing of this offspring.... It is evident from this that every emission of semen, in such a way that generation cannot follow, is contrary to the good for man. And if this be done deliberately, it must be a sin. Now, I am speaking of a way from which, in itself, generation could not result: such would be any emission of semen apart from the natural union of male and female. For which reason, sins of this type are called contrary to nature.[13]

He goes on to explore the need for marriage to achieve the proper upbringing of children:

> Now, a woman alone is not adequate to this task; rather, this demands the work of a husband, in whom reason is more developed for giving instruction and strength is more available for giving punishment. Therefore, in the human species, it is not enough, to devote a small amount of time to bringing up offspring, for a long period of life is required. Hence, since among all animals it is necessary for male and female to remain together as long as the work of the father is needed by the offspring, it is natural to the human being for the man to establish a lasting association with a designated woman, over no short

---

12. Fisher, "HIV and Condoms within Marriage," 329ff., 344–45.
13. Aquinas, *Summa contra Gentiles*, book 3, chapter 122, subsection 4.

period of time. Now, we call this society matrimony. Therefore, matrimony is natural for man, and promiscuous performance of the sexual act, outside matrimony, is contrary to man's good. For this reason, it must be a sin.[14]

This is, in a sense, his natural law argument in relation to sexuality. Later he provides some confirmatory references to Scripture, including Lev 18:27–33, 1 Cor 6:10, Deut 23:17, Tob 4:13, and 1 Cor 6:18,[15] thus covering both the natural law and the faith reasons in relation to sexual morality.

Crucial to the above form of the natural law argument is the relationship of acts to ends ("the purpose of generation, to which purpose the sexual act is directed")—the propagation of the species, including the proper upbringing of children. So we have here what the Church has been inclined to call the inseparable link between sexual acts and procreation within marriage,[16] eschewing acts that exclude the generation of children—that is, all nonmarital acts, as Fisher would have them described. First, Aquinas invokes the natural good of the propagation of the human species. Deliberate emission of semen while preventing the achievement of this good is wrong. Second, he proceeds to say that human generation is fully achieved only through committed and long-term nutrition and education of offspring, for which marriage offers the best context. So emission of semen must be in marriage, directed to human generation, and not be deliberately frustrated.

It is worth noting that prior to the catechesis on the theology of the body[17] by John Paul II, the Church similarly tended to explain the wrong of promiscuity by reference to natural ends or finality of sexuality. Thus, the Congregation for the Doctrine of the Faith explained it in the following way in 1975:

> Experience teaches us that love must find its safeguard in the stability of marriage, if sexual intercourse is truly to respond to the requirements of its own finality and to those of human dignity. These requirements call for a conjugal contract sanctioned

---

14. Ibid., subsection 8.

15. I am grateful to my colleague, Dr. Adam Cooper, for drawing my attention to this passage.

16. Pope Paul VI, *Humanae vitae*, 12

17. The term given to Pope John Paul II's catechesis on marriage and sexuality in his Wednesday audiences and further developed in the encyclicals of Pope Benedict XVI, especially *Deus caritas est*.

and guaranteed by society—a contract which establishes a state of life of capital importance both for the exclusive union of the man and the woman and for the good of their family and of the human community.[18]

Similarly, we find the Congregation for the Doctrine of the Faith also referring to the natural finality of sexuality in relation to masturbation:

> The main reason is that, whatever the motive for acting this way, the deliberate use of the sexual faculty outside normal conjugal relations essentially contradicts the finality of the faculty. For it lacks the sexual relationship called for by the moral order, namely the relationship which realizes "the full sense of mutual self-giving and human procreation in the context of true love."[19]

The basis of the teaching in ascribing a natural end or finality to sexuality based on human experience is very limiting if an interlocutor simply does not accept the claim. Contemporary culture has so banalized sexual intimacy to be, at best, romance. Consequently, there is an apparent inability or unwillingness to recognize sexuality as having a purpose or end that transcends the individual or the individual couple. This approach also lacks pastoral relevance because it is unrelated to a couple's vocational motivation within marriage and their desire for transcendence.

What is important in this is not to so circumscribe natural law that it must ignore transcendence and the Creator or propositions that have their source in reasoning about the Creator. Natural law does not have to be based on atheistic beliefs or agnosticism. Natural law is distinguished by an epistemology that recognizes the role of reason in testing propositions, and it is reasonable to have concluded that there is a creator and that our relationship to the creator matters to us and to the creator, and to take that into account in natural law reasoning. It is important that the First Vatican Council asserted and Pope John Paul II reaffirmed in *Fides et ratio* (52): "If anyone says that the one, true God, our creator and lord, cannot be known with certainty from the things that have been made, by the natural light of human reason: let him be anathema."[20]

One might, for the purposes of a discussion with an atheist, attempt an explanation of a moral issue on atheistic or agnostic premises, but that

---

18. Sacred Congregation for the Doctrine of the Faith, *Declaration on Certain Questions Concerning Sexual Ethics*, section VII.

19. Ibid., section IX

20. *Dei Filius* (Dogmatic Constitution on the Catholic Faith), Canon 2 (1).

would not do justice to reason if it was thought that a reasoned approach must ignore the reasonableness of belief in, and understanding of, the creator from our experience of all creation, including ourselves, as human beings, and reasoning about our relationship to the creator and the purposes of our created existence. In fact, an atheist or agnostic would not expect a believer to behave as though God did not exist.

Contemporary thinking in relation to a theology of the body is not beyond philosophical analysis. It has its basis in Scripture and it understands marriage in terms of the Genesis account of creation, but its propositions about human and divine love and the human vocation to give witness to the Creator's love are philosophically testable. They are bound up with the transcendent which should not be beyond philosophy. In doing so we can approach our secular society with something much deeper and stronger, much more appealing than the emptiness and affective vacuity of the finality of a human act asserted as self-evident in human nature without affectivity and lacking a transcendental context.

Important in this context is to undertake a philosophical analysis of love, especially its agapaic and erotic aspects[21] and the role that affectivity plays in a full account of morality, especially sexual morality as part of and not separable from our vocation to love the Creator and to give witness to his love. It is not beyond us as philosophers to explore what is implied by a "Trinitarian anthropology" and its significance for our understanding something of the nature of divine love as a love not just between God and all creation, but also between the Persons of the Holy Trinity. We might not venture so far in dialogue with an atheist or agnostic, but we are better off explaining a full meaning of love and affectivity and Christianity's positive approach to the human body and sexuality than selling it short with lame claims about human nature and the natural finality of human acts (devoid of a context of divine love). The life, suffering, and death of Christ are a compelling love story, and we would be both fools and hypocrites to ignore the centrality of Christ in understanding what we mean by love and hence what we mean by sexual morality.

The condom issue within marriage for disease prophylaxis needs to address the vocation of married couples and to explain that for a Christian the baptismal vocation is to give witness to divine love. The love between the Persons of the Holy Trinity, the love between the creator and all creation, and the love between Christ and humanity is a love that is both

---

21. In his *Deus caritas est* Pope Benedict XVI discusses the agapaic and erotic aspects of divine love.

unitive and creative. The baptismal vocation of a married couple is to give witness to that unitive and that creative love. That witness is especially important in their marital intimacy. The two-in-one-flesh dimension of that intimacy in its completeness is a witness to both unitive and creative aspects of divine love. To deliberately remove the two-in-one-flesh aspect through the use of a condom would fundamentally alter the meaning of the marriage act and its witness to divine love. The marriage act would lose its vocational meaning. What is important in this analysis is the transcendental meaning of the marriage act. The marriage act expresses something beyond the couple themselves. It is expressive of their relationship to the Creator and anchors the family in that vocation.

THE RELATIONSHIP BETWEEN FAITH AND REASON

The church magisterium has taught extensively about the relationship between faith and reason and the importance of not obscuring the fact that men and women are always called to direct their steps toward a truth that transcends them. Much modern philosophy, with its emphasis on judging by pragmatic criteria based essentially upon experimental data and the scientific method, has tended to abandon the investigation of being, and rather than make use of the human capacity to know the truth has preferred to adopt determinism, placing emphasis on the ways in which the capacity to reason is limited and conditioned (*Fides et ratio*, 4).

Pope John Paul acknowledged that philosophical thinking has succeeded in coming closer to the reality of human life and its forms of expression, but that it has also tended to pursue issues—existential, hermeneutical, or linguistic—at the expense of ignoring the ethical questions about personal existence, about being and about God (*Fides et ratio*, 6). We do ourselves and those with whom we wish to dialogue a disservice if we make the same error.

In seeking to discover the truth, a Christian philosopher ought not to ignore the fact that Revelation introduces an understanding of the truth that "impels reason continually to extend the range of its knowledge until it senses that it has done all in its power, leaving no stone unturned" (*Fides et ratio*, 14). In other words, natural law requires us to consider propositions introduced by Revelation. A philosopher pursuing a natural law understanding does not accept a truth on the basis that it has been revealed, but does not ignore propositions sourced to Revelation. Rather, he or she tests a proposition, whatever its source, as a matter of reason. The partnership between faith and reason includes a role for reason to test what is taught as a matter of faith, and this is its autonomy. The approach taken by Popes Benedict and John Paul II to the natural law and tradition recognizes this autonomy but does not base natural law on atheistic or agnostic assumptions. One of the contributions that natural law makes is to defend the reasonableness of conclusions that have their source in faith.

John Paul II taught that through the light of reason human beings can know which path to take, but they can follow that path to its end, quickly and unhindered, only if with a rightly tuned spirit they search for it within the horizon of faith. He concluded that "reason and faith cannot be separated without diminishing the capacity of men and women to know themselves, the world and God in an appropriate way" (*Fides et ratio*, 16). Quoting Scripture (Prov 1:7; cf. Sir 1:14) he went on to say that human beings attain truth by way of reason because, enlightened by faith, they discover the deeper meaning of all things and most especially of their own existence, and he concluded that fear of the Lord is the beginning of knowledge (*Fides et ratio*, 20).

As Christians, the life, suffering, and death of Christ are central to our belief, and it is important that we acknowledge that reason cannot exclude the mystery of love that the cross represents. To the contrary, the cross can give to reason the ultimate answer that it seeks (*Fides et ratio*, 23). There is a path we can choose to take that "begins with reason's capacity to rise beyond what is contingent and set out towards the infinite" (*Fides et ratio*, 24).

Important for this discussion is whether we understand natural law in terms of what is fitting for the human nature as Suárez had it (see above) or whether the primary questions for us to address are: Does life have a meaning? Where is it going? Is natural law properly about the purposes of our existence, for which we act? (*Fides et ratio*, 26).

The harmony between the knowledge of faith and the knowledge of philosophy is that faith asks that its object be understood with the help of reason; and at the summit of its searching reason acknowledges that it cannot do without what faith presents (*Fides et ratio*, 42).

Faith and reason are not separate in the tradition. Aquinas recognized that nature, philosophy's proper concern, could contribute to the understanding of divine Revelation. Reason is set free by faith from the fragility and limitations deriving from the disobedience of sin and finds the strength required to rise to the knowledge of the triune God (*Fides et ratio*, 43).

In considering the many different approaches to natural law, it is important to note that the Church has not adopted a particular philosophy but recognizes that philosophy must remain faithful to its own principles and methods. A philosophy that did not proceed according to its own principles and methods would serve little purpose. At the deepest level, the autonomy that philosophy enjoys is rooted in the fact that reason is by its nature oriented to truth and is equipped with the means necessary to arrive at truth. At the same time, a philosophy conscious of this as its "constitutive status" in reason cannot but respect the demands and the data of revealed truth (*Fides et ratio*, 44).

There are very practical matters to resolve about how to conduct oneself as a Catholic bioethicist, philosopher, or theologian in the public forum in which much of bioethics is conducted. The NNL explains the issues as a matter of reason on the basis of seeking to win support for the NNL approach without expecting an audience to listen to claims made from a faith perspective, or even that admit of the existence of a deity. This appears to be the approach that Finnis adopted in his seminal work *Natural Law and Natural Rights* referred to earlier.

It seems that, as a matter of recent history, that approach is a failure. The UK is probably the clearest example of a concerted effort to take that approach by Catholic intellectuals, and the UK probably leads the way in the Western world in terms of adopting public policies that actively exclude religious views and natural law concepts, particularly the rejection of the Pauline principle (moral ends can never justify immoral means) and moral absolutes. The latter are at the core of natural law explanations, and in rejecting them, UK public ethics has, for instance, tended to reject any notion of sexual ethics between adults other than that there be consent between parties.

As mentioned earlier, a problem with an anthropocentric natural law approach for a Christian is that we can be seen to be fraudulent in not admitting our religious beliefs and their influence upon our understanding of anthropology. A second problem is the very personal issue of presenting something that is not adequate, given that the approach would exclude the person of Christ and a reasoned examination of the New Law. In other words, the approach lacks what we have been taught by Christ and, in particular, the nature of Christian love and the foundational belief that human happiness is found only in outreach to others and making a gift of oneself in love.

For instance, the marriage analogies for the relationship between God and his people and Christ and His people give a particular meaning to human love that is normatively quite different from the outcomes that derive from an exclusive focus on a non-transcendental idea of human flourishing. Without that meaning, our responses and our solutions to moral questions are quite inadequate. So what is offered to the secular dialogue, as an anthropocentric natural law, may sound false to secular others and, in fact, is false, by our own standards. The NNL project, represented by John Finnis and, as we shall discuss, by Germain Grisez, has proved to be a failure and seemingly was doomed from the outset, because their accounts appear to leave out so much that is necessary to articulate a coherent natural law which includes the role of the transcendent within human reason. The atheistic or agnostic assumptions on which they appeared to be based deny any role for reason in assessing our relationship to the creator, the nature of the creator, what the creator's love may want for us, and ultimately what our final end may be, knowledge of which would give purpose and meaning to our existence.

Natural law, philosophy, and the role of reason are an important part of our tradition, but that does not mean that they had to be carried out in such a way as though there were no creator and the historical figure of Christ and his teachings did not exist. Philosophy can explore the propositions we may have received by faith, but does so as a matter of reason and not as a matter of authority. The difference is in epistemology, not in the content of the propositions to be tested by reason.

GRISEZ'S ARGUMENT WITH AQUINAS

Grisez rejects St. Thomas's claim that the ultimate end of man is communion with God, the beatific vision. Grisez instead argues that our ultimate end is integral communal fulfillment. Thus Grisez's natural law is anthropocentric rather than theocentric and this has grave consequences for his casuistry. It is my view that Grisez's analysis of the moral act, and hence his casuistry, suffers from the position that he takes on the ultimate end in which he disagrees that the ultimate end of human acts is God alone.[22] In this Grisez not only disagrees with St. Thomas, but he is also at odds

22. Cf. Grisez, "Natural Law, God, Religion, and Human Fulfilment"; "The Ultimate End of Human Beings."

with *Veritatis splendor*, first in terms of the nature of the Decalogue and secondly in terms of the specification of the nature of the object of the moral act.

The use of the distinction in St. Thomas between the interior and the exterior act that Grisez invokes in addressing some moral conflicts is worth exploring. In particular it is worth exploring the nature of the moral act in relation to our ultimate end.

In relation to the Decalogue and the Beatitudes, Pope John Paul II says,

> *The Beatitudes* are not specifically concerned with certain particular rules of behavior. Rather, they speak of basic attitudes and dispositions in life and therefore they *do not coincide exactly with the commandments*. On the other hand, *there is no separation or opposition* between the Beatitudes and the commandments: both refer to the good, to eternal life. The Sermon on the Mount begins with the proclamation of the Beatitudes, but also refers to the commandments (cf. *Mt* 5:20–48). At the same time, the Sermon on the Mount demonstrates the openness of the commandments and their orientation towards the horizon of the perfection proper to the Beatitudes. These latter are above all *promises*, from which there also indirectly flow *normative indications* for the moral life. In their originality and profundity they are a sort of *self-portrait of Christ*, and for this very reason are *invitations to discipleship and to communion of life with Christ*. (*Veritatis splendor*, 16)

In relation to the object of the moral act, the pope stated,

> The reason why a good intention is not itself sufficient, but a correct choice of actions is also needed, is that the human act depends on its object, whether that object is *capable or not of being ordered* to God, to the One who "alone is good," and thus brings about the perfection of the person. An act is therefore good if its object is in conformity with the good of the person with respect for the goods morally relevant for him. Christian ethics, which pays particular attention to the moral object, does not refuse to consider the inner "teleology" of acting, inasmuch as it is directed to promoting the true good of the person; but it recognizes that it is really pursued only when the essential elements of human nature are respected. (*Veritatis splendor*, 78)

It is my contention that by not requiring the object of the act to be capable of being oriented by the will to God as an act of love, Grisez significantly shifts the grounds for determining the specification of the moral act and this has grave implications for his casuistry, particularly in relation to double effect reasoning.[23] This is not to say that he adopts the position of the proportionalists in which the intended end can override evil in the object of the act if it is proportionate. Rather, Grisez's position is due to the specification of the object itself and how the concept of direct intention is applied. If the specification is determined by the ultimate end, and the ultimate end is not God alone but includes integral human fulfillment, then that changes the way in which the object is specified. He writes, "Since the self-evident principles of practical reasoning direct us indiscriminately toward the well-being and flourishing of ourselves and everyone else, we reasonably take as our ultimate end an inclusive community of human persons along with other intelligent creatures and God..."[24]

An important aspect of Grisez's analysis of the ultimate end is that he claims that God alone is not sufficient, but that we must consider all the aspects of human fulfillment and not just our relationship to God. This is quite different from St. Thomas's position in which God is the ultimate end, and love of neighbor (and thus the goods of human flourishing) is integral to the love of God. In Grisez's analysis, love of God is part of human fulfillment and not its sole end. Placing human fulfillment first in this way has consequences for specifying the nature of the object of the moral act because it affects the interior meaning of the act and hence the application of double effect reasoning. Instead of a participative theonomy, as proposed by John Paul II in *Veritatis splendor* (cf. 41), Grisez proposes anthropocentrism.

There would also seem to be conflict between this dependence on a philosophical analysis of integral communal fulfillment as the ultimate end and the teaching of John Paul II when he identifies and critiques claims to the "sovereignty of reason."

> Some people, however, disregarding the dependence of human reason on Divine Wisdom and the need, given the present state of fallen nature, for Divine Revelation as an effective means for knowing moral truths, even those of the natural order, have actually posited a *complete sovereignty of reason* in the domain of

---

23. Classical double-effect reasoning allows us to accept evil or harmful side effects provided they are not directly willed and are not disproportionate.
24. Grisez, "Ultimate End of Human Beings," 55.

> moral norms regarding the right ordering of life in this world. (*Veritatis splendor*, 36)

I shall argue that double-effect reasoning, in assessing the object of the act, must not treat humanity as though it existed in isolation and did not depend on God, or that our good is not inextricably bound to our ultimate end of communion with Him. It was significant that in the analysis of the Decalogue in the Sermon on the Mount, Jesus gave so much more meaning to it—for example, by extending the fifth commandment to include anger and the sixth commandment to include adultery of the heart. The New Law is a law of love and not just a law of obligation.[25] To follow Jesus demands so much more of us than the narrow treatment of the object of the act in terms of human fulfillment would suggest. The theological virtues are relevant, and not just the cardinal virtues (which can be understood anthropocentrically), because the ultimate end is God alone and our love for Him should inform every act. What kind of morality is it that lacks the virtue of love? Could I be an authentic Christian and not present an understanding of the virtue of love informed by the life, suffering, and death of Christ?

ST. THOMAS AQUINAS AND THE MORAL ACT

Central to an analysis of the moral act is the concept of intention, which St. Thomas is careful to explain, not in terms of the action itself but in terms of the mind or will which moves to the end. The intention is an act of the will.[26] Second, he argues that the will belongs to the intellect, whose object is universal "being" and "truth." He describes the intellect as moving the will, presenting its object to it.[27]

In explaining what is specific to human actions, St. Thomas accounts for free will as "the faculty and will of reason." Therefore those actions are properly called human that proceed from a deliberate will and in the actions of man the object of the will is the end and the good. He concludes by claiming that all human actions must be for an end.[28] Following Ambrose he asserts that moral acts properly speaking receive

---

25. See Pinckaers, "The Return of the New Law to Moral Theology."
26. *Summa Theologica*, I–II, 12,1.
27. Ibid., 9, 1.
28. Ibid., 1, 1.

their species from the end, for moral acts are the same as human acts.²⁹ Finally, he asserts that the ultimate end is God: ". . . we speak of man's last end as of the thing which is the end, thus all other things concur in man's last end, since God is the last end of man and of all other things."³⁰

That analysis of intention and intentional acts provides the basis for the distinction between interior and exterior acts. Referring to the above analysis he writes,

> Certain actions are called human, inasmuch as they are voluntary. . . . Now, in a voluntary action, there is a twofold action, viz. the interior action of the will, and the external action: and each of these actions has its object. The end is properly the object of the interior act of the will: while the object of the external action, is that on which the action is brought to bear. Therefore just as the external action takes its species from the object on which it bears; so the interior act of the will takes its species from the end, as from its own proper object. Now that which is on the part of the will is formal in regard to that which is on the part of the external action: because the will uses the limbs to act as instruments; nor have external actions any measure of morality, save in so far as they are voluntary. Consequently the species of a human act is considered formally with regard to the end, but materially with regard to the object of the external action. Hence the Philosopher says (Ethic. v, 2) that "he who steals that he may commit adultery, is strictly speaking, more adulterer than thief."³¹

This paragraph is important, for it qualifies the distinction between interior and exterior acts, referring to the species of the act as both formal and material. It would not be true to claim that the exterior act is irrelevant to the species of the act. The latter is the application of the distinction that has made been made in the use of Grisez's analysis of craniotomy in the defense of an apparent direct abortion allegedly carried out by staff at the then-Catholic St. Joseph's hospital in Phoenix, Arizona, which I have discussed at length elsewhere.³² The moral defense claimed that the act can be determined by the interior act alone.³³ That would suggest no

29. Ibid., 1, 3.
30. Ibid., 1, 8.
31. Ibid., 18, 6.
32. Tonti-Filippini, *About Bioethics*, 4:180–227.
33. Lysaught, "Moral Analysis of a Procedure at Phoenix Hospital."

morally significant relationship between the exterior act and the interior act. However, referring to the above passage, St. Thomas has more to say about the specification of the act. He writes,

> A fourfold goodness may be considered in a human action. First, that which, as an action, it derives from its genus; because as much as it has of action and being so much has it of goodness. . . . Secondly, it has goodness according to its species; which is derived from its suitable object. Thirdly, it has goodness from its circumstances, in respect, as it were, of its accidents. Fourthly, it has goodness from its end, to which it is compared as to the cause of its goodness.[34]

Later in the same article he writes,

> Thus it may happen that an action which is good in its species or in its circumstances is ordained to an evil end, or vice versa. However, an action is not good simply, unless it is good in all those ways: since "evil results from any single defect, but good from the complete cause," as Dionysius says (Div. Nom. iv).

The above references in St. Thomas precede and are connected to what he says about double effect and the latter needs to be understood in the general context of his theory of the moral act. About double effect he says,

> It is written (Exodus 22:2): "If a thief be found breaking into a house or undermining it, and be wounded so as to die; he that slew him shall not be guilty of blood." Now it is much more lawful to defend one's life than one's house. Therefore neither is a man guilty of murder if he kill another in defense of his own life. . . . Nothing hinders one act from having two effects, only one of which is intended, while the other is beside the intention. Now moral acts take their species according to what is intended, and not according to what is beside the intention, since this is accidental. . . . Accordingly the act of self-defense may have two effects, one is the saving of one's life, the other is the slaying of the aggressor. Therefore this act, since one's intention is to save one's own life, is not unlawful, seeing that it is natural to everything to keep itself in "being," as far as possible.[35]

In *Quaestiones Quodlibetales*, Aquinas writes that some kinds of human acts "have deformity inseparably annexed to them, such as

---

34. *Summa Theologica*, I–II, 18, 4.
35. *Summa Theologica*, II–II, q. 64, 7.

fornication, adultery, and others of this sort."[36] Aquinas thus explicitly affirms that some actions are intrinsically evil, and corresponding to them are absolute moral norms.[37] In this Pope John Paul II would seem to have concurred when he wrote, "If acts are intrinsically evil, a good intention or particular circumstances can diminish their evil, but they cannot remove it. They remain 'irremediably' evil acts; *per se* and in themselves they are not capable of being ordered to God and to the good of the person" (*Veritatis splendor*, 81). The pope also writes in the same document,

> Reason attests that there are objects of the human act which are by their nature "incapable of being ordered" to God, because they radically contradict the good of the person made in his image. These are the acts which, in the Church's moral tradition, have been termed "intrinsically evil" (*intrinsece malum*): they are such *always and per se*, in other words, on account of their very object, and quite apart from the ulterior intentions of the one acting and the circumstances. (*Veritatis splendor*, 80)

What is important here is that the objects are incapable of being ordered toward God, not because they are a destruction of human goods understood anthropocentrically and in that sense hostile to integral human communal fulfillment, but rather because they radically contradict the good of the person made in His image. The consideration of one's neighbor stems from one's ordering toward God. The first part of the Decalogue importantly informs the second part.[38] Love of God informs love of neighbor. The function of our reason in seeking to assess the moral act begins with our love of God, with God alone as our ultimate end.

RETURNING TO GRISEZ (AND FINNIS AND BOYLE)

The difficulty with Grisez's version of natural law becomes apparent in his treatment of difficult moral issues in which the specification of the object of the moral act matters to the outcome. Consider his treatment of the craniotomy issue. Finnis, Grisez, and Boyle[39] claim that craniotomy in

---

36. "Quaedam enim sunt quae habent deformitatem inseparabiliter annexam, ut fornicatio, adulterium, et aliae huiusmodi, quae nullo modo bene fieri possunt." Aquinas, *Quaestiones Quodlibetales*, 9, q. 7, a. 2.

37. Ibid.

38. I am grateful to Adam Cooper for this insight.

39. Finnis et al., "'Direct' and 'Indirect.'"

the circumstances of arrested labor is not direct killing and thus permissible contrary to the position that had been held by the Magisterium.[40]

Grisez is a strong critic of proportionalism, but one could be forgiven for wondering how his analysis of the subjectivity of the human act is not open to the same criticism that he made of proportionalists: that it involves separating moral intent from psychological intent.

A concern I have with the Finnis, Grisez, and Boyle analysis of the account of the moral act in *Veritatis splendor* is that they seem to interpret the document in a way that provides a strained interpretation of both St. Thomas and *Veritatis splendor*. The latter states, "By the object of a given moral act, one cannot mean a process or an event of the merely physical order, to be assessed on its ability to bring about a given state of affairs in the world" (*Veritatis splendor*, 78).

Finnis et al. say of this passage, referring to St. Thomas, that the species of the moral act as good or bad is not found in its species *in genere naturae* but in its species *in genere moris*. They argue that it is necessary to get beyond common-sense accounts of what is being done and factors such as causal sequences, which gives an unreflective priority over the perspective of the acting person.[41]

---

40. The craniotomy discussion has puzzled me in relation to why it ever came to be presented as a case of save the mother or both will die. Caesarean section has been with us for literally thousands of years—hence its name. Until relatively recently (the advent of antibiotics, aseptic technique, intrauterine stitching, transverse incision, blood transfusion), it had a high mortality rate for the mother. In the 1800s, maternal mortality following caesarean section may have been as high as 85 percent. However, there was also always the possibility of symphysiotomy, which involves severing the ligament that joins the two parts of the pelvis, thus increasing the diameter of the birth canal. That is still done as an alternative to caesarean section in developing countries where the resources or skills to undertake a caesarean section safely may not be available. The choice was always a choice between endangering the child or endangering the mother, never quite a vital conflict in the way in which it has been presented of certain fatality either for the mother or for both mother and child. In fact, those involved were often choosing between, on the one hand, craniotomy, which would kill the child, and on the other hand, grave or at least significant risk to the mother's life and health if they took one of the alternatives—caesarean section or symphysiotomy. It is thus puzzling how craniotomy ever came to be described as the only alternative to the death of both mother and child. Thus in times past complications of delivery raised serious problems. Now, where medical facilities are available, such difficulties are rare—most difficult cases are prevented by timely surgery, with in this case the options being caesarean section or symphysiotomy as described.

41. Finnis et al., "'Direct' and "Indirect,'" 22–23.

However, they seem to deny any role at all for the physical reality in determining the psychological reality. The issue is certainly to assess the act from the perspective of the acting person, but the latter cannot be completely unrelated to the reality of what he or she does. My concern is that in claiming that the narrowing of the child's head is the immediate object in order to save the life of the mother, the description omits a large part of what would be in the mind of the surgeon. "Narrowing the baby's head" is only one aspect of this and is not an adequate description of what the surgeon intends to do. Bear in mind what the surgeon does—he or she thrusts an instrument into the head of the child and evacuates the child's brain. Finnis et al. assert that a surgeon performing craniotomy, "resisting the undue influence of physical and causal factors that would dominate the perception of observers, could rightly say 'No way do I intend to kill the baby' and 'It is no part of my purpose to kill the baby.'" They say that the killing in this case is not brought about as a chosen means and thus is not the immediate object in the sense defined in *Veritatis splendor*.[42]

I cannot see that there can be a separation between the moral description of the act and the clear psychological intent, which is to dismember the head in a way that is death-dealing in itself, not as a side effect. They argue that the death is not necessary and therefore is not intended. The doctor would do the same if the baby were already dead. But the fact that the death is not needed does not make the act any less an act that directly kills. There is a false distinction being made between moral and psychological intent. The major problem in the Finnis et al. analysis is that they permit a moral narrative that is psychologically strained, so strained as to be totally implausible as a way in which anyone would actually reason. The acting person who reasoned like that could only be self-deceiving. The act of penetrating the head of the child and drawing out the contents cannot realistically be an act that is not perceived as an act of killing by the acting person. It so dramatically is an act of killing.

According to Finnis, Grisez, and Boyle, the morally relevant description of the act is narrowing the head of the child by dismembering it. The object, they claim, is to facilitate delivery and save the life of the mother. However, the direct object is the dismembering, and that is synonymous with the death of the child. Note that Finnis et al. are not claiming that the surgeon attempts forceps delivery and in so doing causes

42. Ibid., 23

dismemberment. That would be quite different. They are proposing a separate procedure, the primary function of which is to dismember the head of the child. That would involve a very different set of instruments from those normally used to deliver a child.

This is not like St. Thomas's example of seeking to stop a thief and the injury inflicted in the attempt causing death. The dismemberment intends death. There is no other outcome possible.

There is a difference between this case and the types of cases for which double-effect reasoning ordinarily applies, where the death is clearly a side effect, such as bombing a military installation and killing citizens who happen to be in the vicinity, or removing a gravid cancerous uterus resulting in the loss of life of the child. The procedure involves no assault on the child. In the case of dismembering a child to save the life of the mother, the death is integral to what is chosen rather than beside it. The death is synonymous with the act that is necessary to achieve the end of saving life. Someone who dismembers a child but describes their act according to the preferred consequence of saving life and not as a killing is deceiving himself as to the nature of the act. A morally relevant feature is that the desired consequence is only part of the reality of what is deliberately chosen. To say that in dismembering the child, which is clearly the immediate object, "I did not intend the death" is plainly untrue. This case, it seems to me, is quite unlike removing the gravid but cancerous uterus. In the latter case the act results in death, but the act is clearly separable from the death in that the latter is a side effect and therefore beside the intention. Death is not a side effect of dismembering a baby, it is the main event.

Finnis et al. argue that their account differs from previous accounts that have led the Magisterium to find teaching that supports craniotomy to be unsafe. The difference lies in their rejection of the position that they attribute to Henry Davis SJ and which appears in most accounts of double-effect reasoning:[43] that the good effect must follow at least as immediately and directly as the evil effect. It seems that this principle is an attempt to capture, in part, how it is that the evil in the act is indirect. It is a notion that extends beyond direct lines of causality; that is, the Davis principle does not claim that the impermissible evil is a means to the good, but rather that it precedes or is more immediate than the good.

---

43. Ibid., 19–20.

This is, of course, the case with craniotomy. The dismembering and thus the death precede and are more immediate than the removal of the child that results in the saving of life. The latter is secondary to the procedure to dismember. Finnis et al. argue that the traditional principle (the Davis principle) is a mistake, referring to the soldier who throws himself on a grenade to save others. We applaud his heroism, they argue, but his body being destroyed is more immediate than the grenade not doing injury, or as much injury, to his fellows.

The soldier's case is different from the craniotomy case both because it is his life and not someone else's that is lost if the grenade explodes, and because the loss of life and the saving of life are in fact synonymous. His object is to shield the others; when he does so shield them he saves their lives when the grenade explodes and at the same time loses his. His life is not lost until the grenade explodes, and that is precisely when lives are saved. In the craniotomy case we have a dismembering of the child, and then the removal made possible by the dismembering and thus the resolution of the problem. It is a pre-emptive strike to effect removal.

As examples of this reasoning, Finnis et al. then cite the mention in *Evangelium vitae* of double-effect reasoning in relation to pain relief and refusal of burdensome life support where death is a side effect. The encyclical says that in those cases the death is not willed or sought. But both of those cases are quite different from Finnis et al.'s account in which the evil is more immediate than the good. In the instances in *Evangelium vitae*, the pain relief and the lessening of the burden of treatment are more immediate than the death. If in fact the death was expected to precede lessening of the burden or the relief of pain, then death would appear psychologically to be the immediate object (rather than the lessening of the burden). Rather than demonstrating their narrative of the moral act, the encyclical would seem to indicate difference from it.

There is something of a connection between the Finnis et al. account and proportionalism in that both seem to override the significance of direct killing. In Finnis et al., the moral narrative overrides the psychological narrative of direct killing. In the treatment of the moral act by Richard McCormick,[44] the evil of direct killing is overridden by a commensurate reason. It seems to me that Finnis et al.'s account strengthens McCormick's position by substituting a moral narrative in place of the

---

44. McCormick, "Proportionalism," 193–94.

psychological narrative. In both narratives, what is psychologically direct killing is not considered to be morally relevant.

Pope John Paul II rejects as erroneous any theory "which holds that it is impossible to qualify as morally evil according to its species—its 'object'—the deliberate choice of certain kinds of behavior or specific acts, apart from a consideration of the intention for which the choice is made or the totality of the foreseeable consequences of that act for all persons concerned" (*Veritatis splendor*, 79). The pope then goes on in the next paragraph to say, "The primary and decisive element for moral judgment is the object of the human act, which establishes whether it is *capable of being ordered to the good and to the ultimate end, which is God.*"

In rejecting judging the morality of the object of an act by the totality of foreseeable consequences, the pope seems to be rejecting proportionalism of the kind espoused by such writers as Richard McCormick. However, in rejecting judging the morality of the object of an act by its intention only, the pope would seem to have been addressing the type of treatment of double-effect reasoning espoused at that time by Grisez and others in which they, in effect, separate moral intention from psychological intention.

Part of the reason for being able to classify the object in that way is Grisez's anthropocentrism. The question he asks is not whether this act is capable of being oriented toward God (whether it expresses love for God), but whether it is consistent with or aimed toward integral communal fulfillment. Significant in the craniotomy analysis is that the case is presented as the child being unable to survive, whether or not there is intervention in this way. It is implied that nothing changes with respect to the integral fulfillment of the child, but it is possible by intervening to save the mother and act for the benefit of her integral fulfillment. Missing in that analysis is the meaning of the intervention in the context of the love of God and the ultimate aim of God alone. The theological virtues of faith, hope, and love imply a relationship to God in which we accept our inferiority as creatures and our dependency on our Creator. Such an understanding is not consistent with a morality that depends on reason alone.

CONCLUSION: TOWARD A MORE THEOCENTRIC ENGAGEMENT

This critique of the anthropocentric approach taken by Grisez, and of the defense of that approach by Finnis and Boyle, suggests that as bioethicists we should participate in public debate openly as Christians rather than try to engage in an exercise of pure reason. I would suggest that we should be open about our faith because subterfuge is beneath our dignity and would only breed suspicion, in any case. But more than that, I think that the answers given without the finality of communion with God and without the affectivity of the theological virtues and the meaning and application given to them by Jesus will necessarily be inadequate.[45]

In a pluralist society we can approach this by insisting on being willing to listen to others, to encourage their contribution from their own cultural beliefs and to test our own Christian concepts, and in that way pursue common ground by seeking to identify human goodness and the virtues. That provides a mutually respectful pathway toward seeking human transcendence together in recognition of our differences but also our commonalities. Second, if we engage in public debate as an exercise in reason without Christ we will find ourselves dissatisfied because we will have excluded the New Law.

The latter is an approach that I found successful when I chaired committees undertaking public enquiries. I asked the members to identify their culture of birth, what their parents believed. That then set us free to offer propositions drawn from our different cultures. It also allowed us to aspire to the ideal of the relationship between doctor or nurse and patient, rather than a minimalist view.[46]

---

45. This view is well explained by Servais Pinckaers in his "Return of the New Law to Moral Theology."

46. This experience is discussed in my *About Bioethics*, 1:145–65.

chapter 10

The Family in the Life and Mission of the Church

OWEN VYNER

INTRODUCTION

In a seemingly prescient statement Romano Guardini once declared, "The Church is awakening in souls."[1] This declaration appeared to anticipate the Second Vatican Council's focus on the nature of the Church. At the same time, the Council spoke of another church, the church of the home. It must be asked, however: has an understanding of the "domestic church" awakened in the souls of Christian families? It would seem that families often do not think of themselves as a church. Thus, when the Church speaks of the family as a domestic church, does she run the risk of removing herself from the experience of the laity?

Because the family is a communion that participates in the mystery of Christ and the Church, the family truly is a church. The ecclesial identity of the family is not a parallel layer of existence that stands over and above the natural family. In the same way that marriage between baptized Christians is a sacrament, the Christian home is a church. This is one of the significant theological insights of the Second Vatican Council.

---

1. Guardini, *Church and the Catholic*, 11. This quote is the popular rendering of Guardini's celebrated phrase. The actual phrase, "The Awakening of the Church in the Soul," originates from a chapter heading in Guardini's book.

The question remains: how does one speak of the family as a domestic church? In the first place, such a discussion must include the sacramental life of the Church. Christ acts in and with his Church through her sacramental life; so too the domestic church. As such, the sacraments in-form the identity of the domestic church. Secondly, there will need to be reference to the Church's life of worship. The Eucharist is the "source and summit" of the Christian life and therefore the life of the domestic church. Finally, the Church exists to evangelize.[2] If the family is truly an actualization of the Church, the mission of preaching the gospel will similarly be integral to the essence of the Christian family.

This chapter will therefore present a theology of the domestic church along the axes of communion, worship, and mission. These are characteristics of the Church and must be essential to the domestic church. It will also propose some pastoral recommendations for strengthening the family precisely as a domestic church. However, to begin this reflection on the family, it will first be important to discuss the development of the term "domestic church" in the Second Vatican Council and the post-conciliar period.

VATICAN II AND THE POST-CONCILIAR PERIOD

The recent reappropriation of the family as an ecclesial reality is a significant development in the Church's theological reflection. The retrieval of the term can be attributed largely to the efforts of an Italian bishop, Pietro Fiordelli (1916–2004), who had worked in the Christian Family Movement. During a discussion on the nature of the Church, Fiordelli made the following intervention: "it painfully seems to me . . . that in all of the documents nothing is to be found by way of a special chapter which concerns another state in the Church which is of the greatest nobility and sanctity . . . namely the state of sacramental marriage."[3] This intervention

---

2. Paul VI, *Evangelii nuntiandi*, 14.
3. Quoted in Atkinson, "Family as Domestic Church," 594.

provided no small amount of dissension from those present.[4] Nevertheless, Fiordelli was asked to make a written intervention that would be subsequently considered in the draft for the future document *Lumen gentium*. The final text of *Lumen gentium* eventually affirmed the notion of the family as a domestic church, although the language is more cautious, referring to the family as a church in an analogous manner: "In what might be regarded as the domestic Church, the parents, by word and example, are the first heralds of the faith with regard to their children" (11).[5]

Despite the apparently limited nature of the appropriation of the term "domestic church" in the Council's reflection on the family, the Council was able to provide an interpretive framework for the postconciliar period. From this point on, the Magisterium's teaching on the family would center on its ecclesial nature rather than solely considering the family from a natural perspective. The Council's adoption of the term resulted in the reintroduction of a concept that had been absent from the Church's thinking for fifteen hundred years.[6]

It is the pontificate of St. John Paul II that has provided the most systematic reflection on the nature of the family as a domestic church. John Paul's "Magna Carta" on the family, *Familiaris consortio*, represents a genuine development in the Church's understanding of the family. Whereas *Lumen gentium* applied an ecclesial hermeneutic to the family in analogous terms, John Paul would locate the ecclesial nature of the family in its very being.

For John Paul, the family is a domestic church due to its real participation in the mystery of Christ and the Church.[7] The family shares in Christ's priestly, kingly, and prophetic mission through the sacraments of baptism and ultimately marriage. It is Christ himself, who dwells within

---

4. Fahey, "Christian Family as Domestic Church," 86. It is recounted that Cardinal Alfrink, who was presiding over the session, interrupted Fiordelli, arguing that the topic of marriage was not relevant to the current discussion. Fiordelli responded that marriage and family were indeed at the very heart of the life of the Church.

5. The Council's decree on the laity, *Apostolicam Actuositatem*, would use similar language to describe the family: "The mission of being the primary vital cell of society has been given to the family by God himself. This mission will be accomplished if the family, by the mutual affection of its members and by family prayer, presents itself as a domestic sanctuary of the Church . . ." (11).

6. Atkinson, "Family as Domestic Church," 597–98.

7. John Paul II, *Familiaris consortio*, 17: "Hence the family has the mission to guard, reveal and communicate love, and this is a living reflection of and a real sharing in God's love for humanity and the love of Christ the Lord for the Church His bride."

the family, who determines its identity and mission. Related to the christological foundation of the family is its ecclesial essence. The family is not simply a social reality akin to the Church but is in fact a sacramental, and therefore efficacious, manifestation of the Church: "The Christian family constitutes a specific revelation and realization of ecclesial communion, and for this reason too it can and should be called 'the domestic Church'" (*Familiaris consortio*, 21).

This overview of the development of the understanding of the family as a domestic church is admittedly limited. There is still considerable theological reflection that must be done. Additionally, the reappropriation of the concept has not been without challenges.[8] Still, it is hoped that this book in particular and the work of The John Paul II Institute in general will provide the theological and anthropological foundations for the renewal of the family. The vision of the person in this book is Trinitarian and christocentric. God is gift itself, an eternal exchange of love. The human person is created in the image of God, as male and female and according to the order of gift and love. Consequently, the person's corporeality is not reducible to a biological fact; rather, the sexual complementarity of man and woman is the sacramental expression of the person's capacity to give himself in love and to form a communion of persons. In the present chapter this Trinitarian and christocentric understanding of the person will be applied to the family, especially within the context of the sacramental foundations of the domestic church. In the subsequent sections this chapter will consider the family as a particular manifestation of ecclesial communion, the life of prayer and worship in the Christian home, and the participation of the family in the Church's mission of the evangelization.

---

8. Atkinson, "Family as Domestic Church," 600–603. Atkinson has suggested that there are three main challenges to the reception of the term. First, the modern reductionist worldview is epistemologically incapable of understanding an anagogical vision of family life. Second, there is the problem of theologically grounding the concept of the family as a church. Atkinson contends that there is still work to be done, specifically in the areas of the Church's theologies of baptism and creation as well as the ancient Semitic notion of corporate personality. Finally, he considers the greatest threat to be the misappropriation of the concept. This is a particular issue given the continued breakdown of the family and the concomitant emergence of alternative family structures. The danger is that the term might be utilized in such a way as to render it almost meaningless.

COMMUNION AND THE IDENTITY OF THE FAMILY

The family is a communion whose primordial model is to be found in the divine Communion of Persons, the Blessed Trinity.[9] Furthermore, because authentic conjugal love is "caught up" into this divine Communion, the family both receives divine life and participates in it.[10] In this section, we will discuss the animating principles of familial communion, namely, the sacraments of Initiation and the gift of the Holy Spirit poured out in the sacramental celebration of marriage.

There is considerable debate regarding the question of the sacramental foundation of the domestic church. The discussion revolves around the question whether it is baptism or marriage that "makes" the Christian family a domestic church. Florence Caffrey Bourg argues that the magisterial emphasis on marriage as the foundation of the domestic church does not address the fundamental issue that one becomes a Christian through baptism. Bourg notes that while *Familiaris consortio* outlines the bonds between the universal Church and the domestic church, at no point is baptism mentioned.[11]

This, however, is a false dichotomy that sets marriage and baptism in opposition to each other. While *Familiaris consortio* does indeed refer to marriage as the "specific source and original means" of holiness for spouses and the family, it does so in reference to marriage as a "taking up again" and a making specific the graces of baptism (56). The dichotomy presented by Bourg does not take into account that baptism is the immersion into the Son's death and resurrection, his total *yes* to his Father and his giving of himself to his Bride. Baptism is already therefore the entrance into a mystery that is nuptial. The sacrament of marriage takes up again and deepens the nuptial mystery expressed in baptism. Also, as marriage is a sacrament of Christ's union with the Church it reveals the spousal nature of the sacraments. Thus there is no opposition between marriage and baptism as foundations of the domestic church.

It would seem then that the question is not whether baptism or marriage is the foundation of the ecclesial nature of the family but how is it that the sacraments of Initiation form the communion of the family.[12] The

---

9. John Paul II, *Letter to Families*, 6.

10. *Gaudium et spes*, 48.

11. Bourg, "Family as Domestic Church," 61.

12. The focus on baptism or marriage has the further negative effect of isolating baptism as a source of the domestic church. In doing so, this focus separates baptism

ecclesiology and sacramental theology of the great Jesuit Henri de Lubac (1896–1991) provide an excellent starting point for this discussion.

De Lubac famously stated that the Eucharist makes the Church.[13] For the Christian, the Eucharist completes what has begun in baptism. Through the one Spirit, the Christian has been baptized into one body, the Church. In partaking of the one bread and chalice, and by the action of the Holy Spirit, there is a perfecting of this unity.[14] Thus the Eucharist is the source of unity within the Church, making of her one body. Through the sacrament of marriage, Christian spouses participate in and make present the spousal union of Christ and the Church. The Eucharist draws husband and wife more deeply into this mystery, perfecting their union and strengthening the bonds of familial communion.

This drawing of the Christian into a more profound union with the Body of Christ is not irrelevant to the life of the family. On the contrary, the fruit of an intensely sacramental and eucharistic life is unity. The Eucharist becomes the soul, the life-giving principle, of the family as communion. As the soul of the family, the Eucharist enriches family (and spousal) prayer, concrete acts of service, and those activities that build up family unity (e.g., the family meal). In turn these acts that bring about communion are directed toward the unity efficaciously realized in Holy Communion. Thus the Eucharist is both the source of family communion and its summit (cf. *Lumen gentium*, 11). In the Eucharist, Jesus is truly at work in the family: he is both the source of their actions (cf. Gal 2:20) but also the object of their actions (cf. Matt 25:31–46).

---

from confirmation and the Eucharist. The question of confirmation's contribution to marriage and family is indeed complex. It would be beyond the scope of this chapter to explicate in detail the role of confirmation in a conjugal spirituality. The work of the sacramental theologian Liam G. Walsh, however, does provide a useful starting point. Walsh discusses confirmation as the "sacrament of the messianic, eschatological quality of the gift of the Holy Spirit" (*Sacraments of Initiation*, 200). Confirmation brings to perfection the grace of baptism and initiates the Christians into a mission of the Church in the eschatological age. For married persons this is also the grace to witness to the Paschal Mystery.

13. Lubac, *Corpus Mysticum*, 88. "Now, the Eucharist is the mystical principle, permanently at work at the heart of Christian society, which gives concrete form to this miracle [the Church]. It is the universal bond, it is the ever-springing source of life. Nourished by the body and blood of the Savior, his faithful people thus all 'drink of the one Spirit,' who truly makes them into one single body. Literally speaking, therefore, the Eucharist makes the Church."

14. Lubac, *Splendour of the Church*, 107.

Related to this is the role of the Holy Spirit, who is the bond of the spouses and the family. The Holy Spirit is understood as the source (*fons*) of spousal love. This has been made explicit in the addition of an epiclesis (the priest's petitioning of the Father to send the Holy Spirit) inserted into the nuptial blessing in the *editio typica altera* (revised edition) of the Rite of Marriage. In this epiclesis, the Father is petitioned to send forth upon the spouses "the grace of the Holy Spirit, so that, with your love diffused in their hearts, they may remain faithful in the conjugal covenant."[15]

The *Catechism of the Catholic Church* makes similar reference to the Spirit as the source of love. With reference to the epiclesis in the sacrament of marriage, the *Catechism* states, "The spouses receive the Holy Spirit as the communion of love of Christ and the Church. The Holy Spirit is the seal of their covenant, the ever available source of their love and the strength to renew their fidelity" (1624).

The Holy Spirit is the source of spousal and familial communion. The Spirit is constantly at work in the domestic church, making the family "one" as the Father and the Son are one (cf. John 17:21).

Thus far, the focus of this chapter has been on the role of the spouses in forming a domestic church. However, it must be asked: do children contribute anything to the ecclesial nature of the family? This has to be answered in the affirmative. When Christian parents welcome the child in Christ's name, they also welcome Christ (cf. Matt 18:5). In doing this, they welcome not only the Son but the Father and the Holy Spirit. It is the Holy Spirit, the Giver of Life, who blesses the couple with the child. Thus we see that the same Spirit who is the source of spousal communion is also the source of the fruitfulness of the couple. The Holy Spirit works within conjugal love to enrich, deepen, and expand this communion through the gift of children. In this way, through co-operating with grace, biological fruitfulness becomes sacramental of spiritual fecundity. Through Christ and by the action of the Holy Spirit, the child is welcomed as a source of God's blessing and a means of a deepened participation in Trinitarian communion.[16]

15. *Ordo Celebrandi Matrimonium*, 74. ". . . emitte super eos Spiritus Sancti gratiam, ut, caritate tua in cordibus eorum diffusa, in coniugali foedere fideles permaneant." My translation. The *editio typica altera* has never been translated into English, so that the current Rite of Marriage (1969) used in Australia and other English-speaking countries does not have an epiclesis.

16. A word must be mentioned here regarding those couples who experience the cross of infertility. It is important not to reduce spiritual fruitfulness to biological fruitfulness. The point is that the couple must cooperate with God in their openness

There are, of course, many challenges that strike at the heart of the family as a communion. Individualism, materialism, and the lack of forgiveness all threaten the unity of the domestic church. In the final chapter of this book, Cardinal Ouellet diagnoses the most basic source of these problems as a crisis of the gift of self. The person is created to participate in communion through a sincere gift of self. Through an exaggerated individualism the person becomes both unwilling and unable to commit himself in love to another. However, as Ouellet also stated, the crisis of the gift of self can only be overcome by a rediscovery of the person's call to communion and participation in God's own life. Consequently, this sacramental vision of the family as a domestic church becomes even more pertinent than ever. It is within the life of the domestic church that the sacraments (in particular the Eucharist) and the gift of the Holy Spirit really accomplish the unity that they signify.

WORSHIP: CONVERSION, SACRIFICE, AND VIRTUE

In the Liturgy, the Son draws us into the worship of the Father in the communion of the Holy Spirit. This worship is ultimately a conversion of the heart. In the words of Pope Emeritus Benedict, the dialogue between the priest and the faithful that begins the Eucharistic Prayer is "an interior event; conversion, the turning of our soul towards Jesus Christ and thus towards the living God."[17]

Thus the beginning of the priestly office of the family is conversion. The turning away from sin and turning toward the Lord is a renewal of

---

to life. This openness to children is the source of the couple's fruitfulness. As Adrienne von Speyr wrote, "Every Christian marriage is blessed by God and is fruitful in him, whether through the blessing of children, or the blessing of sacrifice. If God chooses the second alternative, the spiritual fruitfulness of marriage is increased and widened out invisibly so that it flows into the whole community" (*Word Becomes Flesh*, 101). Commenting on this statement, Cardinal Marc Ouellet added, "In [the] case [of infertility], the fruitfulness of spouses approaches, by way of sacrifice, the supernatural fruitfulness of virgins" (*Divine Likeness*, 122).

17. "In the early Church there was a custom whereby the bishop or the priest, after the homily, would cry out to the faithful: '*Conversi ad Dominum*'—turn now towards the Lord. . . . Fundamentally, this involved an interior event; conversion, the turning of our soul towards Jesus Christ and thus towards the living God. . . . Linked with this, then, was the other exclamation that still today, before the Eucharistic Prayer, is addressed to the community of the faithful: '*Sursum corda*'—'Lift up your hearts' . . . In both exclamations we are summoned, as it were, to a renewal of our Baptism." Benedict XVI, Easter Vigil Homily, March 22, 2008.

the Christian's baptism, which is then fulfilled in eucharistic communion. As we have already discussed, the fruit of communion with Christ is a deepening of the bonds of the family. The turning toward the Lord at the heart of worship is also a willingness to be converted toward one another (cf. 1 John 4:20).

Secondly, turning toward one another is expressed in the love of self-sacrifice. John Paul II said that the essence of the family is specified by love (cf. *Familiaris consortio*, 17). This love, so often actualized in sacrifice, is what the Christian family offers in worship. In the preparatory prayers before the Eucharistic Prayer, the priest says, "Pray, brethren, that my sacrifice and yours may be acceptable to God the almighty Father." The Christian family's offering of its daily sacrifices is the manner in which it participates in Christ's priestly office.

This eucharistic view of the family places sacrifice at the heart of the domestic church. Anyone who is a spouse, parent, or child can testify that among the many joys of marriage and family life are to be found trials. In fact, when man and woman become husband and wife in the Rite of Marriage, the vow to love and honor each other through all of life's blessings and challenges contains the very logic of self-sacrifice. It is these sacrifices, tangible expressions of authentic love, that the family unites to Christ's sacrifice made present at each Mass.

Finally, the family's participation in the Liturgy is brought about through a type of "liturgical asceticism." Originating from the Greek word *askesis*, asceticism refers to training or discipline.[18] The training required to participate in the Mass derives from one's baptism (incorporation into the life of Christ) and takes the form of liturgical catechesis and formation. This formation should occur in a manner that is age-appropriate for each member of the family. For a toddler this might simply involve drawing his attention to the epiclesis and the consecration. For

---

18. Fagerberg, *On Liturgical Asceticism*, 206; Ratzinger, *Spirit of the Liturgy*, 121–23. In his treatment of the question of images in *The Spirit of the Liturgy*, Ratzinger describes the "new seeing" of faith that is born of prayer and asceticism. Although in this instance he is referring to a theology of icons, what is said can be applied in general to the Christian's participation in the liturgy. Drawing on the work of the Greek Orthodox theologian Paul Evdokimov (d. 1970), Ratzinger writes that the icon "delivers a man from that closure of the senses which perceives only the externals" and leads him to "the transcendence of faith." This is not to say that the senses are replaced; rather, they are "expanded to their widest capacity." Through this expanding of the senses man is then able to encounter Christ in the liturgy and to declare with Thomas, "My Lord and my God!" See Evdokimov, *The Art of the Icon*.

older children this can include discussing the scripture readings beforehand and catechesis on the signs and gestures in the liturgy. Liturgical formation is an ongoing process of interior conversion that deepens each family member's full, conscious, and active participation in the Liturgy.

The training involved in liturgical participation also has profound ramifications for the mission of the family. When parents require that their children ask for something rather than simply taking it, they are involved in what psychology refers to as "delayed gratification." The capacity to say "no" to oneself has been reported as an integral determinant of whether a child will succeed at school and in later years.[19] In theological terms, the training to participate in the Liturgy is the purification of *eros*. In his first encyclical, Pope Emeritus Benedict wrote that *eros* calls for "a path of ascent, renunciation, purification and healing."[20] This is precisely what parents are doing in the liturgical formation of their children. Thus, parents say "no" to their children not as an end in itself but in order to serve the deeper *yes* of love. In addition to this, participation in the Eucharist is an encounter with the love that is both *eros* and *agape*. Liturgical formation prepares children for this sacramental encounter with love.

A continual turning toward the other, sacrifice, and growth in the life of virtue are all fundamental to family life. They are also integral to participation in the Liturgy. The worship of God is therefore not something additional that is superadded to family life but takes up and perfects the communion of the family. To speak of the family as a church does not run the risk of making the Catholic Church seem far-removed from the lived experience of the laity. On the contrary, this vision of the family demonstrates that the Church has a profound understanding of life in the home.

It is the Church's Trinitarian theology that provides her with this insight into family life. John Paul II described the life of the triune God as "totally gift" and that in the Communion of the Holy Spirit "God exists in the mode of gift."[21] From this perspective, "gift" becomes the personal mode of being within the communion of the family. In the domestic

---

19. Duckworth and Seligman, "Self-Discipline Outdoes IQ," 939–44.

20. Benedict XVI, *Deus caritas est*, 5.

21. John Paul II, *Dominum et vivificantem*, 10. "It can be said that in the Holy Spirit the intimate life of the Triune God becomes totally gift, an exchange of mutual love between the divine Persons and that through the Holy Spirit God exists in the mode of gift. It is the Holy Spirit who is the personal expression of this self-giving, of this being-love. He is Person-Love. He is Person-Gift."

church, the concrete expression of existence as a gift is conversion, sacrifice, and virtue. This is only possible because in worship, the communion of the family is oriented toward and encounters Divine Communion, an encounter that is ultimately transformative.

MISSION AND THE NEW EVANGELIZATION

As we have already discussed, the identity of the family is that of a communion brought about primarily through the sacrament of marriage. In worship the communion of the family encounters Christ in a transformational way. Having encountered this love, the family is sent out ("Go forth, the Mass is ended") to preach this gospel to the ends of the earth. This is the ecclesial mission of family. The family is "called upon to communicate Christ's love to their brethren, thus becoming a saving community."[22]

The first manner in which the family participates in the Church's mission of evangelization is in its very being as a communion. The specific contribution of the family to the new evangelization is its existence as a community of life and love. This is why John Paul II charged the family with the mission to "become what you are." John Paul was exhorting families to live their communion with greater intensity.

For John Paul, the contemporary context in which this mission takes place is the building of the "civilization of love." To this end, in his *Letter to Families* he spoke of the "fairest" or the "most beautiful" love (*pulchra dilectio*). This is the love that finds its source in God. This love focuses on the dignity of the person; it is the love in which the person finds himself through a sincere gift of self in a communion of persons, and it is the love that grows as a result of the pruning of the Spirit so that it may bear more fruit.[23] In a word, the "fairest" or most beautiful love is the love signified by marriage and the body. In the sacrament of marriage, this love is poured out as a gift into the hearts of the spouses through the grace of the Holy Spirit. Spouses participate in it through their *yes* to each other in

---

22. *Familiaris consortio*, 49: "In turn, the Christian family is grafted into the mystery of the Church to such a degree as to become a sharer, in its own way, in the saving mission proper to the Church. . . . For this reason they not only receive the love of Christ and become a saved community, but they are also called upon to communicate Christ's love to their brethren, thus becoming a saving community."

23. *Letter to Families*, 13.

spousal consent. Families are called to grow daily in it throughout their service of each other.[24]

In welcoming the most beautiful love, families are called to radiate it to others. Through their generous response to life, patient love, fidelity in difficult times, and above all in forgiveness, the family gives prophetic witness to the love that originates in God. As such, from the being of the family flows its prophetic mission.

The prophetic witness of marriage and the family was an integral component of Vatican II and subsequent papal teaching.[25] Christian marriage and by extension the family has the duty to bear witness to faithful and fruitful love. In signifying this love, and through their participation in Christ's love for the Church, Christian families become prophets of the good news of the gospel and therefore witness to Christ's saving death and resurrection.

PASTORAL PROPOSALS

The Church is certainly aware of the "cultural shadows" that plague the family today. This vision of the family is not proposed in a manner removed from the reality of the family's situation but precisely in response to these challenges. There are three interrelated proposals to support the family as a domestic church.

The first is communal support. This can take place through the local parish, at the diocesan level and through various lay ecclesial movements. It is important that families are provided with opportunities to gather together with other families. The focus of these gatherings can be both social and formative. It would seem that this is being done both formally and informally at these recommended levels. The necessity of these gatherings is due to the communal nature of faith. If there is no communal support for the faith, then belief becomes at best tenuous. The pluralistic nature of Western societies only increases this phenomenon. The sociologist of religion Peter L. Berger spoke of the need for plausibility structures that reinforce and make religious faith credible.[26] Parish,

---

24. Cf. ibid., 20: "*For love to be truly 'fairest,' it must be a gift of God*, grafted by the Holy Spirit on to human hearts and continually nourished in them (cf. Rom 5:5)."

25. See especially *Gaudium et spes*, 49, 52; *Humanae vitae*, 25; *Familiaris consortio*, 51; and CCC, 1647.

26. See Berger, "Secularization and the Problem of Plausibility."

diocesan, and lay ecclesial movements can assist in providing these plausibility structures.

The second recommendation is in the formation of seminarians and priests. This formation will need to take place both theologically and practically. Theological formation should focus on the ecclesial characteristics of the family: communion, worship, and mission. The Council and the subsequent pontificates have made significant contributions to a theology of the family. Theologians such as Cardinals Angelo Scola and Marc Ouellet have further developed this theology. It is fundamental that seminarians and priests are provided with the most up-to-date theological reflection on the family in order to guide their pastoral ministry.

The practical formation of seminarians and priests is similarly pressing. It is not always a certainty that a seminarian has experienced traditional family life. However, for men who will be called "father" and who are charged with gathering together the "family of God" (cf. *Lumen gentium*, 28) it is hoped that familial relationships will be part of their lived experience, either through their family of origin or through encountering other families. To this end, one practical suggestion is the "adoption" of a seminarian by a Christian family for the time of his formation. Given the recent crisis of the sexual abuse of children by clergy, such a suggestion presents serious challenges. Implementation of this suggestion will involve prudence. Nevertheless, there is the real danger in the current climate that children will become an object of fear for the priest. Should the priest be removed from the daily life of families, this will result in a diminishment not only for priests but also for families and the Church.

With proper formation seminarians can be assisted in understanding how to relate to children at different stages of development. They can also receive formation on managing their relationships with children and the appropriate contexts for these relationships to take place. Hopefully, the fruit of this formation will be that seminarians and priests feel just as comfortable in the Christian home as in their liturgical ministry.[27]

The final recommendation involves the formation of engaged couples, married persons, and the family. In his book *Divine Likeness: Toward a Trinitarian Anthropology of the Family*, Cardinal Ouellet recommends that preparation for the sacrament of marriage take the form of a prolonged catechumenate.[28] This formation will introduce engaged couples

---

27. See chapter 12 for more on this topic.
28. Ouellet, *Divine Likeness*, 209.

to the mystery of Christ and the Church with the goal of conversion. It is the experience of the author that when the demands of marriage preparation are increased and the engaged couple perceive that they are genuinely receiving value from the classes, they will often respond positively.

Catechesis and preparation for baptism and first Holy Communion are also ideal times to present the Church's theology of the family. Furthermore, providing families with explicit suggestions for building unity are essential. Activities and traditions that focus on the Church's liturgical year are very popular with young children. Many parents feel ill-equipped to respond to the challenge of raising their children in the faith, hence the need to provide them with simple and practical activities. However, it is not enough simply to supply families with instruction. It is precisely action (cooperating with grace), in the area of communion, worship, and mission, that will enable the family to experience itself as a domestic church.

Finally, there must be mention of the sacrament of penance. John Paul II referred to penance as an "infallible and indispensable" means for holiness in the family.[29] Penance is the sacramental encounter with the Father of mercies who, when faced with our weakness, sends his Son and the Holy Spirit for reconciliation and forgiveness. This efficacious encounter with mercy is vital for the family to fulfill its mission as a communion that witnesses to the good news of salvation. John Paul described the importance of penance for the communion of the family in this way: "The celebration of this sacrament [of penance] acquires special significance for family life. . . . The married couple . . . [is] led to an encounter with God, who is 'rich in mercy,' who bestows on them His love which is more powerful than sin, and who reconstructs and brings to perfection the marriage covenant and the family communion" (*Familiaris consortio*, 58).

CONCLUSION

Through the sacramental life of the Church, and the insertion of husband and wife into the mystery of Christ and the Church, the family is truly a

---

29. John Paul II, *Man and Woman He Created Them*, 641. "[Spouses] must draw grace and love from the ever-living fountain of the Eucharist; . . . 'with humble perseverance' they must overcome their deficiencies and sins in the Sacrament of Penance. These are the means—infallible and indispensable—for forming the Christian spirituality of married life and family life."

domestic church. As an instantiation of ecclesial communion, the family is called to holiness and to share in the Church's mission of preaching the gospel. The family does this as a communion of life and love.

The expression "domestic church" articulates the nature of the Christian family as a communion. The term also conveys the family's specific contribution to the Church and society. As such, the recovery of the ecclesial identity of the family by the Council is a key development in terms of the renewal of the Church and her mission of evangelization. The implementation of reform sought by the Council will be inextricably linked to how Christian families live their ecclesial nature. To this end, the strengthening and catechesis of marriage and the family as well as the formation of priests to minister to the domestic church will be vital. Should these tasks be undertaken, then John Paul II's two insights regarding the domestic church—that the family will determine the future of humanity and the new evangelization—will bear fruit in abundance.[30]

---

30. "*The future of humanity passes by way of the family*" (*Familiaris consortio*, 86); and "the future of evangelization depends in great part on the Church of the home" (ibid., 52).

chapter 11

God and *Eros*: Six Implications for Religious Education[1]

GERARD O'SHEA

INTRODUCTION

In recent years, I have often found myself in rural communities speaking about strategies for meeting the contemporary challenges of religious education. This has given me the chance to meet many people who have, in their own way, given heroic witness to their faith. During a recent talk, an elderly lady, long retired from her position as a highly respected Catholic teacher, told me of a struggle she had faced for the whole of her life. "I was always made to feel," she said, "as if all that mattered was my soul, and that my body was little more than some kind of prison that I had to punish and subdue so that I could leave it behind and become something like an angel. It never really made sense to me. Why did God make us this way if what he really wanted was angels?" She articulated the problem very well. This was certainly the kind of training that many Catholics of her generation had received. It was as if God had made some kind of mistake in putting human beings together with both material and

---

1. The chapter is a revised version of an article which appeared as "Human Embodiment and Trinitarian Anthropology—Six Implications for Religious Education," *Studia Ełckie* 15 (2013) 455–66.

spiritual components and we would all be better off if we rejected our corporeal dimension altogether. This approach certainly placed a high value on our spiritual nature—but in the end, it actually made the doctrine of the resurrection of the body almost incomprehensible. Among many other reasons, it was to address misunderstandings such as this that Pope John Paul II set out to develop and explain a theology of the body—to try to lay to rest this Platonic denigration of human physical existence and to affirm the goodness of the material creation. Applying the essential ideas of this book, *God and* Eros, to the field of religious education really requires lengthy volumes of its own. In this chapter, regrettably, I will only be able to touch briefly on some of the main ideas. I will do so by proposing six key areas that need further exploration for the renewal of religious education along the lines implied by the ongoing project of St. John Paul II and his successors.

RELIGIOUS EDUCATION AND THE HUMAN PERSON

The General Directory for Catechesis, a 1997 document from the Congregation for the Clergy, makes a valiant effort to bring together in one place many of the insights from John Paul II's massive corpus of authoritative teaching as it applies to education. One of the terms used in this text is "trinitarian christocentricity."[2] This is an example of what teachers might call "excessive lexical density"—too much meaning packed into too few words! Yet it really does sum up something very important about religious education, namely, that it is about bringing human beings into relationship with the Blessed Trinity, through Christ. This idea is perhaps more familiar in the Liturgy, where prayers are typically addressed to the Father, through the Son in union with the Holy Spirit.

If we take time to examine this process, we will discover that it is an excellent summary of what happens when religious education is working effectively. Sofia Cavalletti, whose insights into catechesis are perhaps unmatched in recent history, made this simple comment when asked to sum up the process of bringing children to God: "Remember the order: first the body, then the heart, then the mind." I will unpack this further in a later section of this chapter, but in a nutshell, it means this: if you want children to learn anything new, the best starting point is to present a concrete object—something that stimulates the senses to "wonder." This

---

2. Congregation for the Clergy, *General Directory for Catechesis*, 99.

wonder sets up a desire to explore further because they have "delighted" in what has been sensed—in this way, the senses give access to the heart. Finally, when the needs of the body and the heart have been met, the experience is encoded into its most abstract form: intellectually in the mind. I speak here of the child, but long experience has revealed something else. It is not just children who work this way—adults do this too. It seems that all human beings, when left free to follow their inclinations, prefer to begin with what is most concrete, then move on to delighting in what they have found, and later put it into intellectual form.

Note the simple Trinitarian structure! We can perhaps look at it differently—we are first attracted by beauty, then drawn into goodness, and finally the truth. These classic transcendental properties of being (truth, beauty, and goodness) have long been associated with persons of the Trinity . . . so to put it in yet another way, Christ—the most concrete of the persons of the Trinity—is associated with the attractive power of beauty. By means of the Holy Spirit (Goodness) he leads us to the Father (Truth). It would seem that for human persons, the *abstract* and *spiritual* are accessed by what is concrete and material. The body has an essential role to play in coming to know God—a role that cannot be dispensed with, a role taken on in the Incarnation by the Son of God Himself. We might say, educationally, that this is the key insight of the Theology of the Body: the beauty of the concrete reality evokes "eros"—the desire that draws us into a search for what lies beyond in two further stages before we arrive at the goal.

RELIGIOUS EDUCATION FOR THE BODY

If we accept the view that human development has a Trinitarian structure that gives a place to the body, heart, and mind, then this must have its implication for religious education. Those who understand human development are in no doubt that the youngest children always begin the process of constructing their own understanding of the world through the senses. One has only to follow toddlers around to notice what is going on. These children are fascinated by the real objects in their environment—they want to touch, to smell, to hear, to see and (often to the horror of their mothers) *taste* whatever they encounter. It is also obvious that they are gripped with wonder in the presence of every new reality they encounter. Cavalletti points out that this fascination with the concrete, even in the youngest children, begins to take us out of ourselves through the vehicle of wonder, which is evoked by "an attentive gaze at reality." Few would dispute that this is the way young children operate—but we can often forget that older children and even adults never really lose this capacity to be "awed" in the presence of beauty and drawn into a transcendent reality. For human beings, the careful contemplation of concrete objects appears to direct us to a spiritual reality beyond ourselves.

This characteristic surely points us to the genuinely human starting point of religious education—attending to the needs of the body through the senses. If we circumvent this step, we are simply not attending to human nature as it is constituted. There is a well-known axiom of good teaching practice, expressed simply as "concrete to abstract." This has also been the understanding of the Church in relation to the sacramental system. In every sacrament, by means of the senses, the human person is drawn into a spiritual reality beyond. If religious education is to be successful, it cannot neglect or omit this essential starting point at any stage of development. The senses of the body have a crucial role to play. For example, in presenting the sacraments, it is usually best to begin with a careful, tactile study of the material elements found in the sacramental rites. Each of these, in its own way, draws the participant into a particular reality made present in the sacrament.[3] Any number of instances can be cited in support of this process as the starting point, but there is a particularly poignant story told in *The Religious Potential of the Child* concerning the use of a simple set of materials—cruets for pouring water and wine into a chalice.

> We will never forget seven-year-old Massimo, who continued to repeat this exercise for so long a period of time. The catechist, thinking that he was doing it out of laziness, came up to him several times to introduce him to some other work; but Massimo's facial expression was intent and rapt and he was trying to explain the meaning of what he was doing as he repeated the various actions. . . . Finally—it was almost at the end of the year—he managed to say: "A few drops of water and a lot of wine, because we must lose ourselves in Jesus" . . . In the end Massimo had known how to express it with words worthy of a mystic.[4]

3. The *Catechism of the Catholic Church* gives quite explicit descriptions of the particular realities that the elements of the sacramental rite stand for in the case of the sacrament of Baptism.

4. Cavalletti, *Religious Potential of the Child*, 92.

RELIGIOUS EDUCATION FOR THE HEART

The Attraction of the Scriptures

It is almost a truism in religious education that the whole project will be futile if we fail to reach the heart—but how? Any teacher knows that it is impossible to force anyone to make a "heart response"—this is an intensely personal decision. Some may try, using coercive, manipulative techniques to get an *apparent* response, but this will ultimately fail. In any case, it betrays the respect for genuine freedom that must lie at the heart of human existence. Yet, this does not mean that we should simply abandon the field altogether. Rather, we must be aware that we are leading the child to a place of encounter rather than a predetermined educational outcome! Cavalletti has some extraordinary insights here. She was herself a professional Scripture scholar at La Sapienza University in Rome. When asked to prepare a child for First Communion, she had hitherto no experience with children, so she did the only thing she knew—she began to share the Scriptures with him. The reaction of the child was something she was not prepared for. Even after two hours, the child was deeply moved and wanting to go deeper. Cavalletti had uncovered one of the key ways in which the heart is won over to God—the Scriptures themselves.

A caution must be issued here. This cannot be used as some kind of technique—Cavalletti is not suggesting that if the children are forced to listen to the Bible, their hearts will be won over. Quite the contrary; any force of this kind is more likely to turn the child in the opposite direction. Nevertheless, if the Scriptures are offered as the place to go in order to build on and explain the experiences of wonder that have been brought about through the senses, they are invested with an attractive power. The child encounters there a *person* rather than a sequence of words. The Holy Spirit is enabled to complete the task of revealing Jesus. Time and again, this approach has shown its worth. Cavalletti and her collaborators have already spent more than sixty years determining exactly which scriptural passages seem to touch the hearts of children—and indeed, adults. In order to enhance the natural processes, the initial presentations can be given using wooden models set within simple dioramas to engage the senses and create the scene.

Ultimately, however, it is the actual words of the Scriptures themselves that seem to have the effect on their hearts. Like most well-meaning adults, Cavalletti began telling biblical stories using her own words or those in a children's Bible in order to simplify the message and "get it across." She quickly discovered that this approach did not seem to have the same effect. Eventually, she decided that it was not up to her to simplify the Scriptures to instruct their minds—something (or in her words, *someone*) else was at work here. Just as the children had been enchanted by their contemplation of real objects, so too were they enchanted by the "real" words. It was after these experiences that Cavalletti articulated the principle of how the Scriptures must be presented to those lacking in experience—"rich food, but not too much of it!" Children were to be allowed to read the Scriptures for themselves, but given the time to slowly reflect on passages that captured their imaginations.

The use of the Scriptures at this level does not usually involve complex intellectual study of the Bible and its principles of interpretation. At this point, we are not trying to create scholars—this is a task for a more advanced stage of development, and too great an emphasis on this intellectual task can actually get in the way of the encounter of the heart. It is a relatively easy matter to correct false impressions that may be picked up when reading and only minimal guidance is necessary at this point. My own teaching of children has verified this approach. When children are allowed to follow the natural processes of human development, starting with the senses, and are then offered the Scriptures, they usually seize the opportunity to move in freedom to a deeper relationship with God. The Bibles are among the most popular items found in our catechetical center. Given the freedom to choose, children go to them again and again and spend more and more time reading passages that interest them. They use the Scriptures for their intended purpose: to know and love Christ. Indeed, to echo the words of St. Jerome, "Ignorance of Scripture is ignorance of Christ."

RELIGIOUS EDUCATION FOR THE MIND

The current consensus of educational theory shares a significant insight with the views of St. Thomas Aquinas, namely, that human beings construct their understanding by moving from concrete realities to abstract concepts, words and propositions. Saint Thomas, of course, goes further. In this view, the whole material universe has a purpose—to reflect some vestige of its creator. By engaging with it, we are able to build up a basic picture of who God is. Once we have engaged with reality, we form words and propositions that describe the experience. This indicates the proper place for the mind in religious education—as the synthesis point for describing what the senses and the heart have already discovered. The words then lead us back to the original encounter and to any subsequent reflections we have had about it. The words used to describe objects, events, and reflections are a means of allowing us to participate mentally in those things; they connect us with our own memories and with a cultural tradition that we may not have personally experienced.

Perhaps a common example will illustrate this best. Consider the initial teaching of reading in one of our first-grade classrooms. Children arrive at school with a wealth of existing experience in their oral language—drawn from the data of their senses and from things that they have already loved. *Playground*, for example, is a word that is likely to conjure up for them a whole world of happy associations and experiences. *Mum* is much more than a word of three letters! So even at the age of five, all three components of human learning have begun to operate effectively and are bringing about an integration of body, heart, and mind. Yet it must be clear that there is also a normal sequence that brings this about—the body-heart-mind sequence.

Often in religious education in the past, we have made the mistake of confusing the final stage (clarifying mental propositions) as the principal task, or even as the necessary starting point, rather than seeing how it should take its proper place in the overall scheme of things. At other times, we have reacted against the sterility of an overly intellectual approach by rejecting it altogether—an outcome that can actually prevent participants from arriving at the truth. Undoubtedly, it is essential to connect children with the authentic tradition of their Church and to provide them with clear teaching regarding what the Church holds to be true. But the reality of God is far greater than the propositions written about Him—even though these be true and necessary for us to know. A comment from Pope Benedict XVI (writing as Cardinal Ratzinger) endorses this view:

> Human words, at any rate the great fundamental words, always carry within them a whole history of human experiences, of human questioning, understanding, and suffering of reality. The great theme words of the Bible bring with them into the process of revelation also, in acceptance and contradiction, the fundamental experiences of mankind. So in order to understand the

Bible aright, one must always also turn to question the history preserved in its words.[5]

By the same token, it is beyond dispute that appropriate texts must eventually be committed to memory, as noted so forcefully by John Paul II in *Catechesi tradendae*: "We must be realists. The blossoms, if we may call them that, of faith and piety do not grow in the desert places of a memory-less catechesis. What is essential is that the texts that are memorized must at the same time be taken in and gradually understood in depth, in order to become a source of Christian life on the personal level and the community level."[6]

What must be kept always in view, however, is the fact that these texts cannot stand in isolation from the body or the heart of those they are meant to serve. Religious education for the mind will always work better if it is preceded first by suitable sensate experience and then a reflective engagement of the heart.

RELIGIOUS EDUCATION AND MORAL FORMATION

Moral formation carries very clear implications when looked at in light of the Theology of the Body and Trinitarian anthropology. Too often, this area can be seen as an extension of the philosophical study of ethics. It is far more than this and just as in other areas of religious development, it involves the sequential interplay of body, heart, and mind.

The youngest children are not capable of living their lives in accordance with self-chosen moral principles. It can be quite amusing to see young parents in a shopping center trying to reason with a two-year-old in terms of the moral principles they should observe! It may sound surprising, but, once again, the starting point for moral formation is the body. From the time children can walk, wise parents will be ensuring that they acquire good habits—that their actions will be limited by moderation in every area of their existence. Their parents will ensure that they eat properly, speak courteously, move safely, tell the truth, treat others fairly, and so on. In none of these areas are they actually capable of acting out of intellectually derived moral principles—they are simply trained to respond in the appropriate way. Parents may even "walk them through" the steps that they are meant to follow. The great Italian educator Maria

---

5. Ratzinger, *Pilgrim Fellowship of Faith*, 71.
6. John Paul II, *Catechesi tradendae*, 55.

Montessori developed a wide variety of teaching tools to assist in this basic moral formation of the body. She referred to it as "practical life" activities and "training in grace and courtesy." These activities consisted principally in learning how to care for their immediate environment for themselves—tidying their table, cleaning up after themselves, and so on. She observed that these basic tasks involving the body were found to be the basis of future moral action. It is impossible for the mind to direct a body that has not been "habituated" in this way to carry out virtuous acts.

Once this task of the body has laid the appropriate foundation, it will be time to move on to the Christian motive for moral activity—love. This, obviously, takes us into the realm of the heart. Only those who love deeply are genuinely capable of sustained moral effort. At around about the age of six years, children become capable of understanding that there can be necessary rules that underpin the way they should act. At this point, they will become focused on rules and regulations about how to behave, about what is fair. This is a natural development, and should be allowed to run its course in a way that enables them to work through to a more mature approach to a resolution of the tension between justice and compassion in appropriate ways.

Parallel with this development, however, is another deep need. Those who would acquire moral virtue need to be given the opportunity to fall in love with God—without coercion or manipulation. The moment when this mysterious personal development takes place is not in the hands of the teacher, or even the parent. It can be said from the experience of many who work with children, however, that there will be a myriad of opportunities for it at this time. Often it is associated with the child's preparation for First Communion. While this development cannot be forced, it appears that it can be aided by offering inspiring, beautiful stories about what human beings can achieve at their best when they act from a motive of love. Once again, the Scriptures offer many opportunities for this, as do the lives of the saints or other literature. Most of all, however, it must be stated that those who are most likely to be capable of love resulting in action are those who have been loved themselves. This kind of love is the second (and perhaps the most important) foundation of genuine moral agency. "If you love me, you will keep my commandments" (John 14:15).

While moral action appears to be primarily an activity of the will, it is undeniable that in the fully developed human being, moral reasoning—an activity of the mind—has a significant role to play. The relationship of intellect and will in the field of moral action has been widely explored and is well summarized by St. Thomas Aquinas in the *Summa Theologica*.[7] The study of ethics in secondary school is a valuable activity—if it is based on the proper foundation of authentic human moral development, starting with the body and moving to the heart before reaching the mind. If, however, it is detached from love or made impossible for individuals because of their inability to make their bodies do what their mind perceives to be right, then there is a problem to be worked through. The educational theorist Jean Piaget and his disciple Lawrence Kohlberg located moral agency entirely within the intellect—if you know the right thing, then you will do the right thing. A vast body of evidence drawn from human experience disproves this baseless optimism. To build an intellectual superstructure on an inadequate foundation will never succeed. If, however, moral reasoning takes its proper place as the mental culmination of stages that necessarily precede it, then clearly it will be the crowning glory of moral agency and allow us to perceive more and more ways of entering into the life of the Trinity by the way we think and act.

THE NATURE OF FAITH

Supernatural Gift and Free Assent

Although it is not directly connected with the Theology of the Body and Trinitarian anthropology, one of the greatest challenges currently facing religious education is the widespread failure to recognize the double dimension of faith itself. G. K. Chesterton has insightfully described a key paradox in Christian thought and practice: "Paganism declared that virtue was in a balance; Christianity declared it was in a conflict: the collision of two passions apparently opposite. Of course they were not really inconsistent; but they were such that it was hard to hold simultaneously."[8]

One manifestation of the conflict is the way in which faith must be held, since it necessarily involves two apparently contradictory dimensions held in dynamic tension. On the one hand, faith is an undeserved gift of God—a theological virtue conferred in the sacrament of Baptism.

---

7. *ST* II-I, q.82, a.4
8. Chesterton, *Orthodoxy*, 99.

On the other hand, it is also involves a genuine human assent, freely given. The insights of Benedict XVI shed some light on this for us. Pope Benedict points out that the act of faith comes about in a different way from the act of knowing: "... not through the degree of evidence bringing the process of thought to its conclusion, but by an act of will, in connection with which the thought process remains open and still under way. Here, the degree of evidence does not turn the thought into assent; rather the will commands assent, even though the thought process is still under way."[9]

He recognized the difficulties in this approach and acknowledged the accusations of philosophers such as Karl Jaspers and Martin Heidegger that faith, by presupposing the answers, leaves no room for questions.[10] In answer, Benedict cites Pascal's observation: "The heart has its reasons that reason does not know." He noted that we are able to give the assent of faith not because of the depth of our own inquiries or the quality of our evidence, but "because the will—the heart—has been touched by God, affected by him. Through being touched in this way, the will knows that even what is not clear to the reason is true. Assent is produced by the will, not by the understanding's own direct insight: the particular kind of freedom of choice involved in the decision of faith rests on this.... The will (the heart), therefore, lights the way for the understanding and draws it with it into assent."[11]

In other words, a religious education class must deal with a very different intellectual process than that involved in a science class. Blessed John Henry Newman brought a great deal of clarity to this interface between faith as a gift and faith as an intellectual process of assent to mysteries beyond human understanding in his classic work *An Essay in Aid of a Grammar of Assent*. Here, Newman described three mental acts associated with the holding of propositions of any kind—doubt, inference, and assent. All three, he insisted, were appropriate human behavior. "We do but fulfil our nature in doubting, inferring and assenting; and our duty is not to abstain from the exercise of any function of our nature, but to do what is in itself right rightly."[12]

---

9. Ratzinger, *Pilgrim Fellowship of Faith*, 23.
10. Ibid., 20.
11. Ibid.
12. Newman, *Grammar of Assent*, 7.

Newman draws attention to the fact that in the case of revealed religion, the holding of certain doctrinal propositions indicates the presence or absence of faith itself. To take up a position of doubt in relation to settled doctrine makes one a skeptic. To give such doctrines a merely conditional acceptance (inference) indicates the position of the philosopher. To offer assent (whether or not one understands it fully, as yet) is to be a believer. Baptized Catholics are believers, having received the gift of faith. To position them in such a way that they are encouraged to take some other stance (either doubt or inference) is to deliberately undermine their status.

Newman makes a further distinction between "inquiry" and "investigation." He insists that *inquiry* is inconsistent with *assent*, since one who inquires is in doubt about where the truth lies. Hence, a believer cannot at the same time be an inquirer.

> Thus it is sometimes spoken of as a hardship that a Catholic is not allowed to inquire into the truth of his creed;—of course he cannot, if he would retain the name of believer. He cannot be both inside and outside of the Church at once. It is merely common sense to tell him that, if he is seeking, he has not found. If seeking includes doubting, and doubting excludes believing, then the Catholic who sets about inquiring thereby declares that he is not a Catholic. He has already lost faith.[13]

In closing the door to *inquiry* in matters of religious faith, Newman was certainly not advocating fideism or anti-intellectualism of any kind. He simply made the necessary distinction between the way in which believers and non-believers need to engage with the data of revelation and faith. He believed that educated Catholics have an obligation to try to understand what they believe and discern the reasons underpinning this belief. To use his own words:

> Inquiry implies doubt and investigation does not imply it; and that those who assent to a doctrine or fact may without inconsistency investigate its credibility, though they cannot literally inquire about its truth... In the case of educated minds, investigations into the argumentative proof of the things to which they have given their assent is an obligation or rather a necessity.[14]

---

13. Ibid., 191
14. Ibid., 192.

On the other hand, Newman saw the dangers involved in encouraging those who had been poorly instructed, or ill-equipped, to assess subtle arguments to place themselves in danger through deliberate exposure to such approaches without proper preparation. Perhaps we could include in this group those who have not been properly prepared in the body (through the senses) or the heart (by means of a personal relationship with Christ founded in the Scriptures and the life of prayer).

> [Some] who, though they be weak in faith . . . put themselves in the way of losing it by unnecessarily listening to objections. Moreover, there are minds, undoubtedly, with whom at all times to question a truth is to make it questionable, and to investigate is equivalent to inquiring; and again, there may be beliefs so sacred or so delicate that, if I may use the metaphor, they will not wash without shrinking and losing color.[15]

In the current circumstances pertaining in religious education classrooms—particularly in secondary schools, these truths constitute a challenge. Much of the school system encourages a method of inquiry that can best be described as systematic skepticism. If such an approach finds its way into a religious education class, it will effectively undermine and denigrate the dimension of faith as a gift, and attempt to evaluate it using inappropriate criteria. Perhaps it is time to subject this kind of critical thinking to a process of critical evaluation to determine whether it is effectively performing a useful role in religious education!

CONCLUSION

The current chapter has sought to draw attention to some of the issues facing contemporary religious education in terms of the theological turn brought about by the Theology of the Body and renewed emphasis on Trinitarian anthropology. The needs of contemporary religious education, of course, are not exhausted by these six issues; there are others—for example, that any authentic religious education in the Catholic tradition must promote a disposition that looks not only inward, at one's own spiritual and physical needs, but also outward, to the needs of others. It is now widely accepted that this outward focus must find expression in an orientation toward New Evangelization and social justice, in authentic relationships, and it must give appropriate place to the role of

15. Ibid., 192.

the community and the family if the project is to be successful. Clearly, further developments in this field lie ahead of us.

chapter 12

Priestly Formation for Celibacy: Nuptial and Trinitarian

ANNA KROHN

INTRODUCTION: THE CONTEXT OF PRIESTLY FORMATION SINCE THE COUNCIL

In his programmatic teaching on priestly formation, St. John Paul II writes that the formation for ordination is "one of the most demanding and important tasks for the future of the evangelization of humanity" (*Pastores dabo vobis*, 6). The importance of priestly formation that is at once sound, integrated, and lifelong has occupied the minds and hearts of many saintly reformers and great theologians in the Church's history. From the patristic to the baroque reforms, writings by saints Catherine of Siena,[1] Pope Gregory the Great,[2] Bonaventure, Charles Borromeo, and Vincent de Paul[3] give testament to a concern for the connection between

---

1. Catherine of Siena, *The Dialogue*. Catherine relates the Lord's displeasure with priests who are "little boys rather than mature men" and attacks Church leaders who make priests "so darksomely, they put them in charge of souls even though they see that they do not know how to take charge of themselves" (257).

2. Gregory the Great, *The Book of Pastoral Rule*.

3. St. Vincent de Paul combined his well-known work for the poor and galley convicts with attention to the thorough formation of priests, including the intellectual, spiritual, and pastoral aspects of their formation. Cf. d'Agnel, *St Vincent de Paul*.

the sacramental and spiritual vigor of the Church and the type of priests she produces.

Since the opening of the Second Vatican Council there has been a sharpened attention to this link and, by the popes at least, focused concern that priestly formation be fed by the ecclesiology and biblically renewed anthropology sketched out firmly by the Council. On this backcloth, John Paul II charted a map for the promotion of integrity in priestly formation, marking out four crucial and interrelated areas: the human, spiritual, intellectual, and pastoral dimensions.[4] These elements are roundly human but also christological and Trinitarian in source and form. Pope Benedict XVI captures the humble beauty of this organically and affectively whole Christ-form when it is lived: "I think of all those priests who quietly present Christ's words and actions each day to the faithful and the whole world, striving to be one with the Lord in their thoughts and their will, their sentiments and their style of life."[5]

Since the Catholic Church is a sacramental and dramatic instantiation of Jesus Christ through time, the quality and holiness of both the common[6] and ministerial[7] priesthood is the context for formation for ministerial ordination.[8] The manner in which all the baptized are priestly calls them, in their distinctive and complementary vocations, to aptly reveal, offer, and represent Christ's love for the world to the Father in their lives, works, and relationships. At the same time, there can be no illusion that for Christians this is anything other than a fragile and grace-dependent drama.

John Paul II, while still a cardinal, urged the church fathers to see that the mission of the Second Vatican Council was to ensure that the fragmentations of sin and modern secularity could be met by a vigorous conversion and transformation to the priesthood of Christ in the moral, existential, and cultural lives of the all baptized: "This is not merely a

---

4. Cf. *Pastores dabo vobis*, 43–59.

5. Benedict XVI, "Proclaiming a Year for Priests," 1.

6. All of the baptized share in the one "royal" priesthood of Christ, which is activated in them through their being immersed in and conformed to Christ through the Holy Spirit so that they might consecrate the world to the Father. Cf. 1 Pet 2:5; *Catechism of the Catholic Church*, 1546; *Lumen gentium*, 31; John Paul II, *Christifideles Laici*, 14–15.

7. *Catechism of the Catholic Church*, 1547; *Lumen gentium*, 10.

8. The complementarity and the respective "authority" of the baptized, evident in the Council documents, was informed by works such as Yves Congar's *Mystery of the Church* (1956) and Henri de Lubac's *Splendour of the Church* (1953).

question of external resemblance but of the fruit of internal participation and the work of the Holy Spirit, which operates in all the baptized to form the attitude which expresses their resemblance to Christ the priest."[9] In this John Paul II and the subsequent popes have understood that neither the Church's institutions nor any of its members can rest upon a notion of being transformed in Christ that is in any way a generic "acting out" of faith, or simple reform of "policy" or of a polishing of appearances.

Since the ordained priest is called to be iconic, to be *persona Christi* by receiving the form of Christ within an essential "existential of faith"[10] in a particularly public and liturgical sense, his conversion to ever greater Christlikeness has deeply personal and soteriological implications. Aidan Nichols captures this elegantly: "The future of the priesthood is pivotal to the life of the Church since that priesthood is the public representation of the difference which the divine ordering of the world makes in Jesus Christ."[11]

THE CRISIS[12] IN PRIESTLY CELIBACY

Historically, crises in the cultural and sacramental life of the Catholic Church as a whole coincide with crises in the theological, pedagogical, and moral lives of her priests. Likewise, the disconnection between the personal and theological, the embodied and the intellectual, the "attitudinal" and the "official," evident in the lives of many contemporary priests, accompanied by depression, "an excessive loss of energy" (*Pastores dabo vobis*, 3) and other symptoms, suggests continuing problems in realizing a convincing christological or charismatic, still less a vigorously human integration for those in priestly formation.

Even more serious is the recent unearthing of cases of clerical sexual abuse of minors and other vulnerable people. Some of these certainly owe something to the perennial weakness of human beings and the breakdown of the sexual norms and behavior of the surrounding

9. Wojtyła, *Sources of Renewal*, 223–25.

10. Ibid., 224.

11. Nichols, *Christendom Awake*, 233.

12. Rather than deploying the term "crisis" in a hackneyed sense, the biblical or moral sense of a "kairos" with its understanding of crisis as a moment of judgment/opportunity seems apt here. The crisis affects people's and societies' cultural imagination and attitudes. One useful discussion of the moral dimensions of this can be found in Melina, *Sharing in Christ's Virtues*, 13–34.

cultures of the time. It is probable that sexual predation of minors within the "helping" professions and entertainment culture has been even more prevalent than among priests or seminarians.[13] But this alone does not explain or excuse the clusters of problems that have been left uncorrected or have been exacerbated during seminary formation, implicating not only the men recruited into the seminary process but also the character of the institutions themselves. The significant incidence of sexual vices and disorders, associated with affective and personality disorders, moral immaturity, institutional cynicism, moral paralysis, and duplicity in the abusive students, priests, and in their superiors, has placed the practice and ideal of "celibacy" at the epicenter of crisis within the Church.

Different commentators both within and outside the Church have attempted to diagnose the reasons for the stark disparity between the ideal and reality of priestly celibacy. A range of interpretative lenses, whether pedagogical, sociological, political, or psychological, have been applied to the problem. Some of these identify the dissonance between the life of chaste celibacy and contemporary sexual "realities" as caused by monastic idealism,[14] resentment,[15] emotional infantilism,[16] sexism, bodily alienation, sexual and other compulsions,[17] "clericalism,"[18] or abuses of institutional control.[19] In some cases a secular political or secular feminist[20] "hermeneutic of suspicion"[21] is applied to shortcomings in male celibacy so as to confirm the authors' underlying and wider dissent from magisterial teaching on sexual morality or ecclesiology. The public culture has made a sinister or comic stock figure of the hypocritical and "nonsexual" priestly caste struggling to control its dwindling power and relevance against an apparent tsunami of more humane, tolerant,

13. As evidenced by reports such as *The Nature and Scope of Sexual Abuse of Minors by Catholic Priests and Deacons in the United States, 1950–2002*, a study conducted by the John Jay College of Criminal Justice (2002).

14. Lamberigts, "Optatum Totius," 25–48.

15. Nelson, "Analysis: Why the Catholic Church Is Mired in More Child Sex Abuse Claims."

16. Sipe, *Celibacy in Crisis*.

17. Plante et al., "Personality and Cognitive Functioning."

18. The position that "assumes that clerics not only are but also are meant to be the active, dominant elite within the Church . . ." Shaw, *To Hunt, to Shoot, to Entertain*, 13.

19. Smyth, "The Land of the Pirates."

20. Sawchuk et al., "Exploring Power and Gender Issues," 499.

21. A hermeneutic identified by such authors as Paul Riceour in *Freud and Philosophy*, 27.

and egalitarian models of sexuality (and priesthoods).[22] Many Catholics, including priests, have been deeply disaffected and alienated by these institutional scandals and by the pervasiveness of secular cultures of sexuality—both of which are powerful countersigns to the gospel.[23]

Some of the academic analyses rest upon a fragmented and nominalistic sexual anthropology, beset by the very dualisms to which they object. On the other hand, some of the criticism is difficult to dismiss entirely since it rightly pinpoints real symptoms, as opposed to the deeper anthropological and theological causes of the problem of celibacy in contemporary clerical and religious life for which instances of child abuse are only the tip of a larger and still present iceberg.

The issues are not confined to scholarly journals or tabloids. Even though many formators and bishops acknowledge the need for a christologically enriched and wholistic formation of seminarians envisaged by *Pastores dabo vobis*, including a more psychological/theological integration in priestly formation and pedagogy, there remains even here a lack of thorough conversance with the anthropology of "integral vision" proposed in the teaching documents since the Council or with sound insights of the human sciences.[24]

Seminarians and recently ordained priests have shared with the author some of their perceptions about problems in their seminary and post-seminary formation.[25] Their observations include: the use of general counseling techniques rather than vigorous or clinical psychological theory,[26] piecemeal formation and support following ordination, the

22. Cihak, "Priest as Man," 75.

23. Cf. Guido, "A Unique Betrayal."

24. There are some outstanding exceptions to this observation: the U.S. Conference of Catholic Bishops' *Program of Priestly Formation* and Creighton University's Institute for Priestly Formation (http://priestlyformation.org/).

25. These observations are obviously the expression of anecdotal and informal opinion, but they have shown some thematic consistency.

26. Throughout the 1970s and 1980s many seminarians were subjected to amateur psychotherapies, undertrained and experimental counseling, and questionable sex therapies. There seemed to be confusion over the differences between spiritual direction, pastoral care, pastoral counseling, and psychology as a registered profession that provides evidence-based therapies, and in particular clinical psychological services. The considerable reluctance and even a residual hostility toward clinical psychology seems to persist in some new wave seminary formators and in some of the "new movements." Cf. Bond, "A Delicate Balance"; Brugger, "Psychology and Christian Anthropology."

secularization of ministry,[27] and the assumption of a gender neutral or "feminized" affective formation which assumes that the masculine Christo-iconic presence in the liturgy is bad faith and mistaken form. Priests and seminarians easily conclude that in a culture of sexual excess, they are offered a consolation prize, a somewhat neutralized "bachelorhood" that allows them time for the finer things or for social recognition.[28]

In a fearful response to the sexual abuse scandals, some seminaries have adopted a culture of "surveillance" rather than mature "supervision."[29] Others seem to believe that the sexual crisis belongs to the past and take an "unworldly" refuge in the belief that the Holy Spirit will iron out deep-seated moral and psychological issues without reference to firm and well-informed moral and psychological advice.

There also persists, in some types of seminary training, attitudes and practices associated with some older seminary cultures, which too little attend to the personal (and especially the sexual) realities of seminary staff and students. Here an overspiritualized and dualistic devotional regime can persist, with an absence of a balanced or realistic ascetical theology and practice, a loss of apostolic typology,[30] manic pastoral activism, and confusion between "otherworldly" renunciation and the biblical reverence for creation.[31]

John Paul II's "theology of the body" and its founding role in the emerging "nuptial mystery" theology (to be discussed further in this chapter) is not widely or systematically understood or promoted in much of the recruitment, formation, and ongoing support of priests. This is in part because there is an often shallow understanding (and sometimes a fear) of the thoroughgoing project of anthropological renewal within the Church among some of the senior priest formators themselves. Sometimes there is a notion that "theology of the body" is only a formulaic series of topics for marriage preparation or for teaching teenagers to

---

27. Acklin, *Unchanging Heart*, 29ff.

28. This was scathingly identified by von Hildebrand in *Celibacy and the Crisis of Faith*, 29

29. This suggests that some seminary formation is more akin to strict boarding school for unruly boys than to sound professional formation relying on peer mentoring with senior supervision, the integration of spirituality with practice-based experience, and assurances of post-training in-servicing and fraternal support.

30. A considered treatment of this can be found in the Balthasarian scholar Dermot Power's *Spiritual Theology of the Priesthood*.

31. Bouyer, *Introduction to Spirituality*, 135ff.

avoid promiscuity rather than a rich theological and existential source for consecrated virginity and apostolic celibacy. Many seminarians say they are keen to learn more about a more affectively and bodily focused anthropology—both for their own sakes and for the very obvious pastoral needs they will face. But some say they feel excluded by the "self-help" or "dating" climate of some popular *Theology of the Body* presentations or are discouraged from engaging in advanced "nuptial mystery" theology because some superiors view it with suspicion. It is dismissed as being continental or exotic or as a passing phase prompted by the Polish pope's charisma—in any case a field that is secondary rather than foundational to the study of either moral or pastoral studies.

RESTORING CREATION AND EROS TO PRIESTLY FORMATION

In his introductory remarks to *Pastores dabo vobis*, John Paul II suggests some reasons why the acceptance and understanding of priestly celibacy and its living have become difficult. Underlying the neglect or misunderstanding of particular tenets of Catholic faith is the substratum of the "social imagination" and cultural ethos of postmodern society, in which the assumptions about the human person and human love have been shaped.

The pope suggests that underlying the incomprehension of celibacy is the widespread atomization and alienation of postmodern "subjectivity" (shrunken to become "subjectivism"[32]), a type of existential consumerism, the "paralysis" of moral responsibility (not merely moral teaching), all floundering within a wider cultural and catechetical vacuum (*Pastores dabo vobis*, 7). Even more deeply, the pope identifies the loss of the Christian anthropological horizon, and even among traditionally Christian people a widespread indifference of "a type of practical and existential atheism."

By the late 1980s Thomas Dubay had explained the extent and effects of this in the late modern era: "Even priests and religious often have a surprisingly superficial grasp of why they are celibate, missing much of what the New Testament says of their vocation."[33] There was certainly intellectual confusion but also uncertainty about the existential meaning and the theological sources and distinctions regarding celibacy,

32. Cf. Wojtyła, *Love and Responsibility*, 153–65.
33. Dubay, *And You Are Christ's*, 15.

continence, consecrated virginity, and the virtue of chastity.[34] In many instances, celibacy was understood only within a naturalistic as opposed to natural and sacramental horizon, devoid of scriptural[35] immediacy or patristic mystical richness.

Dietrich von Hildebrand in the late 1960s wrote that rejection of celibacy betokened a deeper crisis of faith,[36] not only as regards adherence to the Church's particular tenets about priestly life and marriage, but a substantial loss of faith in the world of values and being itself. Von Hildebrand identifies a "utility" thinking and culture that had quickly mutated out of Pelagian or naturalistic teleology in the realm both of marriage and priesthood which in his view had infected many parts of Catholic life and teaching.[37] What is lost is not only the belief in a particular teaching, but the replacement of a "logic" and public identity of "graciousness" by a bureaucratic logic of outcomes, "and pastoral needs that could be tallied and projected by statistics."[38]

In various teachings, Benedict XVI[39] points out that human faith and love are intrinsic to knowledge and (though distinct) underpin our response to our own being, the world, and other persons, and even more to God. With secular fragmentation, Christian claims to a love of transcendent and transforming fire (both its *eros* and *agape*) become simply alien, and knowledge becomes a technology, a rationalistic "survival ration" salvaged after the disconnection between love and knowledge is complete. Dis-"affection" quickly accompanies cynicism, or an apathetic irony locked within "a pragmatic culture eager to embrace sophistry."[40]

---

34. For instance, such a mainstream text as *The Catholic Encyclopedia* offers an easily misconstrued definition: "Celibacy is the renunciation of marriage implicitly or explicitly made for the more perfect observance of chastity." Even though terms such as "renunciation" and "more perfect" may technically belong to an entirely valid ascetic and spiritual tradition that has roots in the Scriptures, the ecclesial context and the affective memory of such terms has been disconnected from a richer and more integrated theological context.

35. The integration of deeper scriptural resourcing for the theology and spirituality of the priesthood as the context for celibacy was affirmed by the Fathers of the Second Vatican Council and by scholars who contributed to the Council. See for instance Congar, *Gospel Priesthood*.

36. Von Hildebrand, *Celibacy and the Crisis of Faith*.

37. Von Hildebrand, "The Crisis of Human Personality."

38. Cardinal Lustiger, cited in Nichols, *Holy Order*, 163.

39. E.g., Benedict XVI, *Deus caritas est*.

40. Hanby, "Logic of Love," 405.

Christian apostolic celibacy is utterly dependent upon a biblical and ecclesial faith, a communal, mystical, apostolic, and liturgical experience in which personal faith and vocation are nourished, even in the face of sin and failing "to believe that love is the truth and meaning of being, which is to believe in turn that the world is creation."[41] "Where one loses the link with the will of the Creator and thus within the Church the link with the will of the Redeemer, functionality easily becomes manipulability."[42] Absent this matrix, celibacy is left high and arid, a depersonalized transcendent. As Benedict XVI writes in *Sacramentum caritatis*, celibacy falls with the depersonalized functionalism of postmodern life: "It is not sufficient to understand priestly celibacy in purely functional terms. Celibacy is really a special way of conforming oneself to Christ's own way of life. This choice has first and foremost a nuptial meaning; it is a profound identification with the heart of Christ the Bridegroom who gives his life for his Bride" (24).[43] Liberal or conservative "utility"[44] loses faith in either the Christ of tradition or the meaning of creation (or both), so that celibacy requires the immolation (or artificial repression) of the priest's masculine, corporeal, erotic, or paternal identity rather than the consecration and fulfillment of it. In each case,[45] the priest is viewed or views himself within an individualistic heroic (but often self-focused) "humanism"[46] or by a fideism that seems inhuman and strained.

41. Ibid., 413.

42. Ratzinger, "Summary of Cardinal Ratzinger's Commentary on *Ordinatio Sacerdotalis*," https://www.ewtn.com/library/priests/ratordsa.htm.

43. Explicit here is a developed theology of nuptial celibacy—a theme proposed in this chapter.

44. Von Hildebrand identified the dangers of "utility" thinking as a distortion of a certain type of naturalistic teleology—and noted that it could infect the practical culture marriage and priestly celibacy. See his *Marriage*.

45. Whether liberal or conservative in stance.

46. Von Hildebrand identifies this ethos of secularized anthropology that infects the Christian world as beginning in the early Renaissance and producing an "anthropocentric" rather than theocentric world view. Von Hildebrand, "The Crisis of Human Personality."

THEOLOGY OF THE BODY AS DEVELOPMENT FAITHFUL TO THE COUNCIL

"It's not only a response to the sexual revolution, it's a response to the Enlightenment."[47]

As a way forward through the anthropological and cultural crises of contemporary life, and by his extensive and synthesizing catechesis titled the "Theology of the Body," John Paul II shows that the source and goal of any education and also of formation is a rediscovery of embodied and existential life within "the mystery of Christ." In a particular way, his catechesis on human love, sacramentality, embodiment, and sexuality rotates about a decisive mystagogical axis around the person of Jesus Christ as both the Lover and Teacher[48] who reveals, enables, and redeems the world of *eros* and creation. Priestly celibacy is not a denial of truth and love but precisely a living dedication and participation in this loving and teaching of Christ.

In restoring the body and love to "theology" (and theology to love and the sexual body), John Paul II did not intend his teaching to be a novel set of personal musings or a merely interesting showpiece of phenomenological biblical exegesis.[49] Nor is it a collection of "teaching as a body of abstract truths" in apologetic defense of certain Catholic teachings. It is first a dramatic invitation to "communication of the living mystery of God,"[50] and it is also an invitation to re-engage wholly with the logic of love and redeemed creation that inspired the saints and the apostles.

These audiences also provide critically important evangelization, clarification, and development of the magisterial insights of the Second Vatican Council and all that it attempted in relation to a renewed theology of human dignity in general[51] and the formation[52] and dignity of

---

47. Christopher West, preface to John Paul II, *Man and Woman He Created Them*, xxvii.

48. This is ably discussed by Michael Waldstein in ibid., 15–18.

49. Waldstein, among others, points out how this "sidelining" of the *Theology of the Body* has been attempted by both "progressive" and traditionalist commentators. Ibid., 16–17.

50. John Paul II, *Catechesi tradendae*, 5.

51. Cf. *Gaudium et spes*, 22

52. Cf. Paul VI, *Optatam totius*, 10. Students to the priesthood should embrace celibacy "not only as a precept of ecclesiastical law, but as a precious gift of God which they should ask for humbly . . . under the inspiration and assistance of the Holy Spirit."

priests[53] in particular.[54] Human dignity was now to be brought back into conversation with the essentially Trinitarian roots of Christianity: "It is within the Church's mystery, as a mystery of Trinitarian communion in missionary tension, that every Christian identity is revealed, and likewise the specific identity of the priest and his ministry" (*Pastores dabo vobis*, 12). In John Paul II's theology of the body, the life of celibacy is not a "nonsexual" behavior but of a piece, and in the form of, a nuptial and "mystagogical"[55] response to a gift of grace and a personalized expression of love for God and others. When the theology of the body is comprehended and appreciated in priestly formation, it provides the grounds for a full-blooded and vigorously enfleshed expression of love.

In his audiences on love, person, and body, John Paul II provides an architectonic basis for an "adequate" and transformed priestly formation to which celibacy belongs and a deeper explanation of *Pastores dabo vobis*' stress on how a more fully human,[56] spiritual,[57] intellectual,[58] and pastoral[59] formation of priests is set within a relational and interpenetrating Trinitarian presence formation. Priestly formation "cannot be defined except through this multiple and rich interconnection of relationships which arise from the Blessed Trinity and are prolonged in the communion of the Church, as a sign and instrument of Christ, of communion with God and of the unity of all humanity."[60]

---

53. The Synod that met in 1990 centered on the topic of priestly formation. For a scholarly discussion of this, see Timothy Costello (now archbishop of Perth), *Forming a Priestly Identity*.

54. Cf. Paul VI, *Presbyterorum ordinis*.

55. The form of exegesis that draws Christians into a participation of the one mystery of Christ pervading the Scriptures, their own lives, and particularly the sacramental and liturgical dimensions of the Church (and of life.) See for instance the classic Bouyer, *Life and Liturgy*, or Louth, *Discerning the Mystery*.

56. *Pastores dabo vobis* 43–44 addresses the psychological, cultural, and genealogical issues of being a human being in contemporary settings.

57. Ibid., 45–51, which provides an extended consideration of priestly spirituality, dedication to scriptural sources, to contemplative and structured prayer, and a christological and eucharistic mysticism.

58. Ibid., 51–57, which provides a restating of the interrelationship of faith and reason central to John Paul II's theology and which also envisages the traditional study in philosophy and theology alongside cultural attunement.

59. Ibid., 58–60. This is expressed here in terms of "communion" ecclesiology.

60. Ibid., 12.

This Trinitarian source and hermeneutic, especially in relation to sexual love, does not rule out a discerning openness to the sound methods and measures of medicine, sociology, pedagogy, or psychology[61] integrated with formation of a "graced" and mature affectivity.[62] John Paul II's audience reflections are also motivated by the obduracy of the hard questions[63] that Paul VI addressed in the midst of the adolescence of the sexual "revolution" and in his attempts to defend the "bright jewel"[64] of priestly celibacy and the Church's teaching on procreation. Pope Paul VI taught that both celibacy and marital love were central to the renewal of the Church, but that in motivation and catechesis they needed to be developed within the christological "*imago*" theology of *Gaudium et spes* 22.[65] In *Sacerdotalis caelibatus* he urged that formation for both expressions of Christian vocation and love be implemented "as soon as possible,"[66] even though his personal sacrifice and urgency were widely rejected or overlooked. The encyclical on priestly celibacy was depicted as reactionary magisterialism, a "betrayal of the spirit of Vatican II" and the creation of a culture of bad faith. A parallel accusation was made of his *Humanae vitae*.[67]

John Paul II comprehended this rejection of his predecessor's prophetic teaching and his attempts to lay bare the cultural and philosophical obstacles to preaching Catholic marriage and priesthood, including Paul VI's diagnosis of distortions in modern priestly reality: "They . . . certainly have reason to wonder how they can coordinate and balance

61. Cf. *Optatam totius*, 11.

62. In professional psychology this is known as emotional, social, and spiritual intelligence skills (EQ and SQ); this also addresses the integration across the bio-psychosocial-spiritual dimensions of a person rather than the fragmentation of long-standing false dichotomies between faith and reason, mind and body, human and spiritual.

63. *Sacerdotalis caelibatus*, 3. Some of the questions that arose at that time revolved around the importance of sexual fulfillment, relational maturity, and the decline in priestly vocations in the West.

64. Ibid., 1.

65. Tracey Rowland identifies this section of *Gaudium et spes* as a hermeneutical key for the Second Vatican Council's renewal of embodied and doxological theological anthropology and a communion ecclesiology: "If one zeroes in on paragraph 22 and treats it as the hermeneutical lens through which the remainder of the document is studied, then the Incarnation is absolutely central and not something that can be distilled." Rowland, "Benedict XVI and the End." See also her chapter in this volume.

66. *Sacerdotalis caelibatus*, 61.

67. A point not lost on von Hildebrand; see *The Encyclical Humanae Vitae*. The "sign of contradiction" in the subtitle of this work comes from *Humanae vitae*, 18.

their interior life with feverish outward activity."[68] Paul VI urged priests to live out their "sacramental brotherhood" with brother priests so that the contours of their ministry remain open to formation and re-formation—grace "rooted in Christ's Pasch" and fired by the work of the Holy Spirit.

For Pope Paul VI, priestly formation took place in "fraternal" complement to the ordinary priesthood of the baptized,[69] while at the same time the priest is a man "set apart" like the prophets (Jeremiah) and St. Paul (Rom 1:1). Far from setting up an opposition between marriage and priestly life, Pope Paul extolled faith-filled families as primal seminaries in which vocations to the priesthood and celibacy are fostered by example and relationship.

Pope Paul also took into account sound advances in psychological, moral, and academic theological formation.[70] He counseled "firmness" in the initial and ongoing screening of seminarians: "An inquiry should be made into the candidate's proper intention and freedom of choice, into his spiritual, moral and intellectual qualifications, into his appropriate physical and psychic health."[71] He urged an honesty about the real difficulties that celibacy presents for candidates to the priesthood; the fostering of a raw clear-sightedness in the seminarian concerning his inner life; a life of "virile"[72] but not "suffocating" asceticism;[73] the importance of time and of trial periods; the development of a rich spiritual life;[74] and ongoing formation in chastity long after ordination.[75]

The "theology of the body" teaching was at least in part motivated by John Paul II's recognition of the importance of Pope Paul VI's teaching

---

68. Paul VI, *Presbyterorum ordinis*, 14.

69. All the baptized "offer spiritual sacrifices to God through Jesus Christ, and they proclaim the perfections of him who has called them out of darkness into his marvellous light. Therefore, there is no member who does not have a part in the mission of the whole Body; but each one ought to hallow Jesus in his heart, and in the spirit of prophecy bear witness to Jesus." Ibid., 2

70. *Sacerdotalis caelibatus*, 64:"The life of the celibate priest which engages the whole man so totally and so delicately, excludes in fact those of insufficient physical, psychic and moral qualities." The pope warns of entertaining "false hopes," etc., and advises thorough moral and psychological screening.

71. *Optatam totius*, 6.

72. *Sacerdotalis caelibatus*, 78.

73. Ibid., 70.

74. Ibid., 75.

75. Ibid., 73.

on such issues as priestly celibacy and his faithful development of the theology of person. But John Paul's catechesis was also motivated by the fact the Paul VI's teaching bridged two styles of theological and philosophical expression.[76] For Paul VI, in discussing celibacy and married love, still employs a language of "natural ends" and "renunciation," employs a use of "desire" that can be confused with concupiscence, urges celibates to be "free from the bonds of flesh and blood,"[77] and warns them to be on guard against "seductions of the flesh."[78] John Paul appreciated that this could be misinterpreted as "angelism" and might not address the "utility" teleology of naturalism.

At the same time, Paul VI acknowledges the importance of emotional freedom, spiritual maturity, the joy of self-giving love, and the "spousal" and "fraternal" dynamic of celibate love. In some places this is clothed in a more scholastic or canonical phraseology, even though it clearly foreshadows (while not fully or explicitly) the interrelationship of sexual identity, the sacramentality of the body and "eros,"[79] and love in the spiritual and moral ideals of priestly celibacy. What Cardinal Wojtyła observed in 1978, on the anniversary of the document *Humanae vitae*, might also apply to Paul VI's document on celibacy: "This anthropological stratum of the document [*Humanae vitae*] does not appear in the form of a systematic exposition, but is rather 'outlined' in it and in this way permeates the whole content and the entire text from beginning to end."[80]

THE THEOLOGY OF THE BODY AND FRUITFUL, LOVING CELIBACY

The Spousal Paradigm of Love

When he defended Pope Paul VI's controversial but definite teaching about the canonicity of priestly celibacy in the Western tradition, the German Catholic philosopher Dietrich von Hildebrand observed that the "purpose and mystery of marriage" was associated with the ecclesial

---

76. See Nicholas Tonti-Filippini's analysis in chapter 9 for some aspects of this matter as it pertains to moral theology and bioethics.

77. *Sacerdotalis caelibatus*, 21.

78. Ibid., 73.

79. For a discussion and definition of love as "eros," see chapter 6.

80. Wojtyła, "The Anthropological Vision of *Humanae Vitae*."

importance and mystery of priestly celibacy, because both in their respective ways presented to the world the "spousal love" of Jesus Christ, foreshadowed in the Old Testament and revealing that "the great gift of marriage is connected with the sacrifice involved in priesthood."[81]

In this and his earlier writings, von Hildebrand recognized the spousal giftlike meaning and the rich dignity of sexuality in both the vocation to marriage and priesthood, and subsequently devoted his phenomenological attention to the importance of the grace-fed sources for the love that sustains them. He had identified in the Council and magisterial teachings that which in the theology and catechesis of Pope John Paul II coalesce and flower into a more explicit theology of human "embodiment" and nuptial/spousal/betrothed[82] love—a love that is foundational to marriage and dedicated celibacy, and watermarked into the heart, consciousness, and body of men and women.

John Paul II captured the essence of this significance, at once sacramental and existential, and draws it up out of its roots in biblical and patristic theology and from the Council's renewal of the *imago Dei* anthropology: "The human body in its original masculinity and femininity according to the mystery of creation ... is not only a source of fruitfulness, that is, of procreation, but has 'from the beginning' a spousal character, that is, it has the power to express the love by which the human person becomes a gift, thus fulfilling the deep meaning of his or her being and existence."[83] It is this engrafted, but often veiled, "spousal" or "nuptial" meaning of the embodied person that proves so problematic to the dualistic and secular anthropologies of modern and postmodern experience. Why does the Church remain insistent that marriage is between one man and one woman? Why only a male ordained priesthood? Why the gravity of celibacy or marital fidelity? Why does the Church care about what we do in the bedroom?

The Church holds to these doctrines and disciplines because she believes that the Creator, Redeemer, and Paraclete are constantly present and revealing in and through Her own spousal form a dynamic and

---

81. Von Hildebrand, *Celibacy and the Crisis of Faith*, 30.

82. Michael Waldstein notes, in his glossary/index to Pope John Paul II's "theology of the body" texts, that the "spousal meaning" (*significato sponsale*) of love, human consciousness, and body is "the single most central and important concept in TOB." See *Man and Woman He Created Them*, 682. For John Paul II's introduction of this pivotal discussion, see 178.

83. Ibid., 257.

meaning that is also truth about authentic human love. There is in this betrothal in truth and teaching an "internal coherence of the Church's understanding across a range of concerns that appear disconnected from the point of view of contemporary secularity."[84] This nuptial or spousal meaning reveals an "inseparable intertwining of three factors: sexual difference, love in its proper sense (relation to other, gift) and fruitfulness,"[85] which is a true but mysterious analogue of the divine love of the Blessed Trinity. In the other direction it is also a firmly earthed, concrete experience of authentic human fulfillment in any vocation, but especially so in the married and priestly consecration of body, heart, life, time, and mind.

If "nuptial mystery" theology dramatically and beautifully revives the logic of love at the heart of creation and redemption, it can hardly be considered an optional extra in the recruitment and formation of men to the priesthood. It is central to the Church's own identity and mission as Mother and Bride to whom the priesthood is in another sense wedded. In Western priestly celibacy and in all Christian monastic priesthood, the manly vitality of the "chosen one" is called to be a sign of Christ's eschatological Wedding Feast. As John Paul II explains in his exegesis of Matt 22:1–14 and Eph 5:25–31, an embraced celibacy is not a renunciation of the goodness of spousality, or a denial of a man's own sexual identity, but rather is a response to an invitation to share in Jesus Christ's own consecration of this precious meaning for the sake of the eschatological "kingdom of God." Those who choose to enter the dramatics of the Bridegroom in this particularly significant and sacramental way "must choose it out of appreciation of its value and not on the basis of any other calculation whatsoever."[86] The Church as Spouse and every member of her life—whether priest, married man, or the person living her baptism in love and virtue—responds to the coming of the Bridegroom "through a communion and a personal gift to Jesus Christ and his Church which prefigures and anticipates the perfect and final communion and self-giving of the world to come" (*Pastores dabo vobis*, 29).

A thorough and ongoing formation and conversion to the "spousal mystery" is also vitally important for the work of the priest, since the priest's representation of chaste, generous, passionate, and self-giving love becomes central to the evangelization, preparation, sacramental/

---

84. Hanby, "Logic of Love," 409.
85. Scola, *Nuptial Mystery*, xxiii.
86. Ibid., 434.

pastoral healing, and enrichment in the marital and sexual lives of those he serves. A priest is called to nourish and to have nourished in himself the very spousal values that are fostered in the life of a husband and father. In another important way, the priest is often the Church's fatherly face and hands in the deeply meaningful or abject experiences of love lost or found. He is not therefore to "act" in some forced or artificial sense with fatherly love and concern. Because God sent his Son to reveal his redeeming concern for the world, the priest shares the fatherly love revealed in Christ.

It is important that those being formed and sustained as priests by the centrality of a spousally formed love have the time and the practical personal resources to have that love intimately nurtured (not repressed or worn down) in both the dimensions of eros and agape: "If loving Christ means getting to know him, it follows that the willingness to undertake committed and careful study is a sign of the seriousness of one's vocation and of the earnest inward search for intimacy with Him."[87]

Forming the Priest's Original Experiences

In this limited space, it is perhaps instructive to sketch the key notion of "original experiences" introduced by Pope John Paul II in his first cycle of audiences in the Theology of the Body triptych of catechetical texts, in order to move toward the deeper foundation of the meaning of celibate life. It is worth remembering that this admittedly daunting corpus was daringly intended for the widest possible audience. It was delivered over many months to an open and random audience that included seminarians, girl guides, elderly pilgrims, Soviet intelligence officers, and curious tourists.

It is true that the opening cycle, "In the Beginning," which treats of the pericope of Christ and the Pharisees (Matt 19:3–8) and the creation of man and woman,[88] does not specifically treat of celibacy or virginity and is therefore "only half the story; it reveals a good deal of the Creator's original plan, but it does not disclose the whole of it."[89] However, the pope's exegesis of the biblical creation texts is vital in establishing the

---

87. Ratzinger, *Called to Communion*, 130.
88. See *Man and Woman He Created Them*, 131–225.
89. Anderson and Granados, *Called to Love*, 199.

conceptual scaffolding of his anthropology, and is now (we here contend) vital for any theologically based formation or education.

John Paul commences with an intriguing exegesis of the scriptural creation accounts, highlighting the second creation account because it pries open an immediacy of language and poetry about human bodily experience and desire. Here the pope proposes a new type of foundation for preaching and catechesis that is both ancient and remarkably fresh. First, it is "original" in an epistemological sense, for while the pope recognizes that experience has a cultural foundation, he stresses that it also and more fundamentally immerses the person into "the whole of reality, in terms not merely of the sum of things in their singularity, but also of the integrated relation among things." David L. Schindler has described this with the phrase "originary experience."[90] John Paul II explains that the reason for his preference for Genesis 2 is that humanity's origins are presented there in language and imagery that is vivid and existential, a dramatic person-to-person narrative.

More important for John Paul II is the fact that original experiences are endorsed by Jesus Christ himself, the *logos* and origin of God's love, who gives this chapter filial authority by directing his hearers[91] to the Creator's "original" shaping and blessing of humanity's "one-flesh" existence and relationship "in the beginning" (Matt 19:3–8). It presents humanity as "freshly minted," wide-eyed in wonder, caught in a metahistorical consciousness in "the oldest description and record of man's self-understanding." "One can say that this depth is above all subjective in nature and thus in some way psychological."[92]

Second, in this affectively touching narrative we encounter "*in nucleo*"[93] (as the pope says) all the most sensitive issues of contemporary man and woman "in the raw" (as it were)—subjectivity, identity, desire, embodiment, existential hunger, the relationship to nature, the world of work and fulfillment—at this point outside of reference to either a systematic moral text or abstract theological speculation. The story also places the hearer "inside" Adam's thoughts and desires as he relates to God the father-gardener who, with infinite "affective" concern and attention, walks in the garden of the world and shapes into life the

---

90. Schindler, "Living and Thinking Reality," 167.
91. *Man and Woman He Created Them*, 141.
92. Ibid., 137.
93. Ibid., 138.

beauteous images of Himself. The concrete and existential immediacy of this narrative, although presented in a mythic and even primitive mode, contains "all the elements of the analysis of man to which modern and above all contemporary philosophical anthropology is sensitive."[94]

The pope identifies in the narrative of creation a loving call from God played in a type of musical chord[95] of three clear and beautiful notes felt and experienced in the heart and bodily experience of Adam and Eve, one that, with contemplative reflection, can still be heard by all humanity through time (despite sin and failing). These notes of universal *original experiences* Pope John Paul II identifies as *a*) original solitude, *b*) original unity, and *c*) original nakedness. Each of these can helpfully be brought into conversation with formation for celibacy in priestly education and ministerial and spiritual support.

CONCLUSION: EXTENDING THE ORIGINAL EXPERIENCES FOR CELIBACY

This music of creation is most particularly audible, a hearing "in Christ" through the sacraments and liturgical prayer. In order to prepare authentic embodied vocation and a mystical ear, it is important that the seminarian and priest (as much as the married man or woman) develop a habitual spiritual and affective life, not merely his intellectual formation, through which his particular personality and temperament can be fulfilled peacefully in these "original experiences." A regular recalling of these experiences also allows the celibate priest to experience his solidarity with all humanity—man or woman, unmarried or married.

John Paul II's exploration and narration of humanity's creation, via these key experiences, offers affective pastoral communication as much as being a sophisticated theological exercise. It addresses the heart and imagination of the hearer/reader before the modern analytical or postmodern skeptical mind can disintegrate the "originary experience"[96] of being human.

The first cited "original experience" is "original solitude." Sometimes those explaining the *Theology of the Body* catechesis leap over this aspect of human experience and explain it away as a type of "glitch" in the

---

94. Ibid.
95. This is a helpful analogy discussed in Anderson and Granados, *Called to Love*.
96. Cf. Schindler, "Living and Thinking Reality."

Creator's work prior to "finishing" humanity with the creation of woman. This is particularly unhelpful for those training for priesthood. For John Paul II's "original solitude" does not resemble the secular liberal notion of the isolated "ego," still less the unsatisfactory idea of "being single." Mary Shivanandan notes that "original solitude has a meaning on its own, separate from its preparation for the creation of woman."[97] It does not simply refer to existential loneliness. It is an aloneness before God as primary spousal love and a solitude for service.

Through the creation narrative, the reader or listener is taken imaginatively through Adam's eyes as he surveys the diversity of creation and then his own body. Adam's body is a sign of his difference to all the other creatures; this "moment" of awareness of aloneness is vital for his self-determination and identity. So too priests should be formed so that they do not become isolationists but have a mature ability to stand "in a stark aloneness with God in Jesus."[98] This priestly form of "original solitude" is important not only for a contemplative religious life, but especially for the apostolic life of a diocesan priest. This monastic heart is not the pursuit of a type of Buddhist detachment, but rather involves an active and intentional returning by the priest to the "vis-à-vis" of an interior life in Christ.

Pope Paul VI also alludes to this experience of solitude in his encyclical on priestly celibacy. He notes that this is the solitude of Christ—not emptiness or aloneness motivated by "proud desire to be different from other men . . . or to show contempt for the world" (*Sacerdotalis caelibatus*, 58). Pope Benedict XVI extends this notion of forming a monastic heart: "The deepening of Christian truths and the study of theology . . . presupposes an education to silence and contemplation, because one must become capable of listening to God speaking in the heart." This solitude also relates to the nuptial gift dramatically exchanged in the story of Adam and Eve. Saint Mother Teresa of Calcutta uses some challenging language in her talk to priests. She says, "The greatest gift that one can give to Jesus on the day when one joins the priesthood is a virgin heart and a virgin body."[99]

Furthermore, Mother Teresa implies that tied up with nuptial giving and priestly fatherhood is not an abstract or idealistic spiritual nakedness,

---

97. Shivanandan, *Crossing the Threshold of Love*, 97.
98. Aschenbrenner, *Quickening the Fire*, 16
99. Teresa, "Priestly Celibacy."

but one that is existentially and physically spousal and eschatological: it is a living sign of the nakedness of Job or of the prophets urging the people of Israel toward the coming of God's kingdom. It is a christological nakedness that exposes the body, mind, and heart of the priest with Jesus Christ, "who makes himself the hungry one, the naked one, the homeless one." Furthermore, the nakedness of the choice of celibacy in this life is a sign of solidarity with the little ones in Christ: "I was naked, not only for a piece of cloth, but I was naked for that dignity of the child of God."[100]

There is nothing timid or infantile about this nakedness of gift. Indeed, in Teresa's words we can see a reconciling and completing of a preferential poverty of service and the royal service of both the cross and the Eucharist. It is no wonder that John Paul II insists on a robust constitutional and "sexual identity" in the man to be priest. He is not to be an atomized or a minor man, one whose masculinity is eschewed and whose fraternal receptivity to women is blocked. His vocation and leadership are complementary to the feminine "authority" of such as Mother Teresa and even more of the Mother of God.

Seminarians should foster a "realistic" and non-sentimental Marian prayer life in which this openness to the feminine is alive—a deep and loving relationship in prayer and service to the Mother of God that is complementary to the priest's masculine and paternal development and entails a healthy (rather than childish) maternal anchor to the man's life. She who was instrumental in forming the human heart of Jesus as he grew into the fullness of his manhood is also an integral part of the formation of the heart of his priests.

That heart is not the place for bureaucratic functionalism or for shrunken emotional life. It is the place in which the "audacity of God who entrusts himself to human beings—who, conscious of our weakness, nonetheless considers men capable of acting and being present in his stead."[101] This in the priestly dimension brings with it a form of "exposure" to the love of God that is both renewing and purifying for the Church and world.

---

100. Ibid.
101. Benedict XVI, "Homily for the Solemnity of the Sacred Heart," 1.

chapter 13

Co-operators of the Truth of the Human Person

MARC CARDINAL OUELLET

INTRODUCTION

In December 2008, Pope Benedict XVI made a first appeal for an ecology of the human person: "What is needed is something like a human ecology, correctly understood. If the Church speaks of the nature of the human being as man and woman, and demands that this order of creation be respected, this is not some antiquated metaphysics. What is involved here is faith in the Creator and a readiness to listen to the 'language' of creation. To disregard this would be the self-destruction of man himself, and hence the destruction of God's own work."[1]

This appeal, reiterated in the encyclical *Caritas in veritate*,[2] elicited both positive and negative responses, prompting Pope Benedict to take up the same idea in greater depth in his address to the German Parliament in September 2011. His masterful presentation of created human nature as the foundation of law will remain in the annals of the contemporary dialogue between the Church and the world as a major contribution to the philosophy of law.

---

1. Benedict XVI, Address to Members of the Roman Curia, December 22, 2008.
2. Cf. Benedict XVI, *Caritas in veritate*, 51.

Benedict XVI's teaching prolongs the powerful impetus given to anthropology by the founder of the John Paul II Institute for Studies on Marriage and Family, St. John Paul II. Both pontiffs transmitted the wisdom of the Church, an expert in humanity, on a large scale. John Paul II's chief contribution was the development of the anthropological perspective of Vatican II's Pastoral Constitution on the Church, *Gaudium et spes*, in order the better to ground the moral teaching of Paul VI's encyclical *Humanae vitae*. We know the dissension provoked by this teaching. Dissent hindered its acceptance especially on the part of those interpreting the Council from within a "hermeneutic of discontinuity,"[3] or of rupture with the preceding tradition.

From its foundation, the John Paul II Institute took its place within the perspective of continuity. It deepened the biblical anthropology of the *imago Dei*, in order the better to ground an ethic of human love in the human person's vocation to love according to his nature as the image of God. In Christ the Redeemer, this image is brought to complete fulfillment.

Here I propose to call to mind both the anthropological challenge of our time and the Church's response to it—a response that this Institute helps formulate through its multidisciplinary search for the truth of the human person.

THE TRUTH OF THE HUMAN PERSON CALLED INTO QUESTION

The spread of secularization in the West has profoundly affected contemporary cultures, provoking not only a crisis of traditional values but also an unprecedented anthropological crisis. In many societies, public life is organized without God, with all reference to the transcendent relegated to the private sphere. Intoxicated with the new power science and technology give him but deprived of a metaphysical perspective, the human person marvels at his technological prowess but no longer knows who he is. He is thus more exposed than ever to man's exploitation of man, to the great detriment of the increasingly impoverished masses. He is even exposed to the influence of anthropological theories that are incompatible with his own identity.

---

3. Cf. Benedict XVI, Address to the Roman Curia Offering Them His Christmas Greetings, December 22, 2005.

In other ages the Church attempted to uphold the religious sense and moral values of societies built on a shared Christian heritage. In our day, she finds herself compelled to re-establish a sense for the human, which is disappearing under the pressure of a relativistic and nihilistic culture. In the moral sphere, sexual perversions proliferate, engendering solitude, isolation, and illnesses stemming from a problematic relational matrix. From this flows a confusion of values and ethical norms that directly affects the domain of education. Hence, too, the need for a revival of education through a new evangelization, which includes a renewed vision of the human and Christian identity that shaped European culture and enabled its worldwide influence.

We might have thought that after the fall of the totalitarianisms of the twentieth century, a return to the religious would allow us to eclipse the Godless humanism that so ravaged European culture. But after the various forms of structuralism that declared the death of man as "subject," feminist ideology again challenged the truth of the human person through its latest product, "gender theory." This theory is built upon the negation of human nature as the basis of all cultures. It reduces sexual difference to a mere cultural dimension that can be constructed or deconstructed. The biological given of maleness or femaleness is secondary; the individual can construct his or her identity at will, even changing from masculine to feminine or choosing a hitherto unprecedented gender indicated by the abbreviation LBGT (lesbian, bisexual, gay, transgender).

If this theory were merely the arbitrary cogitations of a few intellectuals, there would be no reason to be bothered by it. But in fact, it forms the basis of movements of opinions that are carefully orchestrated to transform the legislation and educational programs of nations. Moreover, these movements are officially supported by the politics of the United Nations, along with many other international organizations. We cannot, then, remain indifferent. We must also acknowledge the vigilance and courage of the Holy See for opposing with all possible means this subtle and insidious anthropological heresy, which increasingly penetrates the milieu of education.

Tony Anatrella, a French psychoanalyst and sociologist, explains,

> *Gender theory* is the new ideology that openly serves as a reference point for the United Nations and its various agencies, especially the World Health Organization, UNESCO, and the Committee on Population and Development. This ideology has also become the framework of thought for the European

Commission, the European Parliament, and different member states of the European Union, inspiring legislators of these countries to draft numerous laws concerning the redefinition of the couple, marriage, filiation, and the man-woman relation, particularly in the name of "equality" and "sexual orientations."[4]

This extreme theory is not the only cause of the current malaise, but it is certainly a grave symptom of a larger and deeper crisis touching marriage and the family in our secularized societies. Contraception, divorce, free unions, abortion, and below-replacement birth rates are now such widespread phenomena that they have in effect become the dominant culture in many countries. This "culture" reveals that the individual can no longer manage truly to commit himself in love, with a profound sense for the other as a person. Living as if God did not exist (*etsi Deus non daretur*), he closes in on himself for want of an interlocutor, in an attitude that unveils his more fundamental crisis: a crisis of the gift of self. Everything unfolds as if we have lost our sense for this gift, along with the profound motivation for a stable and even definitive commitment. From this flows the breakup of families, the eclipse of fatherhood and motherhood, the erosion of fraternity, and the multiplication of the disturbing phenomena of drug abuse, violence, and suicide, which demonstrate the gravity of the situation.

All of these phenomena express the profound malaise of our secularized societies. Once God has been relegated to the margins of social life or confined to the private sphere of the individual, promoters of love have no interest in—or have downright contempt for—marriage and the family. The individual finds himself delivered over to his own ephemeral, egotistical desires. Rereading the post-synodal exhortation *Familiaris consortio* thirty years after its publication, we see that many—and more obscure—shadows have been added to the "interplay of light and darkness," as the exhortation described the situation of the family in the world today.[5] But in a kind of contrast effect, the Church's response, cultivated in this Institute, shines forth now more than ever as a prophetic light.

---

4. Anatrella, "'Preface' to Pontifical Council for the Family," 3.
5. Cf. John Paul II, *Familiaris consortio*, 6.

SEEKING THE FOUNDATIONS

In order to respond to the crisis of the gift of self in the present culture, as well as for the sake of a fruitful dialogue with our contemporaries, it seems important to me at this stage of our reflection to mention a few points that Pope Benedict XVI highlighted regarding the dialogue between faith and reason. In the encyclical *Fides et ratio*, John Paul II had called for the passage from "phenomenon to foundation" to be accomplished in our own day.

> Wherever men and women discover a call to the absolute and transcendent, the metaphysical dimension of reality opens up before them: in truth, in beauty, in moral values, in other persons, in being itself, in God. We face a great challenge at the end of this millennium to move from *phenomenon* to *foundation*, a step as necessary as it is urgent. We cannot stop short at experience alone; even if experience does reveal the human being's interiority and spirituality, speculative thinking must penetrate to the spiritual core and the ground from which it rises. Therefore, a philosophy which shuns metaphysics would be radically unsuited to the task of mediation in the understanding of Revelation. (*Fides et ratio*, 83)

Benedict XVI took his predecessor's orientation and applied it to anthropology. In the human person, the "foundation" to which we must return ceaselessly, despite criticisms and negations, is human nature. Pope Benedict affirms,

> Even if the concept of "human nature" seems to have been lost in contemporary culture, the fact remains that human rights cannot be understood without presupposing that values and norms, which are to be rediscovered and reaffirmed and not invented or subjectively or arbitrarily imposed, are innate in the human being. At this point the dialogue with the secular world is of great importance: it must appear clearly that the denial of the ontological foundation of the essential values of human life inevitably ends in positivism and makes law dependent on the currents of thought that predominate in a society, thereby corrupting law and making it an instrument of power instead of subordinating power to law.[6]

---

6. Benedict XVI, Address to Members of the International Theological Commission, December 1, 2005.

Gender theory, imposed from above on parliaments and schools, is a prime example of the danger of the manipulation of law by power.

If the human being cannot discover the foundation of law in his own nature, he risks losing a cultural inheritance built up over centuries of history. This loss will certainly occur if the current positivism imposes itself on society and law. "A purely positivistic culture which tried to drive the question concerning God into the subjective realm, as being unscientific, would be the capitulation of reason, the renunciation of its highest possibilities, and hence a disaster for humanity, with very grave consequences," Pope Benedict affirmed.[7] And he asked, with reason, "In the end, what is more inhuman, and destructive, than the cynicism which would deny the grandeur of our quest for truth, and the relativism that corrodes the very values which inspire the building of a united and fraternal world?"[8]

Forgetfulness of human nature has pernicious consequences. In the face of the latter, it is astonishing to see how eager contemporary society is to acknowledge the nature of plants and animals, while it fails to recognize the same concept with respect to human nature. In his call for a "human ecology," Pope Benedict did not hesitate to point out this surprising contradiction and thus challenge consciences: "Rain forests deserve indeed to be protected, but no less so does man, as a creature."[9] If it is true that we must in fact respect the nature of one or another animal species, "Man too has a nature that he must respect and that he cannot manipulate at will."[10]

Why is that which is so obvious in the animal and vegetable kingdoms so obscure and uncertain in the human being? On this point, Pope Benedict refers to a great theoretician of the legal positivism that seems to have prevailed over natural law: Hans Kelsen. Kelsen affirmed that "nature therefore could only contain norms . . . if a will had put them there. But this . . . would presuppose a Creator God, whose will had entered into nature." When Kelsen goes on to say that "any attempt to discuss the truth of this belief is utterly futile," we are perplexed. Pope Benedict asks humbly, "Is it really pointless to wonder whether the objective reason that

---

7. Benedict XVI, Meeting with Representatives of the World of Culture, September 12, 2008.

8. Benedict XVI, Meeting with the Civil and Political Authorities, September 26, 2009.

9. Benedict XVI, Address to Members of the Roman Curia, December 22, 2008.

10. Benedict XVI, "The Listening Heart."

manifests itself in nature does not presuppose a creative reason, a *Creator Spiritus*?"[11]

Kelsen's position helps us understand why we are led today to reject the foundation that accounts for phenomena. The prestige of the so-called exact sciences dominates our culture to the point of invalidating other forms of thought, such as philosophy or theology. Scientific rationality seems to take up all the space and to deny any value to other areas and degrees of knowledge. To wonder about the foundation that is human nature is to cross the threshold of metaphysics. It is ultimately to wonder about the God who created this nature and gave it its dignity. The splendid edifice the West built up with regard to respect for human dignity shows itself to be extremely fragile once we reject its divine foundation. But shouldn't the stone rejected by today's builders—thus compromising the whole structure—once again become the cornerstone?

With a patience coupled with wisdom and pedagogy, Pope Benedict XVI tirelessly called for a definitive return to the truth of Christianity as the foundation of the real: "At the most profound level its content will necessarily consist—in the final analysis, just as it did then—in love and reason coming together as the two pillars of reality: the true reason is love and love is the true reason. They are in their unity the true basis and the goal of all reality."[12]

What all these texts of Pope Benedict that we have cited share in common is a fundamental illumination of the *Word made flesh*, which allows us to give a framework to the dimensions of meaning provided by science, technology, art, and literature. "In the beginning there was the Word," and not irrationality. And this Word is Love, the Beginning and the End of all reality.

The main reason for the current anthropological crisis is thus the loss of this Beginning and of a right relation to it. This loss of the ultimate foundation occasions more or less anarchic cultural evolutions and the loss of moral, social, and religious points of reference. Rather than giving in to the helplessness of the prophets of doom, however, it is more worthwhile to concentrate on a new evangelization, aided by a dialogue between faith and reason. It is eminently worthwhile to rediscover God, the principle and the foundation of all reality. This is the sense of

---

11. Ibid.
12. Ratzinger, *Truth and Tolerance*, 183.

Benedict XVI's great interventions before the leaders of nations on behalf of a "human ecology."

CO-OPERATORS OF THE TRUTH OF THE HUMAN PERSON

a) Epistemology and Multidisciplinary Study

Conscious of the contemporary anthropological challenge that particularly affects marriage and the family, the Church further develops her teaching in the christocentric and Trinitarian perspective of the Second Vatican Council's Pastoral Constitution, *Gaudium et spes*. This teaching relies on the scientific culture of our age, yet it ceaselessly recalls and defends the contribution of the philosophical and theological wisdom without which anthropology lacks a foundation. In the words of the Council, the Church proclaims the "noble destiny of man" and champions "the Godlike seed which has been sown in him." This motivates her firm commitment and collaboration in "fostering that brotherhood of all men which corresponds to this destiny" (*Gaudium et spes*, 2).

Saint John Paul II gathered the fundamental elements of this teaching in his catecheses on human love and in the publication of the apostolic exhortation *Familiaris consortio*, following the 1980 Synod on the family. The latter document, faithful to the spirit and the letter of Vatican Council II, is like a Magna Carta of marriage and the family. Its theological foundation is the biblical revelation about man, the image of God: "Creating the human race in His own image and continually keeping it in being, God inscribed in the humanity of man and woman the vocation, and thus the capacity and responsibility, of love and communion" (*Familiaris consortio*, 11). The human person's divine vocation to love, taken up and confirmed by Christ, is essentially realized in sacramental marriage and consecrated virginity, the "two ways of expressing and living the one mystery of the covenant of God with His people" (*Familiaris consortio*, 16).

This line of thought was further developed in John Paul II's apostolic letter *Mulieris dignitatem* and in the *Letter to Families*—always in the light of *Gaudium et spes* 22, which affirms that "only in the mystery of the incarnate Word does the mystery of man take on light." In paragraph 24 of the same Constitution, the Council adds that the incarnate Word reveals the Trinitarian communion as the source and supreme archetype of the truth of the human person: "The Lord Jesus, when He prayed to the Father, 'that all may be one ... as we are one' (John 17:21–22) opened up vistas closed to human reason, for He implied a certain likeness between the union of the divine Persons, and the unity of God's sons in truth and charity." This Trinitarian perspective indicates much more than an example for us to follow for the sake of harmonious human relations. It reveals the very structure of anthropology: "This likeness reveals that man, who is the only creature on earth which God willed for itself, cannot fully find himself except through a sincere gift of himself" (*Gaudium et spes*, 24).

The teaching of the John Paul II Institute for Studies on Marriage and Family is based on these perspectives of the Word of God, which provoke a good deal of the enthusiasm of all those who participate in the Institute's life. All the multidisciplinary subjects taught there cooperate and converge to illustrate the truth of the human person and his relations. Whether in scientific disciplines such as biology, psychology, sociology, and law, or the disciplines of philosophy and theology, the truth of the human person emerges in the gift of self. It is a truth founded in human experience illuminated by the Word of God.

In our current context, it is of the greatest importance for the Institute's teaching not only to remain faithful to its sources and tradition but also to treat rigorously and clearly the different epistemological levels that come into play in the study of anthropological questions. In the face of the authority of the exact sciences, which positivism imposes on our secularized Western cultures, it is important to follow the example of Pope Benedict XVI. With him, we must carefully expose the metaphysical foundation, which reaches a deeper dimension of reality than does the sensory experience measurable by the sciences. The human person's very being bears the foundational values of law and ethics that no particular science can establish. These values pertain to a specific rational discipline, philosophy, without which no humanism can come to maturity. The John Paul II Institute cooperates in the truth of the human person to the extent that it engages in the dialogue between the different disciplines, respecting the methods of each and aware of their respective limits. There are what Jacques Maritain called "the degrees of knowledge" with regard to being as a whole.[13] The same holds for the truth of the human person. To keep these degrees together and to show their relation

---

13. Maritain, *Distinguer pour unir*.

to one another and their convergence in anthropology is an unavoidable task in the face of the challenges of our present culture.

b) Trinity and Creation

On the theological level, the culture of the gift of self passes through a deepening of the doctrine of the *imago Dei* and of the relation of this image to its archetype. For the crisis of the identity of the human person in our age will not be overcome merely through a reminder of the natural order and its foundation in God. A further step is needed: we must delve more profoundly into the relationship between the *creating Trinity* and human life in its most essential expressions, such as marriage and the family. I spent a great deal of time exploring this theme while I taught at the Institute, but much remains to be done to clarify the relation between the Trinity and anthropology on the basis of a deeper understanding of the relation between the Trinity and creation.

At this point, the dialogue that needs to take place involves confronting medieval exemplarism, particularly that of Thomas Aquinas, with Hans Urs von Balthasar's notion of "theo-drama," or the dramatic interplay of divine and creaturely freedom. The Angelic Doctor locates the fundamental principle of the procession of creatures within the Trinitarian processions of the Word and the Spirit. And he develops his brilliant account of the divine Persons as subsistent relations:

> If we abstract from the relations, which are really identical to [God's] essence, nothing would subsist in God, properly speaking. There is no essence beyond the Persons, but rather a single essence of the three Persons who create. The three Persons are *unus creator* [one Creator], but *tres creantes*, three Persons creating in virtue of a single essence. . . . The [creature's] relation to God as principle refers us to the Trinity in his unity (in whom this relation must be conceived as a relation of reason), but the relation to God considered as *end* can consist in a relation to a particular Person, the exemplar of the gifts by which we adhere to the holy Trinity.[14]

Balthasar develops this relational perspective in what he calls the *Theodrama*, that is, the encounter and espousal between God and his creature,

---

14. Émery, *La Trinité créatrice*, 316.

through the interplay of divine and human freedom. These two freedoms are bound together in the Total Christ, the Image of God par excellence:

> [W]e can . . . assume that *if* God designs and creates a world, it can only be that he wills thereby to communicate his Trinitarian life of love, which it must therefore reflect. Furthermore, it must not reflect the Trinitarian life in the way a finished, discrete copy reflects its prototype: since God's very essence is communication, the "copy" must continue to be open to the "prototype," there must be a sharing between them.[15]

In this light, the medieval axiom of the unity of the Trinity in God's creative action *ad extra* can and must be developed in a way that brings out more clearly the participation of God's works in the intra-trinitarian relations. The ultimate meaning of creation and salvation would thus reveal itself to be integrated into the very life of God. God's work would "contribute" something to God. While obviously not necessary for his beatitude, this contribution remains nonetheless a supererogatory—but not superfluous—expression of the mutual Love of the divine Persons. Balthasar concludes,

> What does God gain from the world? An additional gift, given to the Son by the Father, but equally a gift made by the Son to the Father, and by the Spirit to both. It is a gift because, through the distinct operations of each of the three Persons, the world acquires an inward share in the divine exchange of life; as a result the world is able to take the divine things it has received from God, together with the gift of being created, and return them to God as a divine gift.[16]

At this ultimate horizon of thought, the human person's end is not only defined by obtaining his own beatitude, but above all through the service of God's glory, that is, of *God's* beatitude. "Seek first God's kingdom and his righteousness, and all these things shall be yours as well" (Matt 6:33). Isn't there something beautiful and great here, something we can proclaim to save men and women from meaninglessness, to help them find themselves by loving with all their heart, all their soul, and all their strength? For to love God and our neighbor in all truth means to give glory to God, not only by imitating his Love but by being one with him.

---

15. Balthasar, *Theo-Drama*, 5:99.
16. Ibid., 521.

Medieval exemplarism profoundly inspired Christian thought, rendering it fruitful for centuries. In our day, it is the existential *analogia amoris* (analogy of love), that is to say, a living participation in the synergy of human love and divine love in Christ, that corresponds even more to the aspirations of contemporary men and women. In this perspective, the value of the relational dimension of the Christian faith and its connection to the proclamation of the kerygma need to be highlighted. For before it is knowledge about God, the Christian faith is receiving and personally adhering to a Word who is at one and the same time a Person. This Word and Person reveals his intimate interior as the tri-personal God.[17] In the modern age, a forgetfulness of being and an epistemological shift have led to a hypertrophy of faith as knowledge, at times to the detriment of faith as relation and a source of relations.

Hence the necessity of developing a relational thinking, radically founded on the reality of the Trinitarian relations. Such thinking already exists; it fills the theology of the saints and emanates naturally from an authentic feminine theology (not to be confused with a certain type of feminism). We mention here Thérèse of the Child Jesus, Conchita Cabrera de Armida, Adrienne von Speyr, and Chiara Lubich, among many others. Thanks to an appropriated catechesis of the Trinitarian Gift, who is "being-gift" par excellence,[18] and who grounds the human person and dwells in him intimately, this relational thinking can renew Christian life and enthusiasm for holiness.[19] Like all their predecessors, contemporary men and women aspire to eternal life. They aspire to a personal communion with the true God. This communion implies imitating God as His beloved children. But above all, it implies loving in union with Him, as we hear in Jesus's priestly prayer in the Gospel of John.

The current anthropological crisis depends on the loss of the Trinitarian principle at the foundation of human existence. On the existential and cultural level, the solution to this crisis can only come from a renewed, living relationship with this principle and foundation. This is why the truth of the human person cannot be sought or discovered except in the love that comes from Him. For the triune God created man in Jesus Christ, the one Mediator. He committed His own glory in the glorification of man, through a union of love with him. Hence John Paul II's cry:

17. Cf. Benedict XVI, *Verbum domini*, 24–25.

18. Bruaire, *L'être et l'esprit*.

19. Cf. Pontificia Academia Theologica, *Relazione? Una categoria che interpella*; Mattheeuws, *Les "dons" du mariage*; Donati, *La matrice teologica della società*.

> Man cannot live without love. He remains a being that is incomprehensible for himself, his life is senseless, if love is not revealed to him, if he does not encounter love, if he does not experience it and make it his own, if he does not participate intimately in it. This, as has already been said, is why Christ the Redeemer "fully reveals man to himself."[20]

CONCLUSION

The John Paul II Institute for Studies on Marriage and Family places all its multidisciplinary resources at the service of a rediscovery of the truth of the human person—a truth that has been called into question by a secularized society. The Institute's mission consists in integrating the complementary contributions of faith, philosophy, and the sciences in a holistic vision of anthropology, in its intrinsic relation to marriage and the family. To my mind, the most pressing task at the present hour is to highlight the relational dimension of faith and to present biblical anthropology as a summit of the degrees of knowledge. This demonstration cannot be accomplished through an appeal to scientific facts. Rather, these facts must be integrated into the fullness of meaning that the Christian faith brings to the lights of science and philosophy. To this end, a differentiation and articulation of the epistemological status of the various disciplines is part of the Institute's task, so that it can aid the Church's proposal of a Christian anthropology at this hour of the new evangelization.

The current anthropological crisis places before the Church the urgent need for a renewal of education on all levels. The milieu of the family, the school, and the university must be rehabilitated by means of an image of God that invites us to relationship, that awakens enthusiasm because it causes a new impulse, a passion and energy for the gift of self and for welcoming others, to spring up in the heart of today's men and women.

Conjugal life, the life of the family, and consecrated life can survive and blossom only through the love that is the gift of self. Formation toward this gift requires a new evangelization, which roots human love more profoundly in the Trinitarian Love opened up to our participation in Jesus Christ. Spouses and families can endure, they can accomplish their sacramental mission in today's world, if Christ is welcomed at the

---

20. John Paul II, *Redemptor hominis*, 10.

heart of their love, together with the gift of Trinitarian communion he bears in himself.

When that happens, united couples and families really become the Church who evangelizes and responds to the anthropological challenges of our age. The Church does not do this by means of a step backwards, but through the grace of a personal encounter with the risen Christ. Couples and families thus evangelized drink regularly from the fountain of the Eucharist. In this way, they become the domestic Church that brings the good news of the family to all mankind.

Bibliography

CHURCH DOCUMENTS

Catechism of the Catholic Church. Rev. ed. London: Geoffrey Chapman, 1999.
Congregation for the Clergy. *General Directory for Catechesis*. Vatican City: Libreria Editrice Vaticana, 1997.
Dei Filius (Dogmatic Constitution on the Catholic Faith). http://www.ewtn.com/library/councils/v1.htm#5.
The Documents of Vatican II. Edited by Walter M. Abbott. Translations directed by Joseph Gallagher. London: Geoffrey Chapman, 1966.
International Theological Commission. "Faith and Inculturation." 1988.
———. *The Search for Universal Ethics: A New Look at Natural Law*. Translated by Joseph Bolin. 2009. www.pathsoflove.com/universal-ethics-natural-law.html.
Ordo Celebrandi Matrimonium, editio typica altera. Typis Polyglottis Vaticanis, 1991.
Pontificia Academia Theologica. *Relazione? Una categoria che interpella*. Vol. 10. Vatican: Libreria Editrice Vaticana, 2012.
Sacred Congregation for the Doctrine of the Faith. *Declaration on Certain Questions Concerning Sexual Ethics*. 1975. http://www.ewtn.com/library/curia/cdfcertn.htm.

PRIMARY SOURCES AND SECONDARY LITERATURE

Acklin, Thomas. *The Unchanging Heart of the Priesthood*. Steubenville, OH: Emmaus Road, 1997.
Anatrella, Tony. "'Preface' to Pontifical Council for the Family." In *Gender: La controverse*. Paris: Pierre Téqui, 2001.
Anderson, Carl, and José Granados. *Called to Love: Approaching John Paul II's Theology of the Body*. New York: Doubleday, 2009.
Andia, Ysabel de. "Eros and Agape: The Divine Passion of Love." *Communio* 24 (1997) 29–50.
Aschenbrenner, George A. *Quickening the Fire in Our Midst: The Challenge of Diocesan Priestly Spirituality*. Chicago: Jesuit Way, 2002.
Atkinson, Joseph C. "Family as Domestic Church: Developmental Trajectory, Legitimacy, and Problems of Appropriation." *Theological Studies* 66 (2005) 592–604.

Balthasar, Hans Urs von. *Explorations in Theology.* Vol. 3, *Creator Spirit.* Translated by Brian McNeil. San Francisco: Ignatius, 1993.

———. *The Glory of the Lord: A Theological Aesthetics.* Vol. 5, *The Realm of Metaphysics in the Modern Age.* Translated by Oliver Davies et al. San Francisco: Ignatius, 1991.

———. *Love Alone Is Credible.* Translated by David C. Schindler. San Francisco: Ignatius, 2004.

———. *My Work: In Retrospect.* San Francisco: Communio, 1993.

———. *Theo-Drama: Theological Dramatic Theory.* Vol. 5, *The Last Act.* Translated by Graham Harrison. San Francisco: Ignatius, 1998.

———. *Unless You Become Like This Child.* Translated by Erasmo Leiva-Merikakis. San Francisco: Ignatius, 1991.

Benedict XVI, Pope/Ratzinger, Joseph. Address of His Holiness Benedict XVI to Members of the International Theological Commission. December 1, 2005.

———. Address of His Holiness Benedict XVI to the Members of the Roman Curia for the Traditional Exchange of Christmas Greetings. December 22, 2008.

———. Address of His Holiness Benedict XVI to the Roman Curia Offering Them His Christmas Greetings. December 22, 2005.

———. *Called to Communion: Understanding the Church Today.* San Francisco: Ignatius, 1997.

———. *Caritas in veritate,* 2009.

———. *The Church, Ecumenism and Politics.* Slough, UK: St. Paul Publications, 1988.

———. "Dependence on God Makes Us Free." *L'Osservatore Romano,* Weekly Edition in English, no. 34, August 22, 2012.

———. *Deus caritas est.* Homebush, NSW: St. Paul Publications, 2005.

———. "The Dignity of the Human Person." In vol. 5 of *Commentary on the Documents of Vatican II,* edited by Herbert Vorgrimler. New York: Herder and Herder, 1969.

———. Easter Vigil Homily. March 22, 2008. http://www.vatican.va/holy_father/benedict_xvi/homilies/2008/documents/hf_ben-xvi_hom_20080322_veglia-pasquale_en.html.

———. "Homily for the Solemnity of the Sacred Heart of Jesus." Mass for the Conclusion of the Year of Priests. Vatican City, July 11, 2010. http://www.vatican.va/holy_father/benedict_xvi/homilies/2010/documents/hf_ben-xvi_hom_20100611_concl-anno-sac_en.html.

———. "The Listening Heart: Reflections on the Foundations of Law." Address to the Bundestag, September 22, 2011.

———. Meeting with Representatives of the World of Culture, Collège des Bernardins. September 12, 2008.

———. Meeting with the Civil and Political Authorities and with the Members of the Diplomatic Corps. Prague, September 26, 2009.

———. *Pilgrim Fellowship of Faith.* Edited by Stephan Otto Horn and Vinzenz Pfnür. Translated by Henry Taylor. San Francisco: Ignatius, 2005.

———. "Proclaiming a Year for Priests: On the 150th Anniversary of the 'Dies Natalis' of the Curé of Ars." Vatican, 2009. http://www.vatican.va/holy_father/benedict_xvi/letters/2009/docu ments/hf_ben-xvi_l.

———. *Sacramentum caritatis,* 2007.

———. *The Spirit of the Liturgy.* Translated by John Saward. San Francisco: Ignatius, 2000.

---. *Truth and Tolerance: Christian Belief and World Religions*. Translated by Henry Taylor. San Francisco: Ignatius, 2004.
---. *Verbum domini*, 2010.
Berger, Peter L. "Secularization and the Problem of Plausibility." In *The Sacred Canopy: Elements of a Sociological Theory of Religion*, 127–54. New York: Anchor, 1990.
Bond, Anthony. "A Delicate Balance: Clergy-Psychologist Collaboration in Service of Priestly Formation." *Seminary Journal* 2 (2012) 65–78.
Boot, Alexander. *How the West Was Lost*. London: I. B. Tauris, 2006.
Bourg, Florence Caffrey. "The Family as Domestic Church and the Romantic Model of Love." In *Marriage*, edited by Charles E. Curran and Julia Hanlon Rubio, 157–77. Readings in Moral Theology 15. New York: Paulist, 2009.
Bouyer, Louis. *Introduction to Spirituality*. Translated by Mary Perkins Ryan. Collegeville, MN: Liturgical, 1961.
---. *Life and Liturgy*. London: Sheed and Ward, 1956.
Bruaire, Claude. *L'être et l'esprit*. Paris: PUF, 1983.
Brugger, E. Christian. "Psychology and Christian Anthropology." *Edification* 3 (2009) 5–18.
Caffarra, Carlo Cardinal. "Perché la famiglia? Fecondità della via di Giovanni Paolo II." *Anthropotes* 28 (2012) 37–47.
Catherine of Siena, St. *The Dialogue*. Translated by Suzanne Noffke. New York: Paulist, 1980.
Cavalletti, Sofia. *The Religious Potential of the Child*. Chicago: Catechesis of the Good Shepherd Publications, 1992.
Cavanagh, William T. "Eucharistic Sacrifice and the Social Imagination in Early Modern Europe." *Journal of Medieval and Early Modern Studies* 31 (2001) 585–606.
Chaput, Charles. "As Christ Loved the Church: A Pastoral Letter to the People of God in Northern Colorado on Forming Tomorrow's Priests." 1999. http://www.catholicnewsagency.com/document.php?n=235.
Chesterton, G. K. *Orthodoxy*. London: John Lane, 1908.
Cihak, John. "The Priest as Man, Husband, and Father." *Sacrum Ministerium* 12 (2006) 75–85.
Clarke, W. Norris. *Explorations in Metaphysics: Being, God and Person*. Notre Dame: University of Notre Dame Press, 2004.
Cochini, Christian. *The Apostolic Origins of Priestly Celibacy*. Translated by Nelly Marans. San Francisco: Ignatius, 1990.
Congar, Yves. *A Gospel Priesthood*. Translated by P. J. Hepburne-Scott. New York: Herder and Herder, 1967.
---. *The Mystery of the Church*. Translated by A. V. Littledale. Baltimore: Helicon, 1960.
Costello, Timothy. *Forming a Priestly Identity*. Roma: Università Gregoriana, 2002.
d'Agnel, Arnaud. *St. Vincent de Paul: A Guide for Priests*. Translated by Joseph Leonard. London: Oates & Washbourne, 1932.
D'Arcy, M. C. *The Mind and Heart of Love: Lion and Unicorn; A Study in Eros and Agape*. London: Fontana, 1962.
Donati, Pierpaolo. *La matrice teologica della società*. Rubbettino: Soveria Mannelli, 2010.
Dubay, Thomas. *And You Are Christ's: The Charism of Virginity and the Celibate Life*. San Francisco: Ignatius, 1987.

Duckworth, Angela L., and Martin E. P. Seligman. "Self-Discipline Outdoes IQ in Predicting Academic Performance of Adolescents." *Psychological Science* 16 (2005) 939–44.

Émery, Gilles. *La Trinité créatrice. Trinité et creation dans les commentaires aux Sentences de Thomas d'Aquin et de ses précurseurs Albert le Grand et Bonaventure.* Paris: Vrin, 1995.

Evdokimov, Paul. *The Art of the Icon: A Theology of Beauty.* Translated by Steven Bigham. Redondo Beach, CA: Oakwood, 1990.

Fagerberg, David W. *On Liturgical Asceticism.* Washington, DC: Catholic University of America Press, 2013.

Fahey, Michael A. "The Christian Family as Domestic Church at Vatican II." In *The Family*, edited by Lisa Sowle Cahill and Dietmar Mieth, 85–92. Concilium Series 4. London: SCM, 1995.

Feldman, Ruth, et al. "Mother and Infant Coordinate Heart Rhythms through Episodes of Interactions Synchrony." *Infant Behavior and Development* 34 (2011) 569–77.

Finnis, John. *Natural Law and Natural Rights.* Oxford: Clarendon, 1986.

Finnis, John M., et al. "'Direct' and 'Indirect': A Reply to Critics of Our Action Theory." *Thomist* 65 (2001) 1–44.

Fisher, Anthony. "HIV and Condoms within Marriage." *Communio* 36 (2009) 329–59.

Fortin, Ernest. *Classical Christianity and Political Order: Reflections on the Theologico-Political Problem.* Edited by J. Brian Benestad. Lanham, MD: Rowman and Littlefield, 1996.

Grant, Edward. *The Foundations of Modern Science in the Middle Ages: Their Religious, Institutional, and Intellectual Contexts.* Cambridge: Cambridge University Press, 1996.

Gregory, Pope. *The Book of Pastoral Rule.* Translated by George Demacopoulos. Crestwood, NY: St. Vladimir's Seminary Press, 2007.

Grisez, Germain. "Natural Law, God, Religion, and Human Fulfilment." *American Journal of Jurisprudence* 46 (2001) 3–36.

———. "The Ultimate End of Human Beings: The Kingdom, Not God Alone." *Theological Studies* 69 (2008) 38–61.

Guardini, Romano. *The Church and the Catholic, and The Spirit of the Liturgy.* Translated by Ada Lane. London: Sheed and Ward, 1935.

Guido, J. J. "A Unique Betrayal: Clergy Sexual Abuse in the Context of the Catholic Religious Tradition." *Journal of Child Sexual Abuse* 17 (2008) 255–69.

Habermas, Jürgen. "Pre-political Foundations of the Democratic Constitutional State?" In Jürgen Habermas and Joseph Cardinal Ratzinger, *Dialectics of Secularization: On Reason and Religion*, edited by Florian Schuller, translated by Brian McNeil, 19–52. San Francisco: Ignatius, 2006.

Hanby, Michael. *Augustine and Modernity.* London: Routledge, 2003.

———. "The Logic of Love and the Unity of Catholic Truth: Reflections on *Deus Caritas Est*." *Communio* 33 (2006) 400–422.

Hart, David Bentley. "The Anti-Theology of the Body." *The New Atlantis* 9 (2005) 65–73.

Herbert, George. "The Church." In *The Country Parson; The Temple*, edited by John N. Wall, 139–316. New York: Paulist, 1981.

Hittinger, Russell. *The First Grace: Rediscovering the Natural Law in a Post-Christian World.* Wilmington: ISI, 2003.

John Paul II, Pope/Wojtyła, Karol. *The Acting Person: A Contribution to Phenomenological Anthropology*. Translated by Andrzej Potocki. London: D. Reidel, 1979.
———. Address to the Scholars of Lublin University. *Christian Life in Poland*, November 1987.
———. "The Anthropological Vision of *Humanae Vitae*." Translated by William E. May. http://www.christendom-awake.org/pages/may/anthrop-visionjpII.htm.
———. *Catechesi tradendae*, 1979.
———. *Dominum et vivificantem*, 1986.
———. *Familiaris consortio*, 1981.
———. "The Human Person and the Natural Law." In *Person and Community: Selected Essays*, translated by Theresa Sandok, 181–85. New York: Peter Lang, 1993.
———. *Letter to Families*, 1994.
———. *Love and Responsibility*. Translated by H. T. Willetts. London: HarperCollins, 1982.
———. *Man and Woman He Created Them: A Theology of the Body*. Translated by Michael Waldstein. Boston: Pauline, 2006.
———. *Mulieris dignitatem*, 1988.
———. *Pastores dabo vobis: Post-Synodal Apostolic Exhortation to the Bishops, Clergy and Faithful on the Formation of Priests in the Circumstances of the Present Day*. 1992.
———. "The Problem of the Constitution of Culture through Human Praxis." In *Person and Community: Selected Essays*, translated by Theresa Sandok, 263–75. New York: Peter Lang, 1993.
———. *Redemptor hominis*, 1979.
———. *Sources of Renewal: The Implementation of the Second Vatican Council*. Translated by P. S. Falla. San Francisco: Harper and Row, 1980.
———. *The Theology of the Body: Human Love in the Divine Plan*. Boston: Pauline, 1997.
———. "Thinking My Country." In *Memory and Identity: Personal Reflections*, 84–85. London: Weidenfeld and Nicolson, 2005.
———. *Veritatis splendor*, 1993.
Kant, Immanuel. *The Conflict of the Faculties*. Translated by Mary J. Gregor. New York: Abaris, 1979.
Kierkegaard, Søren. *Works of Love*. Translated by Howard V. Hong and Edna H. Hong. Princeton: Princeton University Press, 1995.
Kingsmill, Edmée. *The Song of Songs and the Eros of God: A Study in Biblical Intertextuality*. Oxford: Oxford University Press, 2009.
Kupczak, Jaroslaw. *Destined for Liberty: The Human Person in the Philosophy of Karol Wojtyla/John Paul II*. Washington, DC: Catholic University of America Press, 2000.
Lamberigts, Matthijs. "Optatam Totius—the Decree on Priestly Formation: A Brief Survey of Its History at the Second Vatican Council." *Louvain Studies* 3 (2005) 25–48.
Leto, Pomponio. *Eight Months at Rome during the Vatican Council*. London: John Murray, 1876.
Levada, William. "Celibacy and Priesthood." 2011. http://www.vatican.va/roman_curia/congregations/cfaith/documents/rc_con_cfaith_doc_20111121_levada-celibacy-priesthood_en.html.

Levering, Matthew. *Christ and the Catholic Priesthood: Ecclesial Hierarchy and the Pattern of the Trinity*. Chicago: Hillenbrand, 2010.

———. *Sacrifice and Community: Jewish Offering and Christian Eucharist*. Malden, MA: Blackwell, 2005.

Lewis, C.S. *The Four Loves*. London: Fontana, 1963.

Louth, Andrew. *Discerning the Mystery*. New York: Clarendon, 1983.

Lubac, Henri de. *A Brief Catechesis on Nature and Grace*. Translated by Richard Arnandez. San Francisco: Ignatius, 1984.

———. *Corpus Mysticum: The Eucharist and the Church in the Middle Ages*. Translated by Gemma Simmonds. Notre Dame: University of Notre Dame Press, 2006.

———. *The Splendour of the Church*. Translated by Michael Mason. New York: Sheed and Ward, 1956.

———. *Theological Fragments*. Translated by Rebecca Howell Balinski. San Francisco: Ignatius, 1989.

Lysaught, M. Therese. "Moral Analysis of a Procedure at Phoenix Hospital." *Origins* 40 (2011) 537–47.

Maritain, Jacques. *Distinguer pour unir ou Les degrés du savoir*. Paris: Desclée de Brouwer, 1932.

Mascall, E. L. *The Recovery of Unity: A Theological Approach*. London: Longmans, 1958.

Mattheeuws, Alain. *Les "dons" du marriage: Recherche de théologie morale et sacramentelle*. Brussels: Culture et Verité, 1996.

McCormick, Richard A. "Proportionalism: Classification through Dialogue." In *The Historical Development of Fundamental Moral Theology in the United States*, edited by Charles E. Curran and Richard A. McCormick, 181–99. New York: Paulist, 1999.

Melina, Livio. "Christ and the Dynamism of Action: Outlook and Overview of Christocentrism in Moral Theology." *Communio* 28 (2001) 112–39.

———. *Sharing in Christ's Virtues: For a Renewal of Moral Theology in Light of Veritatis Splendour*. Translated by William E. May. Washington, DC: Catholic University of America Press, 2001.

Milbank, John. *Being Reconciled: Ontology and Pardon*. London: Routledge, 2003.

Mother Teresa of Calcutta. "Priestly Celibacy: Sign of the Charity of Christ." 2005. http://www.vatican.va/roman_curia/congregations/cclergy/documents/rc_con_cclergy_doc_01011993_sign_en.html.

The Nature and Scope of Sexual Abuse of Minors by Catholic Priests and Deacons in the United States, 1950–2002. A research study conducted by the John Jay College of Criminal Justice for the United States Conference of Catholic Bishops. Washington, DC: United States Conference of Bishops, 2004.

Nelson, Sarah. "Analysis: Why the Catholic Church Is Mired in More Child Sex Abuse Claims." *Herald Scotland*, August 2, 2013. http://www.heraldscotland.com/news/home-news/priests-training-contributed-to-but-didnt-cause-sex-abuse.21761445.

Newman, John Henry. *An Essay in Aid of a Grammar of Assent*. Westminster, MD: Christian Classics, 1973.

Nichols, Aidan. *Christendom Awake: On Re-energizing the Church and Culture*. Edinburgh: T. & T. Clark, 1999.

———. *Holy Order: Apostolic Priesthood from the New Testament to the Second Vatican Council*. Dublin: Veritas, 1990.

Nietzsche, Friedrich. *The Essential Nietzsche*. Edited by Heinrich Mann. Mineola, NY: Dover, 2006.
Noriega, José. *El destino del Eros: perspectivas de moral sexual*. Madrid: Ediciones Palabra, 2005.
Nygren, Anders. *Agape and Eros*. Translated by Philip S. Watson. London: SPCK, 1953.
Origen of Alexandria. *An Exhortation to Martyrdom; Prayer; and Selected Works*. Translated by Rowan A. Greer. London: SPCK, 1979.
Osborn, Catherine. *Eros Unveiled: Plato and the God of Love*. Oxford: Clarendon, 1994.
Ouellet, Marc Cardinal. *Divine Likeness: Towards a Trinitarian Anthropology of the Family*. Translated by Philip Milligan and Linda M. Cicone. Grand Rapids: Eerdmans, 2006.
———. "Theological Perspectives on Marriage." *Communio* 31 (2004) 419–33.
Paul VI, Pope. *Evangelii nuntiandi: Apostolic Exhortation on Evangelisation in the Modern World*. Boston: Pauline, 1975.
———. *Humanae vitae*, 1968.
———. *Presbyterorum ordinis*, 1965.
———. *Sacerdotalis caelibatus*, 1967.
Pieper, Josef. *Faith, Hope, Love*. San Francisco: Ignatius, 1997.
Pinckaers, Servais. "The Return of the New Law to Moral Theology." In *The Pinckaers Reader: Renewing Thomistic Moral Theology*, edited by J. Berkman and C. S. Titus, 369–84. Washington, DC: Catholic University of America Press, 2005.
Pink, Thomas. "Conscience and Coercion." *First Things* 225 (2012) 45–51.
Plante, Thomas, et al. "Personality and Cognitive Functioning among Hospitalized Sexual Offending Roman Catholic Priests." *Pastoral Psychology* 45 (1996) 129–39.
Pontifical Commission on Birth Control. "Minority and Majority Opinions." *The Tablet* 21 (1967–68).
Power, Dermot. *A Spiritual Theology of the Priesthood: The Mystery of Christ and the Mission of the Priest*. Edinburgh: T. & T. Clark, 1998.
Pseudo-Dionysius the Areopagite. *The Complete Works*. Translated by Colm Luibheid. New York: Paulist, 1987.
Rawls, John. *Political Liberalism*. New York: Columbia University Press, 2005.
Riceour, Paul. *Freud and Philosophy: An Essay on Interpretation*. Translated by Denis Savage. New Haven: Yale University Press, 1970.
Rowland, Tracey. "Benedict XVI and the End of the 'Virtual Council.'" *Catholic World Report*, April 13, 2013. http://www.catholicworldreport.com/Item/2196/benedict_xvi_and_the_end_of_the_virtual_council.aspx.
Satinover, Jeffrey. *Homosexuality and the Politics of Truth*. Grand Rapids: Baker, 1996.
Sawchuk, Dana, et al. "Exploring Power and Gender Issues Emergent in an Institutional Workshop on Preventing Clergy Sexual Misconduct." *Pastoral Psychology* 55 (2007) 499–511.
Schindler, David C. "The Redemption of Eros: Philosophical Reflections on Benedict XVI's First Encyclical." *Communio* 33 (2006) 375–99.
———. "Towards a Culture of Life: The Eucharist, the 'Restoration' of Creation and the 'Worldly' Task of the Laity in Liberal Societies." *Communio* 29 (2009) 670–90.
Schindler, David L. "Living and Thinking Reality in Its Integrity: Originary Experience, God, and the Task of Education." *Communio* 37 (2010) 167–85.

Schmitz, Kenneth L. *At the Center of the Human Drama: The Philosophical Anthropology of Karol Wojtyla/Pope John Paul II*. Washington, DC: Catholic University of America Press, 1993.

Scola, Angelo Cardinal. *The Nuptial Mystery*. Translated by Michelle K. Borras. Grand Rapids: Eerdmans, 2005.

Shaw, Russell. *To Hunt, to Shoot, to Entertain: Clericalism and the Catholic Laity*. San Francisco: Ignatius, 1993.

Sheets-Johnstone, Maxine, ed. *The Corporeal Turn: An Interdisciplinary Reader*. Exeter, UK: Imprint Academic, 2009.

Shivanandan, Mary. *Crossing the Threshold of Love: A New Vision of Marriage*. Edinburgh: T. & T. Clark, 1999.

Sipe, A. W. Richard. *Celibacy in Crisis: The Secret World Revisited*. New York: Routledge, 2003.

Smyth, Derek. "The Land of the Pirates—Clerical Culture and Sexual Abuse." *The Furrow* 60 (2009) 471–74.

Speyr, Adrienne von. *The Word Becomes Flesh: Meditations on John 1–5*. Translated by Lucia Wiedenhöver and Alexander Dru. San Francisco: Ignatius, 1994.

Teresa, Mother. "Priestly Celibacy: Sign of the Charity of Christ." http://www.vatican.va/roman_curia/congregations/cclergy/documents/rc_con_cclergy_doc_01011993_sign_en.html.

Thomas, Aquinas, Saint. *Quaestiones Quodlibetales*. Torino: Marietti, 1956.

———. *Summa contra Gentiles*. http://dhspriory.org/thomas/ContraGentiles3a.htm#5.

———. *Summa Theologica*. Translated by Fathers of the Dominican Province. 5 vols. Westminster, MD: Christian Classics, 1981.

Tonti-Filippini, Nicholas. *About Bioethics*. Vol. 1, *Philosophical and Theological Approaches*. Ballarat, VIC: Connor Court, 2011.

———. *About Bioethics*. Vol. 4, *Motherhood, Embodied Love and Culture*. Ballarat, VIC: Connor Court, 2013.

Turner, Denys. *Eros and Allegory: Medieval Exegesis of the Song of Songs*. Kalamazoo, MI: Cistercian, 1995.

U. S. Conference of Catholic Bishops. *Program of Priestly Formation*. 5th ed. 2006. http://www.usccb.org/upload/program-priestly-formation-fifth-edition.pdf.

Von Hildebrand, Dietrich. *Celibacy and the Crisis of Faith*. Translated by John Crosby. Chicago: Franciscan Herald Press, 1971.

———. "The Crisis of Human Personality." *Thought* 16 (1941) 457–72.

———. *The Encyclical Humanae Vitae: A Sign of Contradiction*. Translated by Damian Fedoryka and John Crosby. Chicago: Franciscan Herald Press, 1969.

———. *Marriage*. New York: Longman, 1959.

Walsh, Liam G. *Sacraments of Initiation: A Theology of Rite, Word, and Life*. Chicago: Hillenbrand, 2011.

Weigel, George. *Witness to Hope: The Biography of Pope John Paul II, 1920–2005*. London: HarperCollins, 2005.

Werpehowski, William. "Anders Nygren's *Agape and Eros*." In *The Oxford Handbook of Theological Ethics*, edited by Gilbert Meilaender and William Werpehowski, 433–48. Oxford: Oxford University Press, 2005.

Index of Themes

abortion, 14, 35, 125n3, 153, 215
adultery, 7, 44, 49, 50, 68, 71, 152–53, 155
affectivity, 27, 138, 140, 145, 161, 202
anthropology, 4, 26, 65n4, 98–99, 117, 148, 192, 195, 197, 199n46, 208–9, 213, 219–22
  anthropological Crisis, 218, 223–24
  Christian, 224
  scriptural, 60, 224
  theological, 27, 29, 39, 202n65
  Trinitarian, x, xii, 23, 24, 118, 145, 174, 177n1, 184, 186, 189
anthropocentrism, 137–41, 148–49, 151–52, 155, 160–61
asceticism, 8, 11–12, 17, 196, 198n34, 203
  liturgical, 170
autonomy, 12, 64, 126–27, 129, 131n21, 132n23, 136, 139, 147–48
  of the will, 28

baptism, 10, 80, 82, 118, 145,-146, 164, 165n8, 166–67, 169n17, 170, 175, 180n3, 186, 206
beauty, xv, 24, 27–28, 32, 34, 41, 92, 95, 100, 179–80, 192, 216
bible, 43, 45, 73, 93, 181–84. *See also* scripture
bioethics, xii, 18, 136, 148, 204n76
Blessed Virgin Mary, 9, 74–79, 82–83, 99

Body of Christ, 9, 167
body, xii–xvi, 4, 6, 8–18, 39–59, 84, 101–2, 107–20, 145, 159, 167, 172, 177–86, 189, 200–211
  bearer of love, xvi
  enspirited / enfleshed, 4, 201
  language, 53–55
bride, xiv, 68, 70, 76
  of Christ (Church), 10, 46, 81–88, 90, 93, 108, 123, 164n7, 166, 199, 206
Bridegroom, xiv, 3, 10, 70, 81–88, 90, 93, 123, 199, 206
brother, 66, 78–80, 87, 118, 203, 219

Catholic/s, xvi, 4, 7–8, 13–14, 16, 21, 25, 27, 31–32, 35, 39, 42, 63, 86, 96–98, 122–25, 131, 134–35, 140, 148, 153, 177, 188–89, 195, 197, 198, 200, 202, 204
  Church (*see also* Church(The)) xvi, 31, 123–24, 171, 192–93
celibacy, xvi, 5, 7–8, 44, 52, 195, 198–99, 201, 203–7, 209, 211
  consecrated, xvi, 113n18
  Priestly, 193–94, 197, 199–200, 202, 204–6, 210
chastity, xiii, 8, 16, 77, 198, 203
child/ren, 3, 5, 15, 17, 35, 42, 54–55, 60, 62–63, 65–68, 74–76, 78, 80–81, 85, 87, 99, 110–11, 114, 118, 121–22, 142–43, 156n40, 157–60, 164, 168,

INDEX OF THEMES

child/ren (*continued*)
    169n16, 170–71, 174–75, 178–85, 195
    bearing, 7, 65, 122, 211
    of God, xii, 73
    See also offspring
Christian/ity, xiv, 3–4, 6–13, 25–29, 31, 34–36, 39–43, 47, 58, 61, 67, 70, 80–81, 83–88, 91–102, 118, 120n25, 121–22, 125, 128, 131–34, 136, 138–39, 141, 145–48, 150, 152, 160–70, 172–76, 184–86, 192, 197–99, 201–2, 206, 210, 214, 218, 223–24
    personalism, 18
Christocentric / ism, 29, 136, 165, 178, 219
Church (The), xi, xii, xiv–xvii, 3, 5–6, 8–11, 13–14, 16, 20–21, 24–25, 31, 33, 35, 39, 41–42, 55, 58, 75, 79–90, 108, 112, 116–18, 120–21, 123–25, 127–29, 133–35, 137, 143, 148, 155, 162–76, 180, 183, 188, 191–194, 196, 198–99, 201–2, 205–7, 211–15, 219, 224–25. *See also* Catholic Church
    Fathers / Doctors of, 11, 16, 44, 61, 64, 93n3, 127, 133, 192, 198n35
    teaching, 6, 14, 20–21, 25, 39, 41–42, 50n23, 55, 58, 128, 202
civilisation of love, xi, xv, 19, 34, 37, 172
commandment, xiv, 63, 150, 152
communion, xii–xiii, xvi, 9, 15, 39, 41, 46, 48, 52, 60–61, 65n4, 95, 102, 112, 117, 163, 165, 168, 170, 181, 185, 202n65, 206, 219, 223
    familial, 162, 166–68, 169, 171–72, 174–75, 176
    one-flesh, xiii, 46, 54, 62, 89, 108, 121, 142
    spousal, xvi, 5, 167–68

with God, xiii, 56, 60, 138, 150, 152, 161, 201
complementarity, 4–5, 65n4, 76, 86, 165, 192n8. *See also* sex difference
concupiscence, 5, 10, 25, 41, 44, 48, 49–50, 51n23, 55n38, 100, 204
conjugal, 55–56, 144, 166, 224
    contract, 143, 168
    intimacy, 44, 86
    morality, 54
    spirituality, 24, 44, 122, 167n13
conscience, 6–7, 217
consummation, xiii, 70, 76, 89–90, 94
contraception, 6, 14–15, 20, 30, 54–56, 63, 215
    contraceptive mentality, 54
    See also sterilization
Council of Trent, 13
covenant, 56, 66–69, 71–73, 82, 88–90, 168, 175, 219
creation, 3, 10–11, 15, 18, 23–24, 26, 37, 43, 45–46, 48–49, 56, 58, 60–63, 65n4, 66, 73, 75, 86, 98, 100, 109, 112, 116, 145, 165n8, 178, 197, 199–200, 202, 205–10, 212, 221–22
cross, 58, 77–78, 83, 102, 147, 168n16, 211
culture, xiv, xvi, 12, 15, 19–20, 22, 28, 31–34, 36–37, 39, 41, 57, 68, 85, 88, 96, 100, 102, 107, 110, 122, 124, 139, 144, 161, 194–96, 198, 199n44, 202, 213–21
    Catholic, 31–32
    of death, 34, 37, 122

daughter, 40, 74, 118
dignity, xiii, 21, 28, 34, 42, 56, 62, 103, 119, 122, 161, 172, 200–201, 205, 211, 218. *See also* human dignity
divorce, 7, 44, 47, 60, 69, 71, 76, 88, 100, 130, 215

dualism, 4, 8, 11, 13–16, 40, 128–29, 195–96
　Manichaeanism, 11, 40, 49
　Cartesianism, 21, 29, 40, 110
　Gnosticism, 10–11, 40, 58, 99
duality, 40, 102
duty, 27, 121, 173, 187

education, xvi, 6, 32, 109n6, 129, 143, 200, 208–10, 214, 224
　religious, xii, xvi, 177–84, 186–89
Enlightenment, The, 123, 200
eros, xiv–xvii, 3–5, 24, 34, 41n7, 91–103, 112, 171, 177–79, 197–98, 200, 204, 207
erotic/ism, 6, 8, 11, 28, 41, 91–92, 94–98, 100–102, 145, 199
　drive, 3
ethos, xii–xvii, 41n7, 49–50, 197, 199n46
　of the body, 50
eschaton / eschatology, 10, 33, 44, 52–53, 72, 78–79, 83, 88–90, 113n18, 114, 120, 167n12, 206, 211
Eucharist, 9, 79–80, 83, 87–90, 163, 167, 169–170, 172, 175n29, 201n57, 211, 225. *See also* liturgy
euthanasia, 17, 125
evangelisation, xvi, 165, 172, 176, 189, 191–200, 206, 214, 218, 224
evil, 7–8, 10, 12, 33, 35–36, 40, 58, 63–65, 90, 110, 138–39, 151, 154–55, 158–60. *See also* sin
existence, xii–xiv, 49, 52, 57–58, 99, 101–2, 108–11, 113–14, 116–18, 121–22, 128, 137, 141, 145–49, 162, 172, 178, 181, 184, 205, 208, 223

faith, xvii, 9, 14, 52, 93, 102, 118, 125, 128–29, 131–32, 134–35, 137, 140–41, 143, 146–49, 160–61, 164, 170n18, 173, 175, 177, 184, 186–89,
193, 196–99, 201n58, 202–3, 212, 216, 218, 223–24
family, xi, xii, xv–xvi, 5, 8, 14–16, 19, 20, 24–25, 30–31, 60, 63, 66–67, 71, 73, 75, 77–80, 84, 87, 90, 118, 120–21, 122, 144, 146, 162–76, 190, 215, 219, 221, 224–25
　Christian, 26, 163, 165–66, 170, 172n22, 174, 176
　domestic church, xvi, 79, 96, 162–66, 168–70, 173, 175–76, 225
　familial morality, 54
　Holy, 75, 77, 78, 81
　life, 8, 63, 77–78, 165n8, 170–71, 174–75
father, 21, 31, 37, 40, 62, 67, 71, 74, 76–81, 84, 87, 97, 103, 118, 120n25, 142, 174, 207, 210, 215
fear, 16, 30, 48, 56, 133, 147, 174, 196
female, xiv, 3, 5, 12–13, 15–16, 39, 44, 46, 52–53, 57, 61–63, 86, 142, 214
　femininity, 6, 48, 52, 55, 72, 87, 112, 119, 120n25, 205, 211, 214, 223
　sexuality, 12, 15
　woman, 3, 7, 17–18, 24, 26, 35–36, 39–40, 46–48, 55, 60–63, 65, 71, 74–79, 83, 86–87, 90, 93, 99–100, 103, 111, 113–14, 117–18, 121, 142, 144, 165, 170, 205, 207–10, 212, 215, 219
fertility, 15, 68, 168n16
flesh, 5, 9–10, 39, 50–51, 61–62, 65, 73–74, 79, 81, 84, 88, 108, 134, 146, 201, 204, 208
freedom, xvi, 5–6, 17, 20, 22, 26, 28, 34, 36, 50, 51n23, 64, 76, 78, 93, 126, 128–29, 132n23, 134, 181–82, 187, 203–4, 221–22

INDEX OF THEMES

fruitfulness, xii, 25, 62, 71, 111, 119, 121–22, 168, 169n16, 205–206

fulfilment, xiv, 5, 9, 17, 40, 42, 53, 67, 87–90, 94, 102–3, 112–13, 115–16, 120–22, 136–37, 149 151–52, 155, 160, 199, 202n63, 205–6, 208–9, 213

gift, xii, xv, 7, 15, 21, 24–26, 28, 30, 36, 41, 44, 47–48, 50, 52, 56, 59, 63, 76, 91, 93, 98, 114, 117, 121–22, 165–66, 167n12, 168–69, 171–72, 186–89, 200n52, 201, 205–6, 210–11, 221–25

    of self, xiii, 52, 56, 112, 119, 149, 169, 172, 215–16, 220–21, 224

    self-giving, 5, 9, 15, 112, 113n18, 117, 119, 121–22, 144, 171n21

God, xi–xiii, xvi–xvii, 3–7, 9, 11, 14–16, 18, 21–28, 30–33, 35, 37, 39, 41–45, 47–49, 52–53, 55–56, 58, 60–77, 79–95, 97–103, 107–9, 112–22, 125–28, 131, 136–39, 141, 144–53, 155, 160–61, 164–65, 168–75, 177–79, 181–83, 185–87, 198, 200–201, 203n69, 206–24

    communion of Persons, xii–xiii, 48n16, 52, 58, 61, 165–66, 172

    Creator, xv, 6, 21–22, 24, 30, 42, 46, 60, 62, 65, 67–68, 92, 95, 125, 127, 137, 144–46, 149, 160, 182, 199, 205, 207–8, 210, 212, 217–18, 221

    Father, xiii, 3, 21, 24, 26, 28, 37, 47–48, 50, 58, 61, 75, 78–79, 81, 87, 89, 92–93, 114–18, 120n25, 140, 166, 168–70, 175, 178–79, 192, 208, 220, 222

    Holy Spirit, 9–10, 24, 26, 28, 33, 39, 51–52, 56–57, 75, 79, 87, 94, 102, 114, 117, 166–69, 171–73, 175, 178–79, 181, 192n6, 193, 196, 200n52, 203

    Most High, 24, 79

    Son, xiii, 3, 24, 26, 28, 58, 75–79, 82, 87–88, 93, 99, 108, 114, 117–18, 120n25, 126, 168–69, 175, 178–79, 207, 222

    Trinity, xiii, xvi, 6, 20, 23–24, 26, 28–29, 31, 37, 39, 61, 81, 87, 95, 107, 109, 115, 117–19, 122, 145, 178–79, 186, 201, 206, 221–22

goodness, xii, xv, 27, 32, 34, 47, 62, 95–98, 100, 154, 161, 178–79, 206

Gospel, 7, 18, 42–44, 49, 58, 73–78, 80–83, 89, 96, 120n25, 134–35, 163, 172–73, 176, 195, 223

grace, 5, 7, 9, 12, 33, 35, 46, 50, 51n23, 56–57, 64, 73–74, 76, 86–87, 96, 102, 108n5, 114, 116, 118n22, 122, 129, 140–41, 166–68, 172, 175, 185, 192, 201–3, 205, 225

heart, xi, xv, 5, 7, 9, 33, 42, 44, 47–51, 60, 67, 74, 78, 80, 94, 110–12, 121, 126, 139, 152, 168, 172, 173n24, 178–79, 181–89, 191, 199, 203n69, 205–6, 209–11, 222, 224–25

Hebrew/s, 10

    Scriptures, 7

history, xiv, 23–24, 33, 36, 39, 41, 44–45, 58, 65–66, 68, 78, 89–90, 94, 96, 99, 102, 109, 110n8, 112, 115–16, 127, 140, 148, 178, 183–84, 191, 217

homosexuality, 7, 57. *See also* marriage, same-sex

INDEX OF THEMES

human, xi, xiii, 4–16, 18, 20–29,
    31–35, 37–39, 40–53, 56–58,
    61–70, 76–77, 84, 86, 88,
    90–93, 95–103, 108–10,
    112–21, 126, 133, 136–56,
    160–61, 164n7, 165, 173n24,
    176–83, 185–87, 191–93,
    195, 197–202, 205–6,
    208–24
  dignity, 28, 34, 200–201, 218
    (*see also* dignity)
  ecology, 217, 219
  nature, 5, 9–10, 13, 28, 61, 67n6,
    77, 99, 112, 141, 145, 147,
    150, 180, 212, 214, 216–218
  person, 4–5, 18, 20–23, 25, 27,
    29, 37, 47, 48, 50–51, 57, 64,
    96, 98, 101, 103, 108–9, 112,
    120, 165, 178, 180, 197, 205,
    212–14, 216, 219–24
  race, 61, 65–66, 73, 75, 90, 219
husband, 7, 10, 52, 61–62, 64–65,
    67–69, 71, 75, 82–84, 86–90,
    111, 113, 118–19, 142,
    167, 170, 175, 207. See also
    spouse

identity, xii, 39, 45, 47, 78, 111n11,
    113, 115, 117, 133, 163,
    165–66, 172, 176, 198–99,
    201, 204, 206, 208, 210–11,
    213–14, 221
imagination, xv, 22, 27, 94, 96, 121,
    182, 197, 209
imago Dei, 23–24, 29, 103, 117–18,
    138, 205, 213, 221
imago Trinitatis, 107, 118
Incarnation, 9, 23–24, 32–33, 37, 58,
    79, 81, 93, 99, 108–9, 132,
    179, 202n65
individualism, 139, 169
intention, 7, 39–40, 47, 55–56, 63,
    70, 96, 150, 151–55, 158,
    160, 203, 210

Jansenism, 13, 25

Jesus Christ, xii–xiii, 3–4, 7, 9–10,
    18, 23–24, 28, 33–34, 37, 39,
    42, 44–47, 49, 50n23, 51–52,
    55, 57–58, 60–63, 73, 75,
    77–90, 92–97, 99, 101–2,
    108–9, 112, 115–18, 120n25,
    121, 124, 126, 128–30, 134,
    138, 140–41, 145, 147–52,
    161–64, 166–170, 172–73,
    175, 178–82, 189, 192–93,
    199–201, 203n69, 205–11,
    213, 219–20, 222–25
  Lamb, xiv, 46, 83, 89–90
  Word/*Logos*, 9, 23, 45, 58n44,
    73–74, 208, 218–221, 223
Jewish, 7, 67n6, 70, 77, 82–83
  eschatology, 10
John Paul II Institute for Marriage
    and Family, v, x–xii, xvii,
    3–4, 6, 8, 11, 14, 16, 18–19,
    23, 25, 27, 29, 39, 102, 165,
    213, 215, 220–21, 224
joy, xiv, 5, 9, 16, 18, 30, 41, 51–52,
    74, 81, 93, 99, 103, 134, 204

Kingdom of God, xiv, 6–7, 44, 52,
    82, 88–89, 94, 206, 211, 222

liturgy, 44, 87, 118, 169–171, 178,
    196
love, xi–xvi, 3–5, 10, 14–15, 19–28,
    30, 37, 40–42, 47–49, 51–53,
    56, 58, 61–64, 69–71, 78,
    84–86, 91–103, 108–22,
    131, 138, 143–52, 155, 160,
    164n7, 165, 168–73, 175–76,
    182–83, 185–86, 192,
    198–211, 213, 215, 218–19,
    222–25
  agape, 4, 92, 93n3, 94, 96–100,
    102–3, 171, 198, 207
  bodily, xvi, 107
  caritas, 4
  conjugal, 21, 24, 166, 168
  divine, 6, 15, 30, 39, 45, 56, 93,
    97, 101, 103, 112, 114, 117,
    121, 145–46, 206, 223

INDEX OF THEMES

love (*continued*)
    erotic, 14, 56, 70, 95, 101–3
    filial, 4, 114
    human, 24, 26, 38, 56, 97–98, 101, 103, 109, 113–17, 120–21, 149, 197, 200, 206, 213, 219, 223–24
    marital, 6, 202
    parental, 103, 121
    redemptive, 71, 85
    self-giving, 4–5, 14, 40, 204, 206
    sexual, 8, 202
    spousal, 20, 168, 205, 210
    Trinitarian, 23–24, 109, 115, 117–18, 120–21, 224
Lublin Thomism, 20

Magisterium, 8, 29, 31, 131, 137, 146, 156, 158, 164, 166, 194, 200, 202, 205
male, xiv, 3, 5, 15–16, 44, 46, 52, 57, 61–63, 78, 86, 142, 165, 194, 205
    man, 3, 17–18, 24, 26, 36, 39, 40, 46–48, 55, 60, 61–65, 74–76, 86–87, 90, 99, 100, 103, 111, 113, 114, 118, 120–21, 144, 165, 170, 205, 206–9, 211–15, 219
    masculinity, 6, 55, 205, 211
marriage, xi–xvi, 3–8, 10, 12, 14, 16–18, 20, 24–26, 30, 36, 40–44, 47, 52–56, 62–63, 66–71, 76, 81–91, 93, 96, 103, 108, 111–12, 113n18, 114, 116–17, 120–25, 131, 137, 139, 141–45, 149, 162, 163–64, 166–70, 172–76, 196, 198, 199n44, 202–5, 215, 219, 221, 224
    act, 6, 19, 146 (*see also* sex, intercourse; union, marital/one-flesh/sexual/spousal)
    same-sex, 124–25, 132n23 (*see also* homosexuality)
    matrimonial, 6
    privatisation of, 31
    See also spouse

married couples, xi, xiii, 14, 20, 145
Mass. *See* Eucharist
Metaphysics, 21, 26, 95–96, 212–13, 216, 218, 220
    metaphysical horizons, 22
    See also ontology
mind, ix, 3, 11, 16–17, 22, 27, 39, 40–42, 51, 63, 86, 96, 110n7/8, 115, 141, 152, 157, 178–79, 182–86, 202n62, 206, 209, 211, 213, 224
ministry, xvii, 14, 86, 100, 135, 174, 196, 201, 203. *See also* priest
mission, xi, xvi–xvii, 3, 18, 24, 26, 30, 75, 82, 119n24, 123, 134–135, 162–65, 167n12, 171–76, 196, 203n69, 206, 224
monasticism, 8, 96
monogamy, 62, 71
moral, xvi, 5, 10–11, 15–16, 21, 27, 29, 37, 39–43, 47, 49, 50n23, 53–54, 62–63, 65n4, 66, 86, 97–98, 100–101, 121, 124–25, 128–29, 131–32, 137–39, 141, 143–45, 148–60, 184–86, 192–94, 196–97, 203–4, 208, 213–14, 216, 218
    act, 139, 149–52, 154–56, 159
    order, 5, 144
    responsibility, 4, 197
    truth, 57, 312n22
mother, 40, 62, 72, 74, 76–80, 82–84, 87, 99, 103, 110–11, 113–16, 118, 120–21, 156n40, 157–158, 160, 179, 206, 210–211, 215
mystery, 6, 9–12, 23–25, 29, 42, 48–50, 56–58, 61, 63, 76, 84–85, 88–89, 97, 100, 108, 117, 119n25, 126, 141, 147, 162, 164, 166–67, 175, 200–201, 204–6, 219
nuptial, xi–xvii, 24–25, 29, 37, 108n4, 114, 121, 166, 196, 197, 206
    sacred, 4, 6
    spousal, 206

INDEX OF THEMES

Natural Family Planning, 16
natural law, xvi, 5, 20–21, 120, 125, 131–33, 135–41, 143–44, 146–49, 155, 217
New Evangelization, 172, 176, 189, 214, 218, 224
New Testament, 4, 7, 40, 51, 75, 80–81, 84, 88, 92, 114, 121, 128, 197
nihilism, 31, 214
nominalism, 22
nuptial, xi, xiii, xvi, 5, 18, 24, 29, 42, 58, 93, 96, 108, 111–19, 121–22, 166, 168, 199, 201, 205–6, 210
  mystery. See mystery

offspring, 62, 64, 71, 75, 142–43. See also child/ren
Old Testament, 7, 66–67, 72–73, 75, 81, 88, 108, 112n15, 120n25, 205
Ontology, 22, 45, 96, 216. See also metaphysics

pagan, 7–8, 11, 67–68, 97, 186
parent/hood, 14–15, 44, 54, 63, 66–67, 75, 103, 112–13, 121, 161, 164, 168, 170–71, 175, 184–85
partner, 30–31, 129, 132, 134, 136, 139, 147
Pelagian/ism, 27–30, 198
perfection, xiii, 12, 26, 51n23, 55, 76, 87, 111, 119, 129, 150, 167, 175, 198n34, 203n69, 206
Pharisee, 10, 47, 60, 82, 207
phenomenology, 17, 40, 43, 46, 116, 173, 205, 216
philistinism, 31–33
polygamy, 7
praxis, 27, 32
priest, xvi, 9, 14, 42, 71, 74, 87, 101, 164, 168–70, 174, 176, 191–207, 209–11, 223. See also ministry
procreation, xiv, 3–4, 6, 8, 12, 14, 25, 37, 52, 55, 63, 119, 143–44, 202, 205. See also reproduction
prostitution, 7, 68
Protestant, 13, 96–97. See also Reformation
Providence, 21, 30, 61, 95

redemption, 5, 39, 43, 49–50, 51n23, 56–58, 71, 85–86, 98, 101, 115–16, 206
Reformation, 31, 96, 97. See also Protestant
relationship, xvi, 6, 17, 22, 24–25, 27–28, 30–31, 35, 45, 48, 53, 55–56, 62, 65, 67–70, 73, 77, 80–82, 84–85, 94, 108–9, 111–18, 120, 124, 131, 133–35, 137–38, 144–46, 149, 151, 154, 160–61, 174, 178, 182, 186, 189, 192, 201, 203–4, 208, 211, 221, 223–24
reproduction, 3, 6, 2–26, 35, 119. See also procreation
responsibility, 4, 6, 14, 61, 63–64, 101, 134, 197, 219
Resurrection, xiv, 10, 12, 44, 52–53, 166, 173, 178
respect, 6, 9, 10, 12, 15, 21, 76, 125–26, 131n21, 133, 148, 150, 161, 177, 181, 212, 218, 220
revelation, 6, 18, 20, 33, 37, 40, 50, 56–57, 58n44, 61, 72, 75, 98, 101, 121, 132, 137, 141, 146–47, 151, 165, 183, 188, 219

sacrament, xii–xiii, xiv, 3, 5–6, 9–10, 12, 22, 24, 30, 33, 44, 55, 60, 67, 80, 84–85, 88–90, 97, 103, 108, 111–12, 114–18, 120–21, 127, 162–69, 171–72, 174–75, 180, 186, 192–93, 198, 200, 203–4, 206, 209, 219, 224. See also Baptism, Eucharist, Marriage
salvation, 24, 39, 58, 60, 65–67, 72, 78, 93–94, 97, 108–9, 115–16, 140, 175, 222

242 INDEX OF THEMES

Satan, 12
    Prince of this world, 33–34
Scripture xvi, 6, 39, 43–44, 58, 63–64, 66, 69–70, 88, 90, 131, 141, 143, 145, 147, 171, 181–82, 185, 189, 198n34, 201n55
    prophetic literature, 7
    See also bible; Hebrew scripture
secularism, xvi, 16, 123–24, 135, 137–39
sex/sexual/sexuality, ix–x, xiii, xv, 3–9, 12, 14–18, 21–23, 25, 34, 36, 39–43, 50–51, 53, 56–57, 63–68, 70, 75–77, 82, 86–87, 91–92, 94, 96, 100–101, 103, 112, 113n17, 120–21, 137, 142–45, 165, 174, 193–96, 200–207, 211, 214–15
    difference, 4–5, 16, 25, 112–13, 119n24, 214 (*see also* complementarity)
    ethic, 7–8
    intercourse, 54, 68, 76, 122, 142–43
    intimacy, 25, 31, 37, 144
    morality, 8, 29, 35, 143, 145, 194
    revolution, 8, 14, 16, 200
    sin, 66–68
    union, 5–6, 12, 15
sin, 5, 7–9, 48–51, 57, 60, 64–68, 86, 98–101, 110, 112, 115–16, 118, 132, 142, 147, 169, 175, 192, 199, 209
    original, 4–6, 9, 30, 75
    See also evil
sister, 76, 78–80, 118
son, 40, 66–67, 74, 82, 118
soul, 4, 10–13, 15, 17, 94, 162, 167, 169, 177, 191, 222
    faculties of the, 27, 51 (*see also* mind)
Spirit, xiv, 4, 10–11, 13, 48, 51, 71, 80, 102, 119n25, 147, 202, 219

spirituality, 14, 26–27, 29, 94–96, 122, 196n29, 198n35, 201n57, 216
    conjugal, 44, 167n12
    family, 24, 55n38
spouse, 6–7, 24, 55n38, 62–63, 68, 71, 76, 82, 86–88, 90, 108, 117, 121–22, 136, 139, 142, 166–68, 169n16, 170, 172, 175n29, 206, 224
    spousal bond, 6
    spousal imagery, 69–71, 82, 84, 89
    See also marriage; husband; wife
state (the), xvi, 31, 35, 127–29, 131n21, 132n22, 133–35
sterilisation, 14–15, 35, 63, 183. *See also* contraception
Stoicism, 28, 30
suicide, 17, 215
suffering, 5, 9, 43, 57–58, 64, 85, 88, 93, 101, 110, 116, 145, 147, 152, 183

teleology, 139, 150, 198, 199n44, 204
theocentric/ism, xiv, 118, 136, 149, 161, 199n46
theology, xii–xiv, xv, 6, 8, 12, 18, 20, 23, 26, 37, 58, 61, 70n7, 91, 94–98, 107, 129n18, 134, 136, 139, 163, 167, 170n18, 171, 174–75, 198n35, 199n43, 200–202, 204n76, 205–6, 210, 218, 220, 223
    biblical, 42, 45
    liberation, 32
    moral, xvi, 29, 204n76
Theology of the Body, xii–xvii, 14, 18, 23n7, 38–44, 50, 57, 101, 107, 111, 145, 178–79, 184, 186, 189, 196–97, 200–201, 203–4, 205n82, 207, 209
tradition, xvi–xvii, 6–10, 12, 20, 26–27, 29, 39, 43, 55n38, 57–58, 61, 65, 70, 81, 84, 91, 94, 96, 108, 111, 121, 128, 131, 135–36, 139, 147,

149, 155, 159, 174–75, 183,
198n34, 199, 200n49, 204,
213, 220
Catholic, 16, 140, 189
Christian, 12, 29, 93
Trinity, xiii, xvi, 6, 20, 23–24, 26,
28–29, 31, 37, 39, 61, 81, 87,
95, 107, 109, 115, 117–19,
122, 145, 166, 178–79, 186,
201, 206, 221–22
Trinitarian economy, 28
truth, xv, 6, 15, 22, 26–28, 32,
34, 40, 42, 48–50, 51n23,
53–58, 60–61, 71, 73, 81,
85, 87, 102–3, 117, 120n25,
122, 124, 130–35, 140–41,
146–48, 152, 179, 183–84,
188–89, 199–200, 206, 212–
14, 216–20, 222–24
anthropological, 58
ethical, 58

union, 5, 15, 33, 52, 55–56, 61–63,
67, 70, 75, 84, 88, 90, 116,
142, 144, 166–67, 178, 220,
223
marital, 62–63, 67, 70, 75, 142
one-flesh, 46, 54, 62, 89 121, 142
sexual, 5–6, 12, 15
spousal, 5, 167
See also marriage act; sex;
intercourse
universal call to holiness, xiii, 96

Vatican Council,
first, 127, 144
second, 9, 16, 20, 23, 29, 117,
126, 134, 137, 139, 162–64,
174, 176, 191–92, 195,
198n35, 200, 202n65, 205,
213, 219
virginity, 5, 8, 52, 72, 77, 207
consecrated, 197–98, 219
vocation, xi, xiv, xvi, 5–7, 15, 30,
42, 44–45, 47, 52, 54, 61,
96, 103, 113–14, 116, 121,
122, 135, 145–46, 192, 197,
199, 202–3, 205–7, 209, 211,
213, 219
divine call, 5

Wedding Feast of the Lamb, xiv, 76,
82–83, 88, 90, 206
Wife, 46, 52, 61–62, 64, 67–69, 71,
75–77, 82–84, 86–87, 89,
111, 113, 118–19, 167, 170,
175. *See also* spouse
world, xi–xiv, 5, 7–8, 11–13, 19–20,
22–23, 25, 33–34, 37–38,
41–43, 45–46, 49–50, 52–53,
58, 63, 78, 85, 87, 92, 95–97,
99, 102, 109, 111, 113n18,
115–18, 124–26, 128, 131,
134, 137, 147–48, 152, 156,
165n8, 179, 183, 192–93,
198–200, 205–8, 210–12,
214–17, 222, 224

Index of Magisterial Documents

Apostolicam actuositatem, 126n4, 164n5
Caritas in veritate, 212
Catechesi tradendae, 184, 200n50
De ecclesia Christi, 127
Dei Filius, 144n20
Deus caritas est, xvi, 3, 99, 102, 112n14, 143n17, 145n21, 171n20, 198n39
Dignitatis humanae, 126n5, 127, 129
Dives in misericordia, 28
Dominum et vivificantem, 29, 33, 171n21
Evangelii nuntiandi, 163n2
Evangelium vitae, 34, 159
Familiaris consortio, xi, 60, 164–66, 170, 172n22, 173n25, 176n30, 215, 219
Fides et ratio, 140–141, 144, 146–48, 216
Gaudium et spes, 9, 16, 23, 29, 58n44, 111–12, 117, 126–27, 129, 133, 166n10, 173n25, 202, 213, 219–20

Humanae vitae, 14, 20–23, 29, 37, 41–42, 44–45, 54, 143n16, 173n25, 202, 204, 213
Lumen gentium, 126n4, 164, 167, 192n6/7
Mulieris dignitatem, 65n4/5, 86, 111, 117, 119, 219
Optatam totius, 200n52, 203n71
Pastor aeternus, 127
Pastores dabo vobis, 191, 193, 195, 197, 201, 206
Presbyterorum ordinis, 201n54, 203n68
Redemptor hominis, 23 28, 224n20
Sacerdotalis caelibatus, 202, 203n70, 204n77
Sacramentum caritatis, 199
Unam sanctam, 127
Veritatis splendor, 34, 50n23, 137, 141n11, 150–52, 155–56, 160

Index of Persons

Ağca, Mehmet Ali, 19
Albert the Great (St.), 29
Alighieri, Dante. *See* Dante Alghieri
Anatrella, Tony, 214
Anderson, Carl, 114
Aristotle, 12, 95, 109n7
Augustine (St.), 5, 8, 10–13, 27–29, 47, 94–95, 111–12

Balthasar, Hans Urs von, 30, 110, 221–222
Benedict XVI (Pope) / Joseph Ratzinger, xiv–xvi, 3–4, 17, 27, 29, 32–33, 61, 81, 99, 102, 128–29, 136–37, 139, 143n17, 145n21, 147, 169, 170n18, 171, 183, 187, 192, 198–99, 210, 212–13, 216–20
Berger, Peter L., 173
Boersma, Hans, 22
Bonaventure (St.), 27, 95, 191
Boniface VIII (Pope), 127
Boot, Alexander, 31
Borella, Jean, 22
Bourg, Florence Caffrey, 166
Boyle, Joseph, 136, 155–57, 161

Caffarra, Carlo Cardinal, 21
Catherine of Siena (St.), 94, 191
Cavalletti, Sofia, 178–79, 181–82
Cavanaugh, William T., 35
Charles Borromeo (St.), 191
Chesterton, G. K., 186
Clarke, William Norris, 26

Cooper, Adam G., ix, xv–xvi, 143n15, 155n38

Dalrymple, Theodore, 32–33
Daniels, Anthony. *See* Dalrymple, Theodore
Dante Alghieri, 109n7
Darwin, Charles, 40, 99
Davis, Henry, 158–59
De Armida, Conchita Cabrera, 223
De Lubac, Henri, 129, 167
Descartes, René, 13, 10
Dionysius the Areopagite, 95, 154
Domenach, M. J. M, 32
Dominic (St.), 12
Dubay, Thomas, 197
Dupré, Louis, 22

Elliott, Peter J., ix, xv
Evdokimov, Paul, 170n18

Finnis, John, 137, 140–41, 148–49, 155–59, 161
Fiordelli, Pietro, 163–64
Fisher, Anthony, 142–43
Francis (Pope), x, 17
Freud, Sigmund, 20, 35, 40, 99

George, Robert P., 136
Gilson, Etienne, 27
Granados, José, 114
Grant, Edward, 109n7
Gregory the Great (Pope St.), 191
Grisez, Germain, 136–37, 149–51, 153, 155–57, 160–61

INDEX OF PERSONS

Guardini, Romano, 162

Hanby, Michael, 27–28
Hart, David B., 39
Heidegger, Martin, 109, 116
Herbert, George, 57
Hildebrand, Dietrich von, 198, 199n44, 202n67, 204–5
Hittinger, Russell, 21

Jansen, Cornelius, 13
Jaspers, Karl, 187
Jerome (St.), 182
John of the Cross (St.), 94
John the Evangelist (St.), 51, 83
John Paul II (Pope St.) / Karol Wojtyła, xi, xiii, xiv–xvi, 4, 6, 14, 16–23, 25–30, 32–58, 60, 64n3, 65n4, 86, 101–2, 107, 110–14, 116–19, 136–37, 139, 141n11, 143–44, 146–47, 150–51, 155, 160, 164, 170, 171–72, 175–76, 178, 184, 191–93, 196–97, 200–211, 213, 216, 219, 223

Kant, Immanuel, 29, 37, 40, 99
Kelsen, Hans, 217–18
Kierkegaard, Søren, 97
Kohlberg, Lawrence, 186
Krohn, Anna, ix, xvi
Kundera, Milan, 22

Lewis, C. S., 91, 100
Lubich, Chiara, 223
Luther, Martin, 13, 97

Maritain, Jacques, 220
McCormick, Richard, 159–60
Melina, Livio, 29
Milbank, John, 30
Montessori, Maria, 185

Newman, John Henry (Bl.), 187–89
Nichols, Aidan, 193

Nietzsche, Friedrich, xiv–xv, 3, 27, 34–35, 99–100
Norwid, Cyprian, 32
Nygren, Anders, 96–100

Obama, Barack, 35
Origen of Alexandria, 93–94
O'Shea, Gerard, ix, xvi
Ouellet, Marc Cardinal, ix, xvii, 23–25, 30, 117, 120–21, 169, 174

Patterson, Colin, x, xvi
Paul (St.), 7, 9–10, 13, 33, 50–51, 73, 81, 84, 95, 115, 138, 148, 203
Paul VI (Pope), 14, 20, 41–42, 44, 137, 202–4, 210, 213
Pell, George Cardinal, 35
Philip IV of France, 127
Piaget, Jean, 186
Pinckaers, Servais, 152n25, 161n45
Pink, Thomas, 127
Pius IX (Pope Bl.), 126n7, 127
Plato, 12, 92, 132, 178

Richard of St Victor, 95
Rowland, Tracey, x, xv, 202n65

Satinover, Jeffrey, 67
Scola, Angelo Cardinal, 25, 111n12, 112, 117, 119n24, 120, 174
Scruton, Roger, 32–33
Shakespeare, William, 30
Shivanandan, Mary, 210
Silvas, Anne, x, xvi
Speyr, Adrienne von, 169n16, 223
Stafford, James Cardinal, 35
Suárez, Francisco, 140, 147
Sweeney, Conor, x, xvi

Teresa of Calcutta (Bl.), 210–11
Tertullian, 108
Thérèse of the Child Jesus (St.), 75, 223

Thomas Aquinas (St.), 5, 11–13, 17, 20, 62, 95, 140–43, 147, 149, 152, 154–55, 182, 186, 221
Tonti-Filippini, Nicholas, x, xvi, 204n76

Vincent de Paul (St.), 191
Vyner, Owen, x, xvi

Index of Scripture

OLD TESTAMENT

Genesis

1	43
1:26–28	60
1:27	3
1:28	62
1:31	63
2	60, 208
2:18	46
2:23	46, 88
2:24	84
2:25	46
3	63
3:5–8	64
3:15–16	65
4:1	74
4:8, 10	66
4:26	66
5:24	66

Exodus

22:2	154
24:8	88

Leviticus

18:27–33	143

Deuteronomy

23:17	143
24:1–4	69

Tobit

4:13	143

Psalms

36:9	62

Proverbs

1:7	147

Song of Songs

4:9	76

Sirach

1:14	147

Isaiah

54:2	78
54:5	69
55:3	88
66:8	74

Jeremiah

31:1	67
31:9, 20	67
31:31–32	67, 88
31:31–34	69

Ezekiel

16	84

Hosea

1:2	68
2:14–20	69
3:3	71

Malachi

2:14–16	71

NEW TESTAMENT

Matthew

1:19	75
1:20	76
5:20–48	150
5:27–28	50
5:27–30	44
5:28	7
5:31	7
6:33	222
9:14–15	82
12:46–50	78
14:3–12	82
15:17–20	7
18:5	168
19:3	47
19:3–8	39, 207–8
19:3–9	44
19:3–11	7
19:4–6	62
19:8	60
19:10–13	7
22:1–14	206
22:2	82
22:21	128
22:23–33	44, 52
25:1, 5–6, 10	82
25:31–46	167

Mark

7:20–23	7
10:2–12	7
10:21	92
12:17	128

Luke

1:17	74
1:35	79
1:42	74
1:49	74
2:4–5	74
2:48–49	77
2:51	78
7:38	77
7:38–47	92
16:18	7
20:25	128
22:15–16	88
22:29–30	89

John

1:1, 3	45
1:14, 12–13	73
2:1–11	82
3:28–30	81
4:16–18	7
4:24	119n25
4:34	92
6:53	89
6:54–56	89
8:9	77
8:10–11	7
14:15	185
17:21	168
17:21–22	220
19:25–27	78
21:5	81

Acts of the Apostles

1:14	79
2:4	79
4:19	128
5:29	128
16:14–15	80
20:36–38	81

Romans

1:1	203
7:22–24	115
8:23	50
16:3–5	80

1 Corinthians

6:9–10	7
6:10	143
6:12–17	62
6:18	143

2 Corinthians

4:4	61
5:17	46, 73, 89

Galatians

2:20	95, 167
4:4–7	xiii, 115
5:22	51

Ephesians

5	xiv
5:21	119
5:21–33	44, 84
5:22–33	10
5:25	112
5:25–31	206

Colossians

1:15	61

1 Thessalonians

2:11–12	80

1 Timothy

5:1–2	80

2 Peter

1:4	52

1 John

2:1	80
4:8	115
4:16	117
4:20	170

Revelation

2:7	90
7:9	90
19:6–7, 9	xiv, 90
21:2	90
21:5	46, 89–90
21:9	90
22:13	45
22:17	90
22:20	90

www.ingramcontent.com/pod-product-compliance
Lightning Source LLC
Chambersburg PA
CBHW030823230426
43667CB00008B/1346